Praise for *Street Data*

"*Street Data* calls upon readers to 'flip the dashboard' from a focus on big data to a focus on the voices at the margins—those learners and their families who have been most affected by deep-rooted systemic inequities. When we listen closely to these voices with curiosity, courage, and humility, we gain a greater understanding of the meaning and root causes of these inequities, as well as how they can be addressed in ways that transform and heal. Policymakers and educators at every level of the system need this book to forge a path to genuine equity."

—**Linda Darling-Hammond**
Professor Emeritus at Stanford University and
President of the Learning Policy Institute

"For far too long, education leaders have implemented reform strategies without engaging and centering those most impacted—the students. Shane Safir and Jamila Dugan provide an energizing, anti-racist, actionable framework that centers the voices of the most marginalized students as the experts and co-conspirators that we need to create an education system worthy of their brilliance. Read this, share it, and be a part of ushering in this 'new normal' of street-level data to unlock racial justice in our schools."

—**Taryn Ishida**
Youth Organizer and Executive Director
Californians for Justice

"With *Street Data*, Shane Safir and Jamila Dugan have built a conversation more than a framework, wherein students, their communities, teachers, leaders, and systems are interconnected parts of a family unit. As a professor and psychologist, I found myself drawn to the work's human and family-centered focus. Throughout the work, these are linked to an emphasis on building approaches to the art of teaching grounded in listening, making and holding room for all members of the learning family, and setting goals and evolving approaches that begin with the student as their core. Safir and Dugan are engaging us all in a critically important conversation, where the data we gather and share around learning spaces is shaped and centered on the voices and beings of students. It is family systems-centered teaching and learning. It is holistic, and it is necessary."

—**Napoleon Wells**
Assistant Professor of Social Sciences
Claflin University, SC

"Shane Safir and Jamila Dugan have given us a vivid and immensely readable account of what public education could and should be. Rather than quick fixes, the book is rich with real-life examples and immediately actionable equity practices that educators and leaders can use to tackle root causes. The authors have also issued an unspoken but clear challenge to all of us who care about children's learning and development: 'What if policy decisions were anchored in the lived experiences of students, their families, and their educators?' Their call to action is clear and urgent: we must reverse-engineer and radically reimagine our resources, policies, and practices to support the broad conditions in which students can authentically thrive, and most particularly students who are the most marginalized by the current system. The vision of educational justice laid out in the book will not be more widely practiced if we simply rely on individual teachers and principals to push forward alone into the headwinds. It must be supported at systems and state levels, so that it becomes the rule and not the exception."

—**Sophie Fanelli**
President
Stuart Foundation

"*Street Data* issues an urgent, timely provocation to listen to, honor, and be informed by the experiences, wisdom, fears, and aspirations of children and families who have been forced to the margins by our schools and institutions. Rich with stories that affirm our shared humanity and connectedness, Shane Safir and Jamila Dugan offer a humanistic approach and practical guidance for embedding love, equity, curiosity, and courage in our efforts to manifest learning spaces where every young person learns, develops, and thrives.

"Safir and Dugan call on us to free ourselves from old constructs about data for improvement that are rooted in Whiteness as normative and, instead, model ways to integrate concepts of wholeness, justice, deep culture, personal mastery, and agency into our school transformation efforts. This book is an important contribution to all of us who are working to create a world that works for all of us."

—**LaShawn Routé Chatmon**
Executive Director
National Equity Project

"In this absolutely path-breaking book, Shane Safir and Jamila Dugan use the concept of 'street data' as an entry point to a fundamentally different paradigm for schooling. Foregrounding listening, understanding, and loving over counting, measuring, and classifying, *Street Data* illustrates what it would truly mean to develop a humanizing and liberating approach to school transformation. Startlingly fresh in its prose, clear in its convictions, and moving effortlessly between theory and practice, we can only hope *Street Data* will mark the beginning of a new and different era for American education. A spectacular book!"

—**Jal Mehta**
Professor of Education
Harvard Graduate School of Education

"Old systems are crumbling before our eyes as new ones are being built. *Street Data* offers key insights about how to transform data and explore Indigenous knowledge creation for a new world. Shane Safir and Jamila Dugan give us new ways to analyze, diagnosis, and assess everything from student learning to district improvement to policy. This book is a must-read for researchers and practitioners searching for a fresh and deeply authentic model for school transformation."

—Shawn Ginwright
Professor of Education & Africana Studies,
San Francisco State University and
Chief Executive Officer, Flourish Agenda, Oakland, CA

"*Street Data* gives us a vibrant picture of what it means to do school when we authentically center our students. Shane Safir and Jamila Dugan provide inspiration and clear examples of how we can humanize our classrooms and create a more just education system. Critically for change agents, we also find practical advice for supporting adults across the system as they begin to shift their approach to a new normal that builds with and for students. There is no doubt that we need a new way forward and *Street Data* is a trusted map for charting a course for maximum impact."

—Shanna Peeples
Teacher of the Year (2015) and
Author, Think Like Socrates

Street Data

Street Data

A Next-Generation Model for Equity, Pedagogy, and School Transformation

Shane Safir

Jamila Dugan

With Carrie Wilson

Foreword by Christopher Emdin

FOR INFORMATION:

Corwin

A SAGE Company

2455 Teller Road

Thousand Oaks, California 91320

(800) 233-9936

www.corwin.com

SAGE Publications Ltd.

1 Oliver's Yard

55 City Road

London EC1Y 1SP

United Kingdom

SAGE Publications India Pvt. Ltd.

B 1/I 1 Mohan Cooperative Industrial Area

Mathura Road, New Delhi 110 044

India

SAGE Publications Asia-Pacific Pte. Ltd.

18 Cross Street #10-10/11/12

China Square Central

Singapore 048423

Program Director and Publisher: Dan Alpert
Senior Content
    Development Editor: Lucas Schleicher
Associate Content
    Development Editor: Mia Rodriguez
Project Editor: Amy Schroller
Copy Editor: Karin Rathert
Typesetter: C&M Digitals (P) Ltd.
Proofreader: Dennis W. Webb
Indexer: Integra
Cover Designer: Scott Van Atta
Marketing Managers: Maura Sullivan and
                    Sharon Pendergast

Printed in the United States of America

ISBN 9781071812716

This book is printed on acid-free paper.

22 23 24 25 10 9 8

DISCLAIMER: This book may direct you to access third-party content via Web links, QR codes, or other scannable technologies, which are provided for your reference by the author(s). Corwin makes no guarantee that such third-party content will be available for your use and encourages you to review the terms and conditions of such third-party content. Corwin takes no responsibility and assumes no liability for your use of any third-party content, nor does Corwin approve, sponsor, endorse, verify, or certify such third-party content.

Contents

Foreword

I've been called a "street kid" or variations of that term all my life. Each time, it has seemed like a proxy for something more sinister than the words themselves. Somehow I knew that those who hurled those words intended them to harm. The context around their use, the tone with which they were said, the look in the eyes of those who said them all told me that the words meant not smart, not valuable, not educated/learned. The association between the street and what is wrong or bad has always existed. The streets as inherently bad or low-brow lingers in the imagination of the public. We have been taught to stay as far away from the streets as possible, only to look down upon them with a gaze of judgment and distance.

This perception replicates itself inside schools and school systems. Instead of listening to the families and young people we should be designing schools to serve, we listen to numbers and test scores and choose to believe anything but the most valuable source of data in our buildings: human experience. This is why the concept of Street Data is so radical and rife with possibility. It is in the embracing of what is perceived as negative and highlighting the possibility within it that transformation begins. The work then is the embracing of the street. The sitting in and with it until you become aware enough to see it for what it truly is. Most importantly, for those whose relationship to the street(s) has been used as a mechanism for their dispossession—the robbery of their self-worth and devaluing of their genius, embracing and elevating the street, the hood, el barrio becomes an act of restitution for the goal of restoration. That MUST be the goal of education—restitution and restoration.

One of my favorite hip-hop groups is the LOX. They are a trio of emcees from Yonkers, New York, who went from a group of talented high school friends to one of the most well-known groups in hip-hop. They got introduced to the world through hip-hop producer Sean (Diddy) Combs. Combs is, in many ways, the prototypical hip-hop record executive from the 1990's. He was wealthy, flashy, visible, and had a backing from a larger corporation that had invested millions of dollars in ensuring he was successful. He signed the LOX to a record contract, and they wrote songs for him and also released an album entitled Money, Power and Respect. The album, which contained elements of what made the LOX special, also featured a song they wrote and an accompanying video that was the epitome of materialism, lights and flash. While this song made the group a household name, it was not who they were. They also came to recognize that they were locked into an unfair record contract. After some dissatisfaction with the label over their finances and representation in the public, the group decided they had enough with the record label. They were writing songs they were not getting compensated for, and their talents were being squandered for a corporation that did not truly see value in them. Most importantly, they were being asked to be something they were not. They did not feel true to self in the shiny suits that had become the uniform for Puffy's Bad Boy Records and the caricatures they were becoming as they took on the personas he was constructing for them. They asked to be taken off the label. They were not let out of their contract. They decided to bring their case to the streets and have the community advocate for them in a campaign called "Let the Lox Go." They eventually got out of their contract and released a second album named We Are the Streets. This album was an opportunity to embrace all the things they had to leave behind in signing a contract with Diddy. It was a return to an unapologetically raw and truthful perspective that had been washed away when they were under contract with the record label.

In many ways, the current system of education is run no differently than any other corporation like a record company or tech firm. Its chief purpose appears to be generating income at the expense of workers whose talents and labor are used to maintain an existing structure. The students and their families are "under contract" to attend the school, and they become cogs in a machine that presents itself like it is benefiting them, but actually functions to rob them of their individuality. Schools in this corporate climate privilege numbers over people, looking at quantitative outcomes without recognizing the deep insight that comes from stories, anecdotes, experience, and emotion. Just as major companies shred artists from where they come from or only highlight thin slices of who they are in the pursuit of constructing a narrative of violence and dysfunction, schools present numbers and obtuse quantitative data without context that is used to tell tales of underperformance and inability that do not reflect the truth. Street data, like street science and street knowledge, provides street insight—a more robust picture: one that values experience, emotion, perspective, vision, embeddedness, and community over anything else.

Many identify street data, or a street perspective, as being lower or lesser than established ones. I and the authors of this book argue that it is more complex, more layered, and more nuanced. In Part I of the book, Safir and Dugan unpack *why* street data is a transformative, game-changing model that we should embrace now. In Part II, they break down and explore *what* street data is and *how* to leverage it in pursuit of equity, pedagogy, and school transformation. In Part III, they get down on the street level to unpack how this type of data can catapult student and adult learning to new levels. Finally, in Part IV, they argue that street data, not traditional metrics, will help us transform our school cultures into antiracist spaces of deep, meaningful learning.

Street data is more Wakanda like. In the movie Black Panther, Wakanda was a land that had extensive resources and advanced technological assets that were hidden in plain sight beneath a surface that didn't indicate all that lay beneath. It operated on a street level that much of the world could not see. When they saw what Wakanda really was, it was beyond their comprehension. Street knowledge and street data exist in much the same way. They operate at a level not discernable to the untrained and uninformed eye. In this work, we get a primer on how and why we can embark on that different vision. We are offered a lens with which we can see anew.

In my work, I am often asked about why certain young people from urban settings in America have such a hard time in traditional classrooms. As a science educator, the question is often posed in a way that frames the academic challenges young folks may be having in the classroom as a function of the rigors of the subject and the student's inability to engage in rigorous content. What these educators do not recognize, and the perspective that street science offers, is that there are considerations beyond the rigors of the subject matter that lead to what many term as underperformance. It may not be that the academic content is too rigorous. It may mean that the manner of delivery is too simplistic and therefore, disengaging. The challenge is not in understanding the content. Many young people underperform in classes not because the content is out of reach, but because it is challenging to bend yourself to an approach to instruction that is ordinary when your life beyond the classroom is extraordinary.

Street data privileges narrative and lived experience and engages in what Sandra Harding has called a strong objectivity that is reached with an eschewing of objectivity as we currently have come to know it and rather, a deep subjectivity. Street data is about embeddedness. Sitting in and with people and places until one shifts both philosophy and methodology. It is the pursuit of liberation in both theory and practice by recognizing that if the body and soul are colonized by institutional norms, it is impossible for the mind to function at its highest level. Most importantly, it is about operating with a belief in the infinite potential of those who have been told they are less than and radical honesty about the deep flaws in the system as it currently stands. Street data is about radical new beginnings and having the sense of self and purpose to detach from a broken model and embark on building a new one.

—Christopher Emdin

Acknowledgments

Shane

I am indebted to Jal Mehta and John Watkins for inviting me to participate in the Deeper Learning Dozen project. In that beloved community, I met brilliant people from my own country and Canada whose work helped to inspire this book. I honor Tousilum and Rob Qwiyahwultuhw George, Michelle Staples, and all of the elders who led the learning experience I describe at the outset of Chapter 1. Your work is life changing and healing. I honor my dear friends Denise Augustine and Bonnie Johnson-Aten as well as Victor Prussack, Rod Allen, Kevin Godden, Gino Bondi, Nathan Ngieng, Perry Smith, Carla Danielsson, Christine Perkins, Gail Higginbottom, Tamara Mallof, Ben Eaton, Suzanne Hoffman, David Nelson, Pedro da Silva, and my growing community of BC colleagues who continue to push their own practice toward truth, reconciliation, and healing. Please visit them, learn from them, and elevate their work.

To Shawn Ginwright who read early drafts of the opening chapter and pushed me to dig deeper into questions of epistemology and later to locate myself as a white woman educator in the narrative. Your work inspires, and I wish I could go back and get a PhD under your mentorship!

To all the educators, students, and caregivers whose street-level stories animate these pages, I give thanks: Dr. Matt Wayne; Kellie McNair and Jason Juszczak; the real Alyssa and Jackie who bravely shared their story in Chapter 4 for our learning and their own healing; Ailed Paningbatan, Damien Padilla, Krishtine deLeon, and Taina Gomez, among my first students whose legacy helped to shape a pedagogy of voice; Rex de Guia and Lisa Arrastia for copiloting a bold and crazy pedagogical experiment in 1999 that changed our lives; Danielle "Dani" Martin, whose voice sings in Chapter 6; Han Phung, Emma Dunbar, and Chris Maldonado, whose middle school transformation work energized my writing; Matt Alexander, a leader and friend of the highest integrity; and the real Jason R. whose powerful leadership shaped Chapter 9.

To all the scholars of color whose brilliant work is woven into these pages and whose scholarship made this book possible, among them: Ronald Sentwali Bakari, Dr. Serie McDougal III, Claude Steele, Kimberlé Williams Crenshaw, Linda Tuhiwai Smith, Cindy Blackstock, Terry Cross, Paolo Freire, Linda Darling-Hammond, Geneva Gay, Zaretta Hammond, Gloria Ladson-Billings, Bettina Love, Ibram X. Kendi, and Lisa Delpit. To Christopher Emdin, whose work and presence emanate love and the possibility of transformation: for supporting my first book and then writing a beautiful foreword for this book.

To Deborah Meier, my dear friend, who was the first educational leader who believed in me and made me feel worthy of mentorship. Your brilliance and decades-long call to center the power of student ideas has its mark all over this book. I love you dearly.

Alcine Mumby and Joe Truss, thank you for walking through fire with me and staying committed to our mutual liberation. Your ability to dismantle white supremacy while modeling Black joy and brilliance is pure magic. Abby Benedetto: you are one of the most innovative, humble, and pedagogically genius educators I know. Thank you for giving your career to this work and for teaching me how to model cultural humility and ownership of privilege as a white woman.

Dan Alpert, I don't know how I got so lucky as to have you in my corner! I could not have dreamed up an editor like you. You have believed in this project and kept me on course even when circumstances made it extremely challenging. You give the *best* feedback of any editor I have met: never too much or too little. Thank you for shepherding this book to the finish line.

Carrie, thank you for walking this path with me and integrating your powerful model of public learning into the street data framework. Readers will benefit greatly!

Jamila, it has been a privilege to write this book with you and to watch you blossom as a writer. You are brilliant, passionate, focused, and able to hold a vision of a world that doesn't exist while pounding the pavement *daily* in service to your own children and the educators you support. We are all so lucky to learn from you through this book.

Finally, to my precious family: We are perfect in our imperfection. We have walked the globe together finding ourselves and each other, from Jordan to Costa Rica to Spain, Morocco, and México. Manny, listening to you teach your newcomer students with infinite love, patience, and creativity inspires me daily. Maximo, your natural curiosity helped me imagine a pedagogy of voice. Mona, I wrote this book for you: that we might imagine a system that serves and holds and loves and cherishes and cultivates the brilliance of students like you. You deserve that, and I will continue to fight for it.

Jamila

First, I would like to express my deepest appreciation to my family. To my husband, Fredrick Pugh II; children, Gia Milan, Kingston James, Kendrick Samuel—you are my everything. To my father, Kevin Dugan; mothers, Michelle Wright, Dede Dugan, Scheryl Dugan, and Sheree Wright-Cox; brothers, Jelane Dugan, Devin Dugan, Marquez Wright, and Kenneth Preston; aunties; uncles; and extended family, thank you for guiding me across this journey we call life.

To my ancestors . . . thank you for your breath, your spirit, and your constant reminders of what it means to be unapologetically Black. Your lives remind me that I am but one more person standing on the strength of your shoulders. Maya Angelou, Ida B. Wells, Malcolm X, Muhammad Ali, and so many more, you are the resistance I hope to be.

To my sisters . . . there is no way I could do this work without you: Safia Quinn, Isabelle Mussard, Stesha Andrews, Jasmine Carr-Edmond, Elyse Calloway, Alyssa Hernandez, and Dr. Kathy Black. There is no me without your phone calls, straight talk, and the shelter you provide me. To the women of D3 and Sisters in Education Circle, you have brought new light into my life. Dr. Akosua Lesesne, thank you for founding SIEC and holding space for brilliant Black women. To the elders in our circle, you keep my fire lit. Special acknowledgement to Dr. Lisa Delpit—I keep your note close. I am so thankful for it.

To the educators I have worked with across the years and who have inspired my work, this book is truly dedicated to you. Baba Woods and Baba Ustadi, thank you for centering my learning in Our story. Onome Pela-Emore and Megan Monroe, I am so glad to have started my teaching journey with you as my guides. My deepest thanks to every school leader from the Bay Area to Philadelphia, Pennsylvania, and Camden, New Jersey, for allowing me to work alongside you as a coach, colleague, and friend. Your stories enrich my perspective and color my lense on educating our children.

And finally, Shane, thank you so much for trusting me to be your partner in writing this book. It is you who said I need to write, and it is because of that push that I write here and now. So proud of this piece of work!

Carrie

Listening deeply is central to creating cultures of learning for adults, and it is nearly impossible to listen if you haven't been heard. I am forever grateful to Claire Bove for her infinitely generous listening that encouraged seeds of passion to take shape in the world.

My first experience of public learning was Dr. Anna Richert's graduate seminar at Mills College. Her brilliant work in collaborative inquiry is the foundation of Lead by Learning's (formerly Mills Teacher Scholars) practice of public learning.

To the incredibly compassionate and wise Lead by Learning team and advisors who were instrumental in developing the practice of public learning across a variety of contexts in pursuit of a more equitable future: Jen Ahn, Elizabeth Shafer, Sarah Sugarman, Daniela Mantilla, Aija Simmons, Mary Hurley, Malia Tayabas-Kim, Nina Portugal, Pilar Beccar-Valera, and Julia Moss Beers. The inspirational energy from the amazing Judy Halbert, Linda Kaser, and the fabulous work of NOII cannot be overstated.

I am grateful for the caring and visionary leadership of our teacher and leader partners who courageously support their colleagues' learning, and who question their own and each other's assumptions.

Finally, I am grateful to Shane Safir for her enthusiasm around a better way to envision and to nurture the learning of students and their educators and for her generous invitation to share our approach more broadly.

Publisher's Acknowledgments

Corwin gratefully acknowledges the contributions of the following reviewers:

Gary Anderson
Professor
New York University
New York, NY

Sydney Chaffee
Humanities Teacher and Instructional Coach
Codman Academy Charter Public School
Boston, MA

Mirko Chardin
Founding Head
The Putnam Avenue Upper School
Boston, MA

Becki Cohn-Vargas
Consultant and Author
Identity Safe Classrooms, K–5 and 6–12
El Sobrante, CA

Amy Colton
Professional Learning Consultant
Learning Forward
Ann Arbor, MI

Vanessa Peterson
Vice President—Diversity, Equity, Inclusion, and Accessibility
Northwest Evaluation Association
Portland, OR

About the Authors

Shane Safir (lead author) has worked at every level of the education system for the past twenty-five years, with an unwavering commitment to racial justice and deep learning. After teaching in San Francisco and Oakland, California, and engaging in community organizing to launch a new public high school, Shane became the founding principal of June Jordan School for Equity (JJSE), an innovative national model identified by scholar and policy leader Linda Darling-Hammond as having "beaten the odds in supporting the success of low-income students of color" (Darling-Hammond, 2002). For over a decade, Shane has provided equity-centered leadership coaching, systems transformation support, and professional learning for schools, districts, and organizations across the United States and Canada. She writes for *Edutopia, Ed Week, Educational Leadership* magazine and is the author of *The Listening Leader: Creating the Conditions for Equitable School Transformation* (Jossey-Bass, 2017). Shane is thrilled to coauthor this book with Dr. Jamila Dugan, a long-time collaborator who conducted foundational research for *The Listening Leader* and who facilitates equity workshops with Shane, as well as Carrie Wilson, a colleague whose groundbreaking program for teacher-driven inquiry centers street data in the pursuit of equity. Shane is the mother of Mona Luz and Maximo Oisin and married to Emmanuel, a veteran math and science teacher in Oakland, California.

Jamila Dugan (co-author) is a leadership coach, learning facilitator, and researcher. She began her career as a teacher in Washington, D.C., successfully supporting her school to implement an International Baccalaureate program. After being nominated for Teacher of the Year, she later served as a coach for new teachers in Oakland, California. As a school administrator, Jamila championed equity-centered student services, parent empowerment, and co-led the development of the first public Mandarin immersion middle school in the Bay Area. Jamila and Shane began their work together seven years ago during the development of *The Listening Leader,* for which Jamila acted as the primary researcher. Jamila currently serves as an equity-centered leadership development coach across all sectors including nonprofits, public school districts, charter networks, and parochial and private schools. She is an avid supporter of dual-language learning, serving on the boards of Independence Charter Spanish Immersion School in Philadelphia and Parents of African American Students Studying Chinese (PAASSC) in the Bay Area. She holds a bachelor's degree in psychology from Fresno State University, a master's degree in early childhood education from George Mason University, and a doctorate in education leadership for equity from University of California, Berkeley. Jamila is also a loving wife and the mother of three amazing children who remain her constant inspiration for her work.

Carrie Wilson (**contributing writer**) Carrie Wilson's work focuses on the central role of practitioner knowledge and insight in educational transformation. The guiding principle of her work is the role of learning cultures in promoting individual learning for students, teachers, principals, and district leaders. Carrie's experience as a teacher, teacher supervisor, cooperating teacher, facilitator of professional learning, leader of a nonprofit organization, and a leadership coach has informed and inspired her vision of practitioner-driven educational transformation. In her graduate research, Carrie identified the importance of creating a "thinking space" for novice teachers during post-observation discussions. This led her to develop the practice of public learning, featured in Chapter 7, as a key tool in shifting cultures of compliance to cultures of curiosity. As executive director of Lead by Learning (formerly Mills Teacher Scholars) at Mills College, Carrie oversees all aspects of development, including programs that help districts create adult learning cultures through the practice of public learning. She is passionate about supporting educators to challenge each other's assumptions as they become agents for change with a moral imperative to dismantle oppressive and racist systems.

Note to Readers

With the exception of Chapters 2 and 7, the "I" pronoun in this book signals Shane's voice.

Prologue
Data in a Time of Pandemic

As I write this book, we are steeped in a quadruple pandemic: COVID-19, systemic racism, near economic collapse, and shattering climate change. COVID-19 has exploded onto the international stage, forever transforming our educational systems. Teachers are "ramping up" to digital or hybrid learning models. Administrators have repurposed school buildings into food banks and materials distribution centers. States have canceled standardized testing for the academic year, and many universities have canceled entrance testing requirements for current applicants. As we go to press, Yale University announced that all classes will be held as pass/fail this semester, and K–12 schools across the United States have begun to follow suit. Parents with means are hiring teachers to facilitate home schooling pandemic "pods" for their children, further exacerbating longstanding gaps.

At the same time, the unemployment rate is at a historic high. Police brutality and **white supremacy** reveal themselves daily as Black Americans fight for the right to breathe, live, and thrive in a country built on systemic racism. Activists in the growing movement for racial justice are tearing down monuments to Confederate soldiers, architects of Native American genocide and Canadian residential schools, and other symbols of oppression. And the globe reverberates with the invocation that *Black Lives Matter* in a country where, according to 1619 project director and journalist Nikole Hannah-Jones, "Black Americans have also been, and continue to be, foundational to the idea of American freedom. More than any other group in this country's history, we have served, generation after generation, in an overlooked but vital role: It is we who have been the perfecters of this democracy" (Hannah-Jones, 2019).

All of this is laying bare the broken promises at the roots of the education system: Education for all looks increasingly like education for the economically stable and digitally possessed, survival of the secure. Current testing practices continue to dehumanize young people and teachers while leading us further and further from educational equity. In this book, we posit that not only *can* we pursue equity right now, but we have a moral imperative to reimagine what that means. The *end* (increasing test scores and closing an achievement gap, which we will argue in this book is a racialized fiction) no longer justifies the *means* of packet-driven, teacher-centered pedagogy that preexisted but was roundly reinforced by the No Child Left Behind era. We have a chance to imagine a radically different paradigm for equity. We need a new kind of dashboard.

What's beautiful about this moment is that many of the traditional "givens" around the architecture of schooling—lesson plans, gradebooks, subject-matter exams, even classrooms—are being reframed daily, forcing us to rethink what really matters when people are dying from a global threat never before seen in most of our lifetimes. Everywhere, everyone is trying to figure out what education looks like, and our usual beacons of success—test scores, grades, seat time—have evaporated like water off a turbulent pot. While many clamor for a "return to normal," the voices of educators across the globe are converging around a demand for a *new* normal: What would it look like to let go of all of our assumptions and rebuild the system from the bottom up, from the *student* up?

The purpose of this book is to offer a next-generation model of equity and deep learning, emerging from a simple concept: street data. **Street data** is the qualitative and experiential data that emerges at eye level and on lower frequencies when we train our brains to discern it. Street data is asset based, building on the tenets of culturally responsive education by helping educators look for what's *right* in our students, schools, and communities instead of seeking out what's *wrong*. Street data embodies both an ethos and a change methodology that will transform how we analyze, diagnose, and assess everything from student learning to district improvement to policy. It offers us a new way to think about, gather, and make meaning of data. It calls for what Paolo Freire deemed a pedagogy of liberation (Freire, 1970).

Even as the system seems to fall apart around us, **street-level data** are ubiquitous, offering deep insight into student and educator experience. These data fill our hearts and keep us up at night as we witness children's resilience *and* struggle to stay engaged, socially connected, and emotionally well. These data fill our social media feeds and virtual meetings as we see relevant, just-in-time professional learning, teachers calling their students one-by-one to ask, "How are you? What do you need?" and pedagogical thought leaders pushing us to move beyond the "packet" and engage students in deep learning. All of this manifests the creativity, care, and connection that exist and persist inside the system.

If we listen to policy wavelengths, the system is falling apart without its usual architecture. But if we listen to educators on the ground, the system is self-correcting and humanizing itself in a yearning for reinvention. Somehow, even though we are physically and socially distant, we are emerging into new webs of interdependence like never before. It is 2021. The world order is reorganizing itself, and along with it, our education systems are as well. All of this takes me back over twenty years to when I began my teaching career.

I entered the classroom in fall 1997 with a vision of teaching and learning that burst at the seams of my classroom. I took students outside of the classroom as often as I could. My U.S. history students visited Angel Island to study the history of Chinese immigration to California. My American democracy students conducted a mock Congress in which they wrote and debated bills on pressing social issues. (My friend Javier was the president down the hall with veto power. A student named Jorge wrote an LGBTQ rights bill and then came out as gay to the class with a trembling voice when his legislation was mocked—a moment I'll never forget.) My pre-law students developed a project investigating equity in education, visiting five radically different Bay Area public schools to report on the access and opportunity gaps they witnessed. The next year, this project evolved into a partnership with a nearby private school that became the subject of an Emmy-nominated PBS documentary, *Making the Grade* (1999).

Just a few years after I entered the classroom, No Child Left Behind became federal law. With this sweeping policy shift came an eroding sense of possibility—a focus on narrow metrics of success and compliance-driven forms of pedagogy. Drill and kill your students so they succeed on the tests. Adopt pacing guides to ensure teachers stay "on track." If you can't trust your teachers, script the curriculum!

By the time I became a principal in 2003, the tide had turned, and our little public school, June Jordan School for Equity (JJSE), became a counter-cultural symbol and, in many ways, a pariah in the district. (It is ironic to me that JJSE has since been profiled by leading scholars like Linda Darling-Hammond as a model of equity and deep learning.) We were developing discussion-based seminar courses and project exhibitions while school districts began to compete for the best pacing guides, packaged curricula, and "turnaround" strategies. We were shaping a performance-based assessment system while principals across the district monitored teachers for compliance with the Blackboard Configuration, or BBC: a teacher-proof lesson structure meant to be an equity panacea. We lost what one of my first students, the brilliant Ms. Alondra Jones, who got her BA and MSW at Howard University, called the "human element of education."

Yet for the nearly twenty-five years since I first entered a classroom in southeast San Francisco, many of us have held onto an image of what is possible when we reject the rules of a rigged system designed to trap children in poverty and Black and Brown children in a deficit narrative. **We have retained a vision of what is possible when we build classrooms and schools and systems around students' brilliance, cultural wealth, and intellectual potential rather than self-serving savior narratives that have us "fixing" and "filling" academic gaps.**

My early teaching experiences left me with indelible lessons that I hope will bloom in this book:

- There are many ways of knowing and "succeeding" beyond those that dominate American and much of Western education.

- Learning does not require a school building or even a classroom.

- Equity work is first and foremost pedagogical. We must democratize knowledge and rebuild a pedagogy of student voice.

- Student agency is the goal, not test scores.

- Data live *everywhere*—on the streets, in students' homes, in the hallways, in virtual meetings, in phone calls, and in the micro-interactions among teachers and students.

What is the purpose of education anyway? Do we teach and lead to simply reproduce reality, or will we teach and lead to transform it? In the chapters that follow, we probe these questions in greater depth.

We hope to offer you a vision of an educational system that doesn't yet exist—one rooted in human experience and decolonized ways of being, knowing, and learning. We will explore questions of knowledge and epistemology, digging up the roots of the obsession with quantitative data. We will explore questions of teaching and learning, giving you concrete tools to shape an equity-centered instructional vision and a pedagogy of student voice. We will explore questions of adult culture, offering a framework for the types of daily courageous conversations that make antiracist rhetoric real. And we will unpack the principles, processes, and practices of the next-generation paradigm we call street data.

We look forward to taking this journey with you and invite you to step forward with clear eyes, a full heart, and a spirit of inquiry and curiosity.

Why Street Data, Why Now?

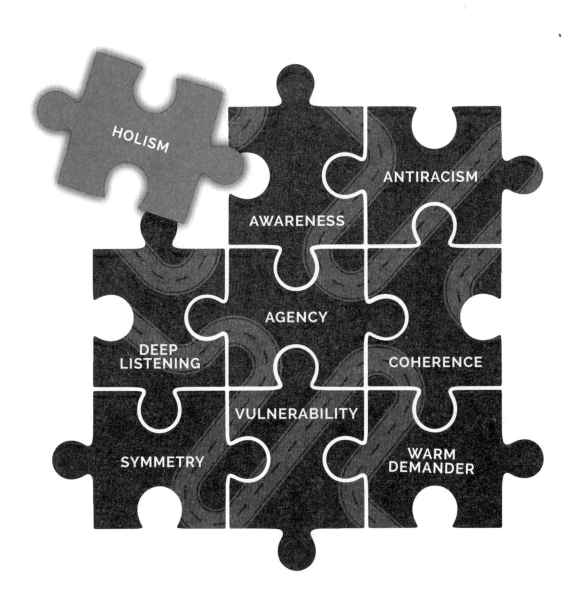

Leading for Equity
Another World Is Possible

1

Reimagine our ways of knowing and learning.

Another world is not only possible, she is on her way.
On a quiet day, I can hear her breathing.

—Arundhati Roy

Reclaiming the Village: Children at the Center

I am seated in a circle, nested among other circles, inside a former boarding school for Indigenous Canadian girls in Duncan, British Columbia—a small town on Vancouver Island. A white cross tops the brick-red steeple on this building, a relic of the Sisters of St. Ann and detail I barely noticed when I walked in. Within these concentric circles sit forty other educational leaders from the United States and Canada, joined by a desire to transform their school districts into spaces of equity and deep learning. I have been asked to speak to the group about listening leadership tomorrow, but for today, I am a learner.

Our guides are First Nations elders and a non-Indigenous woman named Michelle. Tousilum, our main teacher, shares that just entering this building makes his heart heavy: The cross takes him back to being ripped from his family at the age of five to attend a residential school where his music, language, and humanity were robbed from him. Like other elders here, Tousilum discloses that he was abused in the institutions he was forced to attend. He talks about the unimaginable pain his mother must have felt to have her youngest child stolen from her arms. To support his healing, Tousilum pulls out a drum and begins to sing a prayerful song in *Hul'q'umi'num*, the language of the land, calling us to stop and listen, to be still, to remember, to be grateful. I weep silently.

As an educator from Oakland, California, I feel the weight of the history Tousilum invokes—my complicity in knowing so little about Canadian residential schools; my own country's near-erasure of Native American genocide and **settler colonialism** as well as its deep denial of slavery, lynching, and Jim Crow. As the mother of biracial children whose lives straddle histories of immigration, oppression, racism, and privilege, I feel trauma *in my bones* at the thought of my child being ripped from my arms. Having taught U.S. history for many years, I am sitting with the ways I both succeeded and failed to address these histories.

After opening rituals, our teachers direct us to form a Western, colonial society. They position a middle-aged white man at the front of the pyramid. Four men sit staunchly behind him in a row, then another ten men behind them. Women under forty assemble the next row, then myself and other women under fifty. Michelle tells all the "old ladies" over fifty to go to the back room, along with those role-playing the "children," where they can barely see or hear the rest of us. We shape a rigid triangle. "How does it feel to be in this society?" she asks the group.

> The older women shout from the back, "Shut out! Isolated!"

> Women from my row whisper, "Invisible."

The men ahead of me murmur, "Like I have to clamor to get up front . . ."

> Several participants observe, "I can only see the backs of people's heads. I can't communicate with anyone from another group."

Michelle points out that this hierarchical system—a symbolic representation of Western society—fosters not only competition but lateral violence. People are encouraged to transfer their experience of oppression across and down the power structure.

Next, we are directed by our teachers to re-form as a pre-colonial Indigenous community. We pull the chairs to the edges of the room as the elders lay a patchwork of woven blankets in the center. An elder named Linda places a candle at the center of the cloths to symbolize the fire, the heart of the community—the light that shines in each of us and that we must all strive to bring forth in each other. The children of our village are asked to visit a nearby table and choose a "gift" before sitting in a circle around the fabrics. One chooses a canoe for paddling and navigation. Another selects a woven cedar basket for tending, harvesting, and preserving foods like smoked salmon, dried clams, and stinging nettle tea. Others choose a hand-carved rattle for healing and a drum for remembering and singing family histories. The "old ladies" are retrieved from the other room and asked to encircle the children. Next, the aunties, uncles, mothers, and fathers (I'm in that group now) surround the elder women, and finally, the spiritual warriors surround us. I am once again moved to tears, this time by the centering of children and the felt sense of connection.

Rob, or Qwiyahwultuhw in Hul'q'umi'num, lifts an abalone shell filled with burning cedar and begins to walk around the room, using an eagle feather to gently blow the fragrant smoke into the space. He moves the shell behind him to signify that we must always remember where we come from—our path, ancestors, parents, grandparents, villages—and in front of him to symbolize the future. He later tells me, "We are the future of whatever we do to the earth around us. Whatever we do today is going to affect our grandchildren" (personal communication, May 19).

Our teachers explain that in this village, every child has a distinct gift—an aptitude for old words that aren't used very often, an intuition for the medicinal qualities of plants, an affinity for genealogy—and each child will be paired with mentors who will pass their gifts to the next generation. Some will become language keepers, others medicine keepers, other holders of the community's history. The elder women have become the revered center of village life, those who hold community wisdom and are turned *to* rather than banished.

> "Every one of you came from a village like this somewhere back in your history," says Michelle. "How does it feel to be in this community?"
>
> "I feel safe," says one woman.
>
> "Held."
>
> "Like I belong."
>
> "Like I matter."
>
> "I can see everyone."

As we make meaning of our transformation from a rigid hierarchical society to a circular village, the group is overcome by emotion. There is no attempt to contain or "professionalize" it. This is what it means to confront our shared histories of racism, oppression, pain, and possibility. This is what it feels like to connect with each other's humanity.

A Canadian superintendent of mixed ancestry talks about warring between her Indigenous side that wants to feel and express her emotion and her European/Western side that keeps things "buttoned up." She reflects that the educational system taught her to suppress her feelings in order to get to the top of the pyramid. The white man up front tears up as he talks about being a first-generation child of Italian immigrants whose father had a second-grade education: "I too came from a village like this." And the lone researcher in the room, from an American organization that prizes quantitative metrics, reflects, "I've read about 'student-centered learning' for a long time, but this experience completely transformed my understanding."

I reflect on how my life intersects with the societies we formed. I am a white woman of Irish and Jewish descent, married to a Filipino immigrant. I've had the privilege to visit the seaside village in County Galway where my great-great grandfather was born in a stone hut that still stands, overgrown by brush. He was the only sibling of five to immigrate to America and arrive in my now-hometown of Oakland, California, in the late 1800s to raise twelve children. My Irish great-grandmother grew up in the urban village of West Oakland, and my grandfather and mother grew up in Oakland and similar urban villages. My paternal Jewish family hails largely from villages in Eastern Europe that no longer exist, wiped from the earth by pogroms and eventually a Holocaust that scattered Jews to the diaspora. The fact that I can't picture these villages pains me, my only connection being a few words of Yiddish I learned from my grandfather.

Though I will never know what it means to inhabit this world in a Black or brown body, structural racialization and the federal government's policy of redlining urban communities and establishing white suburban enclaves defined my upbringing. In the suburbs, nothing felt real. I experienced deep disconnection—from myself as an aspiring feminist and antiracist with a secret LGBTQ identity, from my peers who largely wanted to remain in the same community, even from my family in many ways. My early efforts to disrupt racism were met not with deaf ears but with outright resistance and rejection at times. I am certain I participated in racism and white supremacy without being aware of it: buying into the white supremacist structure of schooling hook, line, and sinker; earning the grades and test scores to attend an elite university; subscribing to the myth of the meritocracy. My large public school smacked of the Western society: hierarchical, segregated, exclusive rather than inclusive. My brilliant younger sibling dropped out of school after his ways of learning and being were pathologized one too many times.

As a child, I yearned for a village where I would feel seen, known, and loved. It took me many years to find that—to create it really— and many more to dismantle my own internalized racism, sexism, and homophobia (in truth, an ongoing project). Raising children at the intersection of these forces and others continues to shape my understanding of educational equity. I have written this book as an offering: *May we dig up the roots of our deepest beliefs about education that have never served children at the margins.* I have written this book as a healing: *May we nourish a process of truth and reconciliation that frees us all from the grip of white supremacy and restores the inherent dignity and worth of every human being.* I have written this book as a promise: *May I recommit daily to each of you, to the ancestors, and to the long arc of struggle for justice.* I view schools as possibility spaces in which to reimagine society. I don't have "answers" for you—rather ideas and provocations and stories that I hope will ground you in the expansiveness of this moment. As things fall apart, maybe the answers to our deepest challenges lie not in test scores and curriculum guides but in the cultural wealth and wisdom of our villages—both current and ancestral.

I am transported back to the room in Duncan, BC, where I am filled with gratitude for this experience, the wisdom of our guides, and the vision of a child-centered village that manifests my hopes and dreams for education. Looking around me at the faces of leaders from across the United States and Canada, I take in a simple truth: Another world is possible.

The Street Data Paradigm

> *The master's tools will never dismantle the master's house.*
>
> —Audre Lorde

What would an educational system based on this village look like, and how would we create it? It would require a radical reimagining of what we value, what we believe about learning and knowledge itself, and how we think about data and "success." With this book, I hope to tip over the sacred cows that have been overfeeding on the fertile terrain of our school communities: first and foremost, the fixation on big data as the supreme measure of equity and learning.

In a sense, this is an ecological project. We have over-farmed the land and undernourished our students and educators while failing to water the roots of a healthy system: student voice, multiple ways of knowing and learning, and **community cultural wealth**, defined by Chicano/a Studies scholar Tara J. Yosso (2005) as an array of knowledges, skills, abilities, and contacts possessed and used by communities of color to survive and resist racism and other forms of oppression. **For all our talk of being student centered, we have bought into a success paradigm that robs many children of their voices, marginalizes their gifts, and prioritizes measurement and incremental improvement over learning and transformation.**

How do we reorient public education around another set of values and approaches? We begin by reclaiming the village, centering the experiences of children—*particularly* children at the margins—and working to heal the wounds of racism and oppression in our schools. Educators are hungry for an actionable framework for equity that transcends our current toolkit. This book offers fresh ideas and innovative tools to apply immediately. The test-and-punish era incarcerated our collective imagination, and many schools and districts continue to seek off-the-shelf instructional programs rather than build internal capacity and entrust teachers with the art of pedagogy. By contrast, this book will offer you a way to rethink teaching and learning and make your equity visions a reality through the use of street data. The test-and-punish era left behind wounded adult cultures—communities fractured by a blame-and-shame climate and riddled with mistrust, skepticism, and initiative fatigue. *Street Data* will provide you with concrete strategies to listen to and heal your communities.

Street data is a next-generation paradigm that roots equity, pedagogy, and school transformation in what matters most: human experience. Street data reminds us that what is *measurable* is not the same as what is *valuable*. In the United States, parents and educators have stomached twenty years of a rotating cast of policy characters that focus on "standards," "percentages," and "metrics": No Child Left Behind (2001), Race to the Top (2009), Common Core State Standards (2010), Every Child Can Succeed Act (2015), and dozens if not hundreds of local and state counterparts. What has been the result of all these policies?

Despite billions of dollars spent to close purported achievement gaps, the performance of American teenagers in reading and math has flat-lined since 2000, and the achievement gap in reading between high and low performers is widening, according to the latest results of the Program for International Student Assessment, or PISA (Goldstein, 2019a).[1] How do we make sense of the fact that other countries, relying far less on high-stakes testing and embracing progressive pedagogical approaches like performance assessment and play-based learning, continue to blow the United States out of the water? How do we understand seemingly intractable equity gaps?

To paraphrase the late self-identified Black lesbian warrior poet Audre Lorde, we keep trying to dismantle and rebuild the "master's house" with the same faulty set of tools while failing to dismantle the rotten foundation at its base: **systemic racism**. The theory of systemic racism addresses individual, institutional, and structural forms of racial inequality and was shaped over time by scholars like Frederick Douglass, W. E. B. Du Bois, Oliver Cox, Anna Julia Cooper, Kwame Ture, Frantz Fanon, and Patricia Hill Collins, among others. Sociologist Joe Feagin built on this legacy to offer this framing (Cole, 2020).

> Systemic racism includes the complex array of antiblack practices, the unjustly gained political-economic power of whites, the continuing economic and other resource inequalities along racial lines, and the white racist ideologies and attitudes created to maintain and rationalize white privilege and power.

While this definition focuses on **anti-Black racism** in the United States, we can apply many of the ideas to diagnose how racism functions to oppress Indigenous peoples and other people of color, both within the United States and globally. In short, systemic racism is built into the foundation of U.S. society and infuses all aspects of it: law, policy, economy, politics, media, social institutions, beliefs (conscious and unconscious), and certainly education. Despite our talk of "equity" and "culturally responsive education," we continue to base policy and success frameworks on a data model that is narrowly Western, Eurocentric, and racist.

---

[1] It's worth noting that PISA itself is criticized for overemphasizing testing, and there is a movement afoot inside the Organisation for Economic Co-operation and Development, or OECD, to ask students questions about their well-being, including their sense of belonging and life satisfaction.

We have written this book for teachers, educational leaders, and policymakers who recognize that their current approaches are not bearing fruit where the tree is most barren. We hope that whether you are an educator, coach, principal, assistant principal, or superintendent, you will resonate with a data framework that brings you closer to the action, embraces an explicitly antiracist stance, rebuilds depleted reservoirs of trust and good will, and closes the gap between espoused equity values and day-to-day actions. We recommend that you engage the book in study groups, discussing it chapter by chapter as a professional learning community.

Street Data: How Do We Know What We Know?

To understand street data and its potential for transformation, we must first understand the ways in which our current beliefs about learning and equity have been formed. We must explore questions of **epistemology**, or theories of knowledge: How do we know what we know? Why do we value what we value? What constitutes knowledge, and where does the implicit hierarchy of knowledge come from? Let's demystify the ingrained ideas about data that have become normalized in education and orient ourselves to a different conception of knowledge.

In *Decolonizing Methodologies*, Maori scholar Linda Tuhiwai Smith sheds light on the Western theory of knowledge known as **empiricism**—which emphasizes the role of sensory evidence and patterns in the formation of ideas rather than innate ideas or traditions—and its relative, the scientific paradigm of **positivism**. In Western epistemology, "Understanding is viewed as being akin to measuring. As the ways we try to understand the world are reduced to issues of measurement, the focus of understanding becomes more concerned with procedural problems . . . and of developing operational definitions of phenomena which are reliable and valid" (Smith, 2012, p. 44).

Western approaches to knowledge building via research and data collection (often called, in Indigenous critiques, "white research" or "outsider research"') emerge from a larger idea of "the West," which scholar Stuart Hall breaks down into four components:

1. Allowing researchers to characterize and *classify* societies into categories (think "subgroups" in our current data system)

2. Condensing complex images of other societies through a *system of representation* (think "dashboards")

3. Providing a standard *model of comparison* (think "valid and reliable assessments" that allow us to compare the performance of "subgroups" from year to year)

4. Providing *criteria of evaluation* against which other societies can be ranked (think "standards") (Hall, 1992, pp. 276320)

Africana Studies scholar Serie McDougal III discusses the science of knowing, cautioning against scientific colonialism, "which occurs when the center of gravity for the acquisition of knowledge about a people is located outside of that people's lived reality" (McDougal III, 2014, p. 15). He cites Wade Nobles's explanation that scientific colonialism leaves many researchers conceptually incarcerated (a stark image) by using non-African concepts, ideas, and perspectives to study people of African descent. This leads to a host of interpretive problems, including ahistorical analysis, deficit thinking, and failure to give adequate weight to the cultural perspective of the people being studied—the essence of our modern educational data system.

Does this start to look and feel familiar? Can you trace the shadows of the Western hierarchical society from our opening story? Since the birth of standardized testing in the mid-1900s, the field of education has validated an empirical distance when it comes to data. We value knowledge and by extension, data that can be verified by measurement and that is viewed as neutral and "scientific." By the same token, we reject the legitimacy of spiritual, social, and story-centered forms of knowledge.[2] The language of this Western data system has become so naturalized in our discourse that many of us no longer question its legitimacy. Of *course*, we're talking about the "achievement gap," "grades," and "subgroups"! It's the air we breathe.

What if, because of what we've deemed valid and reliable, we have been asking the wrong set of questions? What if the achievement gap itself is a mythology? In reality, we rely on test scores and other quantitative metrics that are deeply entwined with our histories of racism, exclusion, and even eugenics—the movement for controlled selective breeding of human populations born in late nineteenth century England and made famous through Hitler's genocidal master-race

---

[2]My colleague Denise Augustine, a secondee for Indigenous Education with the Ministry of Education in British Columbia, challenges educators to stop using the qualifier "just" before talking about stories and other forms of qualitative data. She names that these are central data points in Indigenous and other non-Western cultures, with profound, unmitigated value.

theory. While this history may seem a far cry from today's high-stakes tests, we can find echoes of pseudo-scientific beliefs in genetic difference throughout American educational history that have been used to justify exclusion and inequity.

In 1779, Thomas Jefferson proposed a two-track educational system, with different tracks for "the laboring and the learned." Scholarship would allow a very few of the laboring class to advance, Jefferson said, by "raking a few geniuses from the rubbish." By the 1830s, most southern states had laws forbidding teaching enslaved African Americans to read. Still, around 5 percent became literate at great personal peril. By 1870, the state of California had devised a formula of ten: When African Americans, Asian Americans, or Native Americans numbered ten students, a school district was empowered to create separate schools for whites and non-white children. (Note the emphasis on classification and separation, a precursor to "subgroups.") (Applied Research Center (ARC) Timeline, 2011)

Fast forward to 1932 when a survey of 150 school districts revealed that 75 percent were using so-called intelligence testing to place students in different academic tracks. By 1948, we see the Educational Testing Service merge with the College Entrance Examination Board, the Cooperative Test Service, the National Committee on Teachers Examinations, and other entities to continue the work of eugenicists like Carl Brigham (originator of the SAT), who did research to "prove" that immigrants were feeble minded. The list goes on and on. Race Forward (previously the Applied Research Center) has a historical timeline of public education available on their website (https://www.raceforward.org/research/reports/historical-timeline-public-education-us).

As we reckon with these histories, we must interrogate our assumptions about knowledge, measurement, and what really matters when it comes to educating young people. What if there were a completely different way to think about all of this? What would a more expansive and culturally sustaining epistemology yield?

Holism: A Core Stance for Street Data

On our globe today, there are two predominant worldviews— linear and relational. The linear worldview is rooted in European and mainstream American thought. It is very temporal, and it is firmly rooted in the logic that says cause has to come before effect. In contrast, the relational worldview sees life as harmonious

relationships where health is achieved by maintaining balance
between the many interrelating factors in one's circle of life.

—National Indian Child Welfare Association
(NICWA), 1997 May/June

How might we begin to reimagine our deep-seated ways of meaning-making and knowing? Indigenous and Afrocentric epistemologies offer powerful worldviews, a term used to describe the collective thought process of a people or culture. Indigenous ways of knowing place value on relationality, intergenerational wisdom, experiential learning, and holism, or holistic learning. (Think of the opening story, in which the children were nested inside a circle of elders and surrounded by the adults of the community.) **Holism** is a core stance that integrates all aspects of learning—the emotional (heart), spiritual (spirit), cognitive (mind), and physical (body)—which are "informed by ancestral knowledge . . . to be passed to future generations" (Blackstock, 2007, p. 4).

FIGURE 1.1 Holism

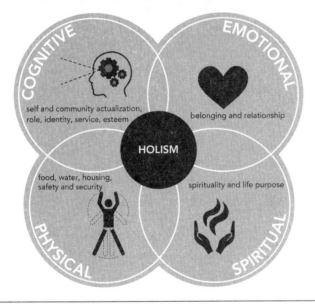

Adapted from the work of Cindy Blackstock and Terry Cross.

In this knowledge system, well-being (not incremental metric progress) is the ultimate goal, and the four elements of heart, spirit, mind, and body cannot be separated. Furthermore, "accountability" connotes *public* accountability to the community, not to a disembodied state or provincial entity. It is much easier for schools to be accountable for student learning and redressing historical harm when surrounded by elders and community leaders rather than anonymized in a "data set" (Blackstock & Bennett, 2007). The First Peoples Principles of Learning, developed by First Nations leaders in British Columbia (First Nations Education Steering Committee, 2015), embody holism and provide a compelling counternarrative to the dominant Western paradigm.

FIGURE 1.2   First Peoples Principles of Learning

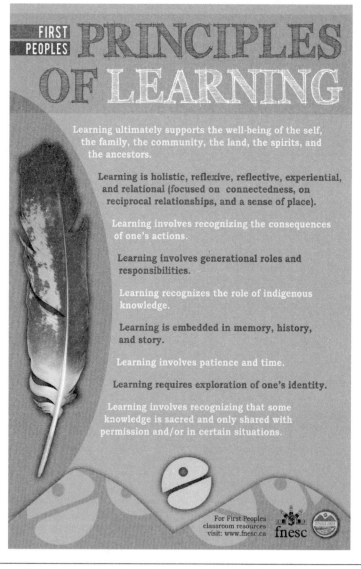

Source: First Nations Education Steering Committee. https://www.fnesc.ca.

Fulbright scholar Ronald Sentwali Bakari writes of an Afrocentric epistemology [that] "is rooted in spirituality, communalism, cooperation, ethics, and morality" (Bakari, 1997, p. 20). Bakari situates the idea of African American liberation at the center of this system of knowledge. This idea of the struggle for the liberation of the *mind* in the face of racism and oppression is an essential concept we will revisit throughout the book and is inextricably linked to deep learning. Bakari reminds us that critical consciousness—a hard-to-measure outcome of deep learning—emerges from collective struggle, the eradication of powerlessness, and being centered in African tradition, thought, and behavior.

It feels important here to note my subjectivity as a white female writer invoking scholars and thought leaders of color, as well as non-European epistemologies. To be clear, my intention is to honor the work on whose shoulders this book stands and to approach these discussions from a place of cultural humility. Throughout the book and in partnership with coauthor Dr. Dugan and contributing writers, I hope to decenter myself as an expert and position myself more as a co-conspirator in the long arc of struggle for social and racial justice.

Street data is a decolonizing form of knowledge that honors Indigenous, Afrocentric, and other non-Western ways of knowing. Street data emerges from human interaction, taking us down to the ground level to see, hear, and engage with the children and adults in our school communities—particularly those at the margins. With this book, we offer you an actionable framework for school transformation. Each section explores a different application of street data, from its capacity to help us flip the dashboard and diagnose root causes of inequity (Chapters 3–4), to its potential to transform learning (Chapters 5–7), to its power to reshape adult culture (Chapters 8–9).

At the heart of the book lies an existential question: Why do we rely on current forms of data, and what would happen if we simply stopped . . . and embraced a new model? To that end, we offer you three beliefs to guide your journey:

- **Data can be humanizing**

- **Data can be liberatory**

- **Data can be healing**

A Road Map for Your Journey

The book is organized into four sections that provide an integrated framework. In **Part I**, including this current chapter, we unpack *why* street data leads to equity and why we should embrace this model now. Having examined questions of epistemology and a vision of holism, we shift our sights in Jamila's beautifully written Chapter 2 to traps and tropes that undermine our well-intentioned equity efforts. We deliberately placed this chapter early in the book because Jamila discusses some of the most common barriers to progress in dismantling inequitable practices. She also helps us consider what it means to develop awareness of the complex dynamics of systemic racism, white supremacy, intersectionality, implicit bias, stereotype threat, and other foundational concepts.

FIGURE 1.3   The Street Data Framework

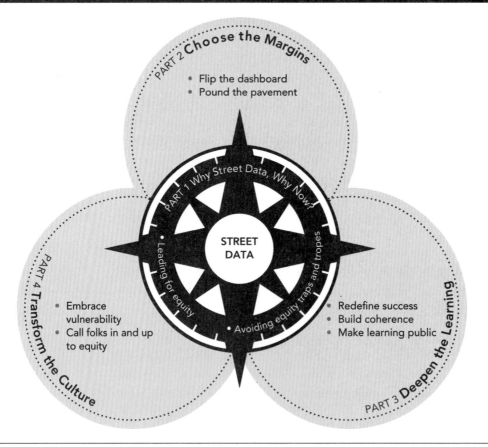

In **Part II**, we explore *what* is street data and *how* to leverage it in pursuit of equity. We consider what it means to "choose the margins" by centering the voices of the most disenfranchised in our communities. In practical chapters on how to "flip the dashboard" (Chapter 3) and "pound the pavement" (Chapter 4), we break down street data fundamentals: what it is, how to gather it, and how it can complement other forms of data to guide a school or district's equity journey. Part II offers an antidote to the pyramid approach: Invert top-down models of data collection and rehumanize the system by collecting and responding to a robust array of street data, in partnership with people at the margins.

In **Part III**, we consider how street data can transform student and adult learning, positing that equity work is first and foremost pedagogical. We braid together critical pedagogy, project-based learning, authentic performance-based assessment, and culturally responsive education into a vision of equitable pedagogy. In Chapter 5, we outline a *pedagogy of voice* in which student experiences drive instruction and student agency becomes our central metric. In Chapter 6, we discuss the conditions that need to cohere for a pedagogy of voice to take root. And in Chapter 7, contributing author Carrie Wilson lays out a model of public learning for educators that will foster symmetry between adult and student experiences.

Finally, in **Part IV**, we look at how street data can transform school culture and build momentum for equity. Chapter 8 offers concrete ways to move through equity transformation cycles with a stance of vulnerability and a commitment to antiracism. We close with Chapter 9, which outlines the type of day-to-day "warm demander" conversations that serve to disrupt systemic racism and bias and ensure that deep learning is accessible to every child. This aspirational chapter teaches us how to call each other *in* and *up* to the promise of equity.

Each chapter includes a principle and a core leadership stance to guide your journey (see Table 1.1). Throughout the book, you will find us toggling between the micro and the macro—from the small interactions between teacher and student or colleague and colleague, to the big implications of street data on how we pursue school and systems transformation.

In order to rebuild the current system, we must acknowledge the wounds we carry from decades of misguided reliance on big data. As educators, many of us have tried to do the right thing inside a

TABLE 1.1   Street Data Principles and Stances

CHAPTER	GUIDING PRINCIPLE	CORE STANCE
Part I: Why Street Data, Why Now?		
1	Reimagine our ways of knowing and learning.	Holism
2	See the barriers; imagine what is possible.	Awareness
Part II: Choose the Margins		
3	Center voices from the margins.	Antiracism
4	Seek root causes over quick fixes.	Deep Listening
Part III: Deepen the Learning		
5	Equity work is first and foremost pedagogical.	Agency
6	Less is more; focus is everything.	Coherence
7	Mobilize a pedagogy of voice for educators.	Symmetry
Part IV: Transform the Culture		
8	Break the cycle of shame.	Vulnerability
9	Every moment is an equity moment.	Warm Demander

broken paradigm and failed. The history of deflating data walks and under-resourced school buildings runs deep, and the wounds we carry are fractal in nature—patterns that replicate across every level of the system, just as the tiniest broccoli flower mirrors the largest floret. At the classroom level, the emphasis on Western ways of knowing has colored our vision of what's possible and reinforced transactional, often-oppressive pedagogies. At the school level, it has stripped many teachers and students of a sense of agency and efficacy. At the systems level, it has reinscribed racial hierarchies and white supremacy by trapping us all inside a false construct of an "achievement gap" that perpetuates a deficit story about students of color.

Until we fundamentally rethink the purpose of accountability, we will continue to rebuild the master's house with the same faulty tools. The big data paradigm privileges a narrow, dysfunctional pedagogy: students in rows "ingesting" content, anxiety over grades (a signature Western classification system), a narrowing of the curriculum in high-poverty schools where children most need access to deep learning. It's going to take a radical shift in approach to inspire the instructional transformation we need: deep, equitable, culturally sustaining learning.

We hope this book will offer you rich ways to describe what you see, hear, and experience every day. Fractal challenges require fractal solutions. Street data can act as a healing balm at every level of the system. This book will explore concrete ways to leverage street data in service of school transformation, from listening campaigns, to performance assessments, to exhibitions of learning, to a pedagogy of student voice. Join us on this journey. Our children and in many ways, our democracy, depend on it. Let's embrace a new way of being, learning, and doing.

GETTING UP CLOSE AND PERSONAL: REFLECTION QUESTIONS

1. "For all our talk of being student centered, we have bought into a success paradigm that robs many children of their voices, marginalizes their gifts, and prioritizes measurement and incremental improvement over learning and transformation" (page 12). What are your reactions to this quote? Do you agree, disagree, or something in between?

2. How has the press for big data and "results" impacted you and your community? What have you gained and/or lost?

3. In the section on epistemology ("How do we know what we know?"), what jumped out at you and why? Where did you find your ideas about data and knowledge challenged?

4. Do you believe the "achievement gap" is a mythology? Why or why not?

5. What resonates with you about the core stance of holism? What might a more holistic approach to teaching, learning, and school culture look like in your context?

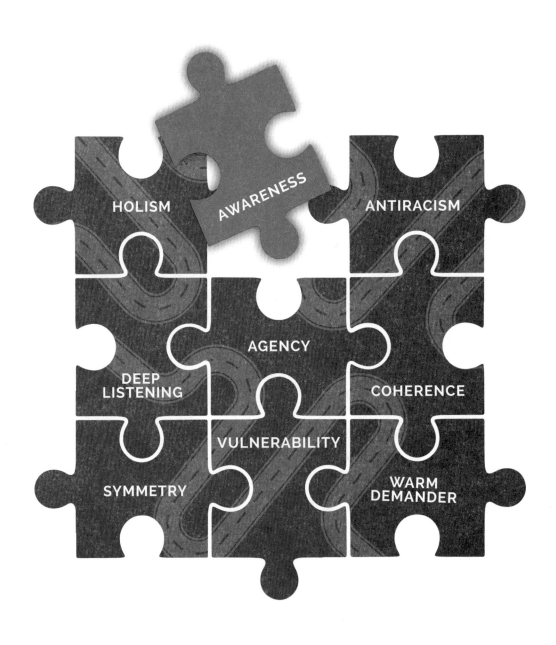

No Shortcut

Avoiding Equity Traps and Tropes

By Dr. Jamila Dugan

2

See the barriers; imagine what is possible.

Abolitionists want to remove what is oppressive, not reform it, not reimagine it, but remove oppression by its roots. Abolitionists want to understand the conditions that normalize oppression and uproot those conditions, too. Abolitionists, in the words of scholar and activist, Bill Ayers, "demand the impossible and work to build a world rooted in the possibilities of justice."

—Bettina Love

Six weeks ago, my dreams for the education system seemed to be fading. My son Kingston, who is considered "on grade level," was beginning to loathe school. He bemoaned not having enough time to run outside since recess had been cut to twenty minutes. *(The school's underlying mental model:[1] We need to maximize "instructional time"; playtime like recess is secondary to covering the standards.)* He felt bored taking notes during math lessons while his teacher lectured at the board. *(Mental model: "Engaging activities" are reserved for elective classes and special projects—engagement is the exception, not the rule.)* Kingston had been

---

[1] Systems theorist Peter Senge defines mental models as our theories about the way the world works that influence our actions and in turn influence the development of our systems and approaches (Senge, 2000).

spending his nightly reading time delving into stories of the Black experience that captured his imagination, but his teacher wrote a note directing him to read "new material" more closely related to the class content. *(Mental model: Standards and curriculum determine what students need to read, not their identity and interests.)*

As a parent and educator, I was becoming exasperated. Why was this happening? How could this Black boy full of curiosity, joy, and potential be starting to dislike school in the third grade? Maybe I should settle for what we've been told is the "right way" to educate students so that Kingston "performs" on his first standardized test at the end of the year. Maybe I should set my dreams aside.

Then, the COVID-19 pandemic erupted and *dis*rupted everything. Suddenly, I had to be an educator, a leader, and a mother to my two children in one house, 24–7, all at once. We had our essentials, and we had each other, but it still felt nearly impossible. It seemed like I couldn't accomplish anything. Our lives were rattled, and internally, I faced a new set of questions about the purpose of education. The reality of trying to educate two small children with limited time felt paralyzing, but it was also a painful reminder of what so many of our students and families go through all the time. It was soul-crushing.

I was transported back to myself as a young woman growing up in East Oakland, California—baffled at how the odds seemed to be intentionally stacked against me, my friends, and my family. I began to feel again the fire, agitation, and inspiration to dream that I had experienced when I first entered the teaching profession. There wasn't going to be a magic potion to help me figure this out. I needed to trust my gut, lean on my community for support, and ride the emotional rollercoaster of bringing my own vision for equity into my home.

As the ups and downs of pandemic life led me to reinvent schooling at home, I realized something: The dream of equitable education for every child is alive and well, but our system is designed for us to forget it. Our system is built to deprive us of imagination, especially when it comes to the learning and liberation of Black and brown children. In the moments of (slightly) less chaos in my household, I became a teacher without the constraints of "schooling," and my vision of child-centered learning reemerged.

Imagine a world where school feeds our innate creativity and where educators and students have the time and space to co-construct a vision for learning, not driven by mandates and test scores but by their deepest hopes and dreams for the future. In this world, students' developmental needs and interests drive instructional design. In this world, deep engagement is not a luxury; it is the baseline for every educator and child who enters the school doors. In this world, we are satisfied not by numbers on sporadic tests but rather by observing a moment of "knowing" in our children. This visceral delight rarely comes from a bubble-in test but from our experience of watching mastery happen in real time.

In this world, school and district leaders would see their work as removing barriers to teacher and student prosperity—like pruning in a garden. The more space, the more everyone thrives. **In this world, teachers share a commitment to cultivating the gifts and talents of their learners *and* they are given the time, tools, and trust to do it. They aren't asked to batch-process students who will be measured by white supremacist standards but to develop students who have the self-concept, competence, and agency to contribute to an ever-changing world. In this world, every student matters.**

This world is possible but challenging to manifest. The pressure and power baked into the DNA of an outdated system makes it feel nearly impossible—especially for those of us serving students and families at the margins of society.

That doesn't mean we aren't trying. Every day, before the pandemic, I walked into schools full of educators doing their best. Regardless of the context, the majority of teachers and principals I encountered wanted the best for themselves, their colleagues, and of course, their students. They could articulate a commitment to excellence and to ensuring that every student gets what they need to thrive. They held onto this commitment even when the educational system worked against their goals. These educators were and *are* operating with a fierce sense of passion and urgency, constantly trying to improve, and working long hours to make a difference in the lives of the people they care about most.

Under intense pressure from external forces, they aspire to be deemed "successful" by entities that are often disconnected from their day-to-day work. Sometimes it's the district or charter office: "We need to get to more equitable outcomes. There's an achievement gap, and we have to improve our test scores." And sometimes, it shows up inside our classrooms: "The curriculum says students have to know all of this material to prepare them for the state test." This could easily have been the behind-the-scenes experience of my son's teacher.

And yet . . .

Something doesn't feel right. There's a constant air of discomfort. In conversation after conversation, we acknowledge that we are suffering. Somehow, the dialogue about the achievement gap doesn't sit right. We talk the talk of test scores, but it doesn't sit well in our spirits. We appreciate the gold star for being a "successful" school, but we question if the success is real. At worst, we internalize a deficit frame—the problem lies in the children, not the system—subscribe to limited ways of defining success, and fall into equity traps and tropes.

So many of us enter the field of education with hopes that our work will meaningfully impact students. However, we are often asked to focus our attention on ways of teaching and learning that aren't always connected to those goals. We take a *satellite* view of student needs rather than being on the *street* in the details and joys of improving the student experience—a framework we will explore in this book.

What if I told you that equity has nothing to do with test scores and traditional metrics? What if I told you that benchmarks are not only a distraction from equity, they are often the very tools used to solidify and *justify* the perpetuation of inequity? What if I told you that trying to measure an equitable experience can happen right here, right now, side by side and in dialogue with the learner? What if we were able to pull out of the current paradigm and use our imagination to lead us to liberation?

Throughout this book, we seek to answer those questions. We will offer ways to flip the paradigm of how we design and measure the success of schooling from the macro or satellite view and take our work down to the micro moments—street data that can help us transform our schools. We must begin, though, with deeper awareness of what gets in the way. We must understand the landmines that lay before us as we attempt to redefine what it means to work toward equity in schools.

Awareness is the core stance of this chapter. Becoming aware of the shortcomings of the oppressive system within which we work is the first step toward dismantling it. Cultivating an awareness of common barriers to equity, such as prioritizing "silver bullet" solutions over deep learning, will take us beyond "good intentions" to meaningful change. This is the subject matter of the remainder of this chapter. With an understanding of some of the traps and tropes, we hope to offer framing vocabulary that will provide a lens to view the complexity of the work ahead.

Defining Terms: Equity, Traps, and Tropes

What does equity mean to us, your coauthors and guides along this journey? We ascribe to a simple definition that requires deliberate action. **Equity** is an approach to ensuring equally high outcomes for all by removing the predictability of success or failure that currently correlates with any racial, social, economic, or cultural factor.

Ensuring high outcomes for all is not a task that can be checked off a list. Equity isn't a destination but an unwavering commitment to a journey. It can be easy to focus on where we hope to land and lose sight of the deliberate *daily* actions that constitute the process. Day to day fires and the weight of the system make it enticing to hold others and not ourselves accountable. Thus, we reorient ourselves to **working *toward* equity**, which requires us to

- Acknowledge that our systems, practices, and narratives are designed to perpetuate disparities in outcomes for marginalized students

- Deliberately identify barriers that predict success or failure and actively disrupt them

- Consistently examine personal identity, bias, and both personal and collective contributions to the creation and/or reproduction of inequitable practices

- (Re) Allocate resources (tools, time, money, people, support) to ensure every child gets what they need to succeed to thrive socially, emotionally, and intellectually

- Cultivate the unique gifts, talents, and interests that every person possesses[2]

Street data—real time, on the ground, systematic information—is our guiding light as we work toward equity. It is going to take a radical shift in our data paradigm to propel the kind of instructional transformation we need: deep, equitable, culturally sustaining learning. The traps and tropes are landmines that exist to deter us from this understanding.

---

[2]This definition is adapted and amended from definitions offered by Promise 54, National Equity Project, and the work of researchers including Bell, 2005; Bensimon, 2005; Brayboy et al., 2007; DeCuir & Dixson, 2004; Delgado & Stefancic, 2012; Gotanda, 2004; Gutierrez & Jaramillo, 2006; Jencks, 1972; Noguera, 2008; Darling-Hammond, 2010; Ladson-Billings, 2006; Lynch & Baker, 2005; North, 2008 (all of these as cited by Galloway & Ishimaru, 2015).

A **trap** is a mechanism or device designed to catch and retain. It quickly allows entry but does not allow exit. A **trope** is a recurring theme we've seen happen before. Over my years as an educator, I have found myself and have watched others unintentionally fall victim to the very circumstances we are trying to change—stepping into oppressive traps and replaying oppressive tropes.

Exhibit A: Traps and Tropes in Action

A while back, I sat with a colleague who was frustrated about the lack of progress she was seeing in her school. Ashleigh shared that student attendance was decreasing, staff frustration with administration was increasing, and despite many hours of collaborative work, classroom instruction had failed to change. I asked her what she was focusing on for the year.

> *We've had inequitable outcomes for our African American and Latinx males for a while, including disproportionality in suspensions and lower passage rates in English, Science, and Math exams. The leadership team agreed this needed to be addressed. We brainstormed and decided to first make sure our vision statement named a commitment to equity so that all of our staff would understand our dedication to the work. We also realized that we needed to be doing work around culturally responsive teaching, bias, and community engagement. We knew we couldn't do all of it at once, so we decided to focus on culturally responsive teaching (CRT). We developed a plan to have our teachers do a book study around CRT, and the leadership team developed a checklist of observable practices we wanted to see in the classrooms. The checklist made our leadership team feel really good that we were finally doing equity work! We started all of our planning sessions by reading our new vision statement and made sure that every teacher was consistently observed, using the checklist. Despite all of that, we saw no real change. I just don't know what I am missing at this point.*

I could tell she was at her wits' end. Ashleigh and I are African American women who have had ongoing conversations about systemic racism and the importance of being change agents. She wasn't short on commitment, resilience, or follow-through. How could she and her team have done so much and seen so little movement?

Exhibit B: Traps and Tropes in Action

Gary, a white male central office leader, and I are close colleagues but have different beliefs about how to support Black and brown students to thrive. Despite our differences, I have appreciated his contributions to my learning over time. Recently, Gary helped a team of educators open a new school that serves predominantly Black students. I asked him to update me on how the school was doing and quickly experienced déjà vu: as Gary spoke, I felt just like I had during my conversation with Ashleigh.

> *You know that I am very excited about this school. The leaders are committed to making sure that students of color have a great place to learn. The idea is that if the school has a strong standards-aligned curriculum and community engagement, students will feel deeply connected and achieve at high levels.*

> *Right now, it's a new school. We are experiencing growing pains. When you look at classrooms, students aren't yet engaged or feeling particularly connected, but the leadership team is working on it. The lead team hired a new dean of culture and they're hoping that he will be able to help engage the families and students.*

I will admit: In talking to Gary, a white man, the reference to hiring a new dean of culture raised my racial antennae. I decided to pull up the website and look at the school demographics. I found that the only Black staff members in this school of 94 percent Black students were the teacher's assistants, two out of fourteen certificated teachers, and, as I had predicted, the new dean of culture. Every other staff member was white. I asked him if he was concerned about the staffing demographics, and he told me the following:

> *Everyone is committed to doing the best work for kids at this school. It isn't right to say that just because someone is not the same race as the students, they can't create a great place for kids to learn. The staff <u>cares</u> about equity. They know that they need to add staff of color, which is why they hired the new dean. They have two awesome trainers coming in during their summer professional development, and they are going to learn about restorative practices, so I fully expect that the classroom and school culture will improve.*

This conversation reminded me of how our prevailing approach to educational reform makes it possible, even likely, to fall into traps and tropes that are harmful to kids, tokenize educators of color, and reinforce the blinders our colleagues wear. We gravitate toward test scores and satellite-level understandings of community needs and take action guided by what we *think* versus what we *know* from those who are most important; students, caretakers, and staff on the street. Gary and his colleagues had good intentions, but I was struck by how they had been undermining their own efforts almost from the start. Thinking back to my conversations with Ashleigh and Gary, their situations were different but evoked the same feeling in me. Ashleigh wasn't seeing results and Gary, by the end of the school year, had lost the two Black teachers, 30 percent of his students, and community partnerships had never come to fruition. Both were working hard, but their progress toward equity had stopped before it even started.

What Are the Equity Traps and Tropes at Play in These Scenarios?

As I reflected earlier, we've been viewing our educational system through a lens and discourse that has reinforced deficit narratives about Black and brown students, promoted narrow definitions of success, and reproduced inequitable outcomes over and over again. We fully *intend* to work toward equity, yet we have internalized the wrong set of change drivers (Fullan & Quinn, 2015; Mintrop, 2016), tipping us over and over again into equity traps and tropes.

In the following section, we examine ten common equity traps and tropes, deconstructing what it looks and sounds like to fall *into* the trap. The following chapters offer a robust guide for getting ourselves out.

Equity Tropes and Traps

TABLE 2.1 Traps and Tropes at a Glance	
TRAPS AND TROPES	DESCRIPTION
Doing equity	Treating equity as series of tools, strategies, and compliance tasks versus a whole-person, whole-system change process linked to culture, identity, and healing

TRAPS AND TROPES	DESCRIPTION
Siloing equity	Locating equity work in a separate and siloed policy, team, or body
Equity warrior	Nesting equity with a single champion and holder of the vision
Spray and pray equity	Engaging "equity experts" to drop in for a training with no ongoing plan for learning or capacity building
Navel-gazing equity	Keeping the equity work at the level of self-reflection and failing to penetrate the instructional core and/or school systems and structures (e.g., instructional planning, student tracking)
Structural equity	Redesigning systems and structures (e.g., master schedule) without investing in the deeper personal, interpersonal, and cultural shifts
Blanket equity	Investing in a program or curriculum rather than building the capacity of your people to address equity challenges as complex and ongoing places of inquiry
Tokenizing equity	Asking leaders of color to hold, drive, and symbolically represent equity without providing support and resources to thrive nor engaging the entire staff in the work
Superficial equity	Failing to take time to build equity-centered knowledge and fluency, leading to behavioral shifts without understanding deeper meaning or historical context
Boomerang equity	Investing time and resources to understand your equity challenges but reverting back to recycled, status quo solutions

1. **Doing equity**: Treating equity as a series of tools, strategies, and compliance tasks versus a whole-person, whole-system change process linked to culture, identity, and healing

    In the first story, Ashleigh struggled to see progress as a result of the investments her team was making. Her team accelerated from a commitment to addressing inequities in their building to immediately taking action—following a well-prescribed program for creating change. When something is not working, you "do" something else. We've been taught to find the framework, the new observation checklist, or the new teaching approach and to implement it without deeply understanding what we are doing and how it connects to our overall goals. In Ashleigh's case, the team uncovered that there was racial disproportionality in their suspensions and standardized test data. With this information, they identified a problem and found a "solution": pursuing culturally responsive teaching in book groups. Scholars have long cautioned against this approach. Working toward equity is not a journey of implementation. The work requires us to understand the specific ways inequity plays out in our context, to engage in praxis—the integration of constant reflection and action (Freire, 1970)—and to engage in a continuous cycle of learning. (Chapters 3 and 7 will illuminate how street data can animate and fuel such a cycle.) "Doing equity" reduces the complexity of our work to a set of straightforward tasks without thinking about the school as a complex ecosystem requiring a holistic approach to change.

2. **Siloing equity**: Locating the equity work in a separate and siloed policy, team, or body

   Look at the strategic plans of many organizations and schools working toward equity: You will likely find a policy, new "equity" vision statement, or a newly formed task force designed to increase equitable outcomes. These task forces may generate good ideas and even strong plans. Siloing equity happens when these task forces are disconnected from the overall work of the school or system. For example, if the equity task force sets priorities for increasing staff diversity but the broader staff cannot articulate those goals, then working toward equity in the task force is likely a siloed effort. If the task force meets as a unit but never engages with any other body in the system—*especially* those related to instruction—the work toward equity is likely siloed. Siloing equity leads us to believe that equity is separate from instruction, which is separate from culture, which is separate from every other aspect of student experience and learning.

3. **Equity warrior**: Nesting equity within a single champion and holder of the vision

   The equity warrior is an incredible educator, often treated as a martyr for their work. This person is eager to push their colleagues and school forward and willing to take on significant additional work to bring the team along. Unfortunately, the equity warrior can easily become the default holder of the school or system's vision for equity, allowing colleagues to opt out, stay inside their comfort zones, or refuse to invest in their own equity learning, which is critical to the change effort. When "siloing equity" is at play, this person is often asked to be the lone voice for change. In the example of hiring for staff diversity, the school administration may ask the equity warrior to join the hiring committee and ask at the end, "So what do you think of this candidate? Are they an 'equity teacher'?" Despite the school or district's espoused commitment to equity, it's the warrior's job to make it happen. The equity warrior can be elevated for their contributions or sometimes obliterated for them. In either scenario, the work rests on their shoulders, and if they are not present, the work tends to fizzle out.

It is hard to be an equity warrior regardless of your identity. However, it is important to name that not all equity warrior experiences are created equal.

Tropes Within the Equity Warrior Trap: The Great White Hope and the Lone Ranger of Color

The Lone Ranger of Color

Racism puts enough burdens on educators of color; white colleagues can't also expect them to end it.

—Clarice Brazas and Charlie McGeehan

This trope can be hard to spot in its early stages. A school team is excited to elevate the leadership of a staff member of color and shower them with praise for taking on the work. As time goes on and the work gets deeper, the burden on the Lone Ranger of Color begins to increase. The Lone Ranger asks colleagues to demonstrate coalition and cross-racial leadership for equity, only to have white colleagues treat these requests as an add-on ("I already have too much on my plate."). They are asked to be the resident culture and behavior specialist when white colleagues are unsure what to do. At worst, they're encouraged to bring ideas to the table, but when they step into their power and express a dissenting view, they have the devastating experience of being subtly or overtly reprimanded. There is nothing worse than turning a passionate advocate into a lone soldier in charge of carrying the weight for everyone.

The Great White Hope

The White Savior Industrial Complex is not about justice. It is about having a big emotional experience that validates privilege.

—Teju Cole

The Great White Hope trope rests in a savior mentality—the belief that it is this person's responsibility to rescue students of color from an oppressive situation or even from themselves. This leader has been to antiracism conferences, read equity-focused literature, and is committed to the cause. The trap is to view this leader as an equity "expert" rather than a dedicated, lifelong equity *student*. We are in dangerous territory when this leader is elevated for their warriorship while silencing the leaders of color around them. Sometimes, the leader may have a decisive approach to school improvement, much like Gary and his colleagues, but proceed to cherry-pick approaches to fit their (often misguided) perspective around what is "right" for kids. This leader may be valorized in a way that leads to the behavior we saw in Gary's white colleagues—a stance that says, "We know more than you. We are here to save you." This is a song of the colonizer's tongue: "As long as you listen to me, you shall be set free." If the leader is called out for this behavior, they can often become defensive and begin to attack those attempting to bring awareness to their entitled position (often, the Lone Ranger of Color). This leader must be vigilant in developing awareness of their positionality in the work, as they have the potential to undermine working toward equity under the guise of heroism. White leaders must be careful of their approach to leadership and see much of their work as uplifting the voices of others, holding other white people accountable, and taking action in coalition with people of color.

4. **Spray and pray equity**: Engaging "equity experts" to drop in for a training with no ongoing plan for learning and capacity-building

   Gary and his colleagues felt strongly that if they had summer trainers come in to help their staff learn about restorative practices, the staff would become more equity centered. Many of us are convinced that if we just get the right trainer, including someone like myself, everything will be "fixed." A common refrain Shane and I hear is, "If we just train our teachers around their implicit biases, then they will treat students better." While such training may benefit staff, training without a commitment to ongoing learning and development will likely result in temporary or no change. Sleeter (1992) found that even when teachers receive long-term daily training for a full six weeks, change in their practice dissipates within three months. Authentic commitment to working toward equity requires a comprehensive approach to capacity-building, including coaching, reflection, and collaborative learning processes, which we'll discuss in Chapters 5, 6, and 7. Imagine breaking all of your bad habits after a one-day training. Highly unlikely.

5. **Navel-gazing equity**: Keeping the equity work at the level of self-reflection and failing to penetrate the instructional core and school systems and structures (e.g., master schedule, tracking)

It would be unfair to say that there aren't schools and organizations across the country doing deep work around issues of equity. Another trap that we can fall into, though, is having our deep work live in one part of a complex puzzle. Navel-gazing equity may look like a staff that completes training around bias, privilege, and identity but never takes that work into any other domain of the school. How do bias and privilege show up in our academic counseling systems, disciplinary procedures, grading, and so forth? Transformation requires investment in personal and interpersonal development, awareness and creation of shared cultural practices, and the redesign of inequitable systems—all at the same time. I've seen countless schools and districts make heavy investments into personal transformation work for themselves and their staff, but if you ask them what systems or structures they've changed as a result, there is often a long pause . . . followed by silence. If you ask them how their adult *culture* has shifted, another pause. It is easy to spot navel-gazing equity when a group of staff members participate in bias training and then proceed to engage in instructional and leadership planning in a business-as-usual fashion without applying the personal work to transform the system.

6. **Structural equity**: Redesigning systems and structures (e.g., master schedule) without investing in the deeper personal, interpersonal, and cultural shifts

Structural equity is the converse of navel-gazing equity. Many eager educators are ready to radically change their systems—so much so that they figure out the biggest shift they can make to disrupt an inequitable system—for example, exchanging the use of suspensions for restorative justice. There is clear research that suspensions can cause great harm to students (Losen & Gillespie, 2012), and making systematic shifts to counteract those effects is a courageous move. However, many leaders fall into the dangerous trap of making a seismic shift without recognizing the political, social, and cultural impact of the change. Does our staff understand and agree with the new approach of restorative justice? Are we well-grounded in both the theory *and* the practices? What instructional and leadership practices will need to change to make this more than a cosmetic shift? How much time will we need to invest in starting and reinforcing the shift? How will we need to engage our families in the change process? People don't accept changes simply because they are executed at a structural level. There must be an equal investment in the interpersonal, cultural, and social dimensions for all of the players involved in the process. Moves like eliminating suspensions, de-tracking, or extending the school day may be a result of thoughtful research and great intentions, but we set ourselves up to flounder if we fail to align structural changes with the deep learning our teams must do to actualize them.

7. **Blanket equity**: Investing in a program or curriculum rather than building the capacity of your people to address equity challenges as complex and ongoing places of inquiry

   Ever heard the phrase, "There is an app for that"? Well, if you want to achieve equitable outcomes, there is apparently a curriculum for that. Students aren't learning at similar levels. *Great, this new curriculum will fix that.* Students don't feel safe and valued. *Great, there is a program for that.* While curriculum can be a helpful tool, schools across the country have made sweeping investments in buying new curriculum, hoping that if educators just follow the material, all students will achieve. This trap can cause leaders to become hyper-focused on accountability and implementation, completely forgetting that if equity could be addressed by curriculum, we would have solved our nation's greatest challenge years ago. Whether you opt to use curriculum as a tool or not, our work requires stitching together a quilt with many different textures and features. A blanket will not do.

8. **Tokenizing equity**: Asking leaders of color to hold, drive, and symbolically represent equity without providing support and resources, nor engaging the entire staff in the work

   In my earlier example with Gary, I shared that when he mentioned his mostly white staff had hired a new dean of culture, my racial antennae went up. I was worried that the school had fallen into a trope that can emerge from the mental model of the Great White Hope leader: "I know everything about leadership and instruction, but culture, climate, and the behavior of our students? We'll leave that to you, expert leader of color." A mostly white team of educators is hired, and one of the few people of color, usually a Black or brown person, is thrust into the "culture" role and implicitly asked to be the Lone Ranger of Color. This may be the security guard, the parent liaison, or the teacher who is given the "difficult" class. These are extremely important positions, but when a staff is predominantly white and the few leaders of color have to play these roles, a dangerous, implicit message is sent: "You are responsible for dealing with 'these' students."

Tokenizing equity can also look like asking a staff member of color to take on the equity initiative because we assume it is personally important to them. "I know how much equity work means to you. You've helped us realize a lot of our missteps, so I am wondering if you'd be willing to lead our equity task force." I've heard this type of refrain too many times, and it does nothing but deplete our colleagues' internal resources, reinforce oppression, create Lone Rangers, and leave educators who have racial privilege with little responsibility to change.

9. **Superficial equity**: Failing to take time to build knowledge and fluency around issues of equity, leading to behavioral shifts without understanding deeper meaning or historical context

Superficial equity essentially amounts to grasping any equity-centered practice with little understanding of its origins, its purpose, and how to engage in it with depth and authenticity. In both Ashleigh and Gary's example, there was clear evidence of this trope. In moving through the "doing equity" trope, Ashleigh's team decided to "do" culturally responsive teaching (CRT). CRT isn't something to "do"; you can and should not attempt to engage in culturally responsive teaching or any practice without understanding its history, building deep knowledge of its meaning, and practicing the work on your own. In Ashleigh's school, CRT was reduced to practices on an observation checklist, which created a superficial attempt to move toward equity. In Gary's example, educators developed a vision for an equitable, community-based school that served 94 percent Black students but led the school with a 90 percent white staff. It is nearly impossible to demonstrate to families, students, and staff that your pledge is authentic when your behavior demonstrates a lack of understanding of what you are committing to and doing.

10. **Boomerang equity:** Investing time and resources to understand your equity challenges but reverting back to previous mental models in ways that lead to unintentionally harmful solutions (e.g., measuring progress toward equity solely through state testing exams)

Boomerang equity may be one of the hardest tropes of all to disrupt. It is the trope that feeds itself back to the econometric, test-driven education frame we seek to dismantle. Many organizations and schools may actually arrive at a deep under-standing of why they are facing equity challenges. However, boomerang equity happens when we move from a deep under-standing of our challenge (i.e., increased suspensions for Latinx students) to immediately brainstorming solutions that mirror everything we've ever tried before. "Our Latinx students are being suspended because they aren't engaged. To help them get engaged, we must increase their confidence in school and the support we offer." Here is where it boomerangs. "Let's pull them out for intervention. This way, we can help them read more. We will assess them every six weeks and by the end of the year, we should see less suspensions and higher achievement on the state exam." In this example, we've gone from promising analysis to harmful decisions leaving the team who did such thoughtful work back to where they started.

The dominant narrative about what schools are and how they should treat students—especially those of color—has got us beat. Our sense of urgency gets in the way of understanding complex-ity, and it feels too hard to disrupt the current state of things. Reflecting deeply about how we are contributing to our predic-ament takes too much time. We ingest such a constant prescrip-tion of how to create equitable change that we sometimes miss the forest for the trees. Another world is possible. I've experienced it as a student. I've felt it in classrooms that I will never forget, and now, I've worked with friends and colleagues to recreate schooling for our own children during an unprecedented pandemic. The potential impact couldn't be any more clear.

Awareness: A Core Stance for Climbing Out of the Traps and Tropes

The core stance for this chapter is awareness. One of the things that makes the traps and tropes so seductive is the way we've been taught to engage with change—our discourse and approaches reflect a lack of understanding of how complex our challenges really are. In Ashleigh's case, the leadership team went from a concern around Latino male achievement to a checklist for culturally responsive teaching. Gary's team diagnosed the problem as students failing to meet standards and decided they needed a new school to boost test scores. Equity challenges require us to build awareness of our default discourse and behaviors that lead us to approach the work as if it is complicated rather than complex.

If we are to meaningfully shift our paradigm toward street data, there are specific concepts we must tune into. In the Fluency First sidebar, you'll find a few essential terms we will use throughout the book to bring complexity to the work and become more aware of the traps and tropes.

FLUENCY FIRST: CORE CONCEPTS

Complex Versus Complicated Challenges

Complicated Challenges

The solution to the challenge is not immediately obvious but can be known prior to taking action. These challenges are hard to solve but can be addressed by assembling the right technical expertise. Examples of complicated challenges include

- Designing a middle school master schedule to de-track classes

- Increasing diversity by hiring more staff of color

Complex Challenges

The solution to the challenge is not known and can only be seen or known during or after the action unfolds. Equity challenges are complex in nature. There is no set of steps or algorithm that will tell you how to respond. Examples include

- Shifting the adult culture so that de-tracked classrooms feel inclusive for every learner

- Creating an inclusive and collaborative staff culture in which Black, Indigenous, and brown staff are valued, empowered, and able to be authentic

White Supremacy

White supremacy is the global system that confers unearned power and privilege on those who become identified as white while conferring disprivilege and disempowerment on those who become identified as people of color. While white supremacy is a system of beliefs and structures created by white people, it can also infiltrate the ideologies and actions of people of color as well. Luis Urrieta (2010) explains, "whitestreaming" begins in schools through a curriculum that is founded

(Continued)

(Continued)

upon the "practices, principles, morals, and values" of white supremacy (Aronson & Boveda, 2017).

Anti-Black racism:

A feature of white supremacy, anti-Blackness is a two-part formation that both strips Blackness of value (dehumanizes) and systematically marginalizes Black people. This form of racism is overt, historical, and embedded in all of our institutions. Beneath anti-Black racism lies the covert structural and systemic racism that is held in place by anti-Black policies, institutions, and ideologies. Anti-Blackness is also the disregard for Black institutions and policies privileging outside practices over Black traditions.

Defining anti-Black racism is important as white supremacy is not a system of oppression that operates under a "one size fits all" approach. Instead, it targets people differently depending on how much capital it takes from a particular community and how much power and brutality it wields over them. In other words, the difference between anti-Blackness and white supremacy is that anti-Blackness in the United States is a more pervasive, systematic and brutal form of white supremacy (Council for the Democratizing Education, n.d.).

Settler colonialism:

A feature of white supremacy, settler colonialism involves the removal and erasure of Indigenous peoples in order to take land for use by settlers for permanent use. According to Laura Hurwitz and Shawn Borque's *Settler Colonialism Primer*, "This means that settler colonialism is not just a vicious thing of the past, such as the gold rush, but exists as long as settlers are living on appropriated land and thus exists today."

Settler-colonialism plays out in the erasure of Indigenous presence and the ongoing dispossession of land and other resources from Indigenous peoples. For example, American schools rarely teach about Native Americans, past or present; when they do, information is often distorted or incomplete.

Students are rarely taught about contemporary Native peoples who have survived the settler-colonial process and continue to thrive, create, practice their traditions, and live modern lives (A. Morris, 2019).

BIPOC

Black, Indigenous, and People of Color (BIPOC) is used to highlight the unique relationship to whiteness that Indigenous and Black (African Americans) people have, which shapes the experiences of and relationship to white supremacy for all people of color within a U.S. context (BIPOC Project, n.d.).

Intersectionality

Intersectionality is a theory and way of framing the various interactions between race, gender, and other identities as well as explaining how systems of oppression interact with each other in complex ways to impact people's lived experiences. Intersectionality acknowledges the nuances of our human experiences based on how the social world is constructed. For example, it is often assumed that diversity will improve students' schooling experience by simply adding a person of color to staff. Intersectionality asks us to consider, for example, what it means for a Latino male teacher who attended the school in which he works to work alongside a majority of white female staff who live outside of the city. Another example is how LGBTQIA youth of color experience particular intersections of oppression in schooling that marginalize them and have deleterious effects on social, academic, and mental health (Crenshaw, 1989, 1991).

Implicit Bias

Implicit biases stem from implicit associations we harbor in our subconscious that cause us to have feelings and attitudes about other people based on characteristics such as race, ethnicity, age, and appearance. These associations are activated involuntarily and without individual awareness as they develop over the course of a lifetime beginning at an early age through exposure to direct and indirect messages. In addition to early life experiences, the media and news programming are often-cited origins of implicit associations (Kirwan Institute, 2015).

(Continued)

(Continued)

Stereotype Threat

Stereotype threat is a theory developed by social psychologist Claude Steele to describe how the performance of women, people of color, and others often dips in the face of the psychic threat of being viewed as inferior. As this threat persists over time, students may feel pressured to protectively disidentify with achievement in school. This protects the person against the self-evaluative threat posed by the stereotypes but may have the by-product of diminishing interest, motivation, and ultimately, school achievement (Steele & Aronson, 1995).

Stereotype threat is an unappreciated source of classic deficits in standardized test performance suffered by Black students and other stereotype-threatened groups such as those of lower SES and women in mathematics (Herrnstein, 1973; Jensen, 1969, 1980; Spencer & Steele, 1994).

VOICES FROM THE STREET

Students

"Yesterday, my math teacher was saying if you're Chinese or Vietnamese, it's easier for you to learn math than if you're Latino. This is an example of him not knowing that he is essentially discouraging students of Latin descent. The non-Asians were joking around, 'Maybe that's why I'm stupid.' I am not sure all of our teachers know the harm this can cause."

—High school student, San José, California

It is our hope that reading the equity traps and tropes allows you to see the ways in which the system has set us up for false starts. Our intentions may be spot on, but if we aren't aware of our discourse, understanding, and the moves we are making, we are liable to reinforce the system we seek to dismantle. In summary, we argue that there are no shortcuts when it comes to leading for equity. If we hope to transform our institutions into vibrant spaces of learning for every student, we must revisit the fundamental purpose of education and commit to a long-term change process.

GETTING UP CLOSE AND PERSONAL: REFLECTION QUESTIONS

1. Which traps and tropes sound or feel familiar to you?

2. How does the author's series of provocations around how we approach working toward equity align with or challenge your beliefs?

3. Where do you see a trap or trope playing out in your school or organizational context?

4. What traps or tropes might students and families identify in your context? Are they the same or different from the ones you identified? Why might that be?

5. How does reading the essential terms influence your understanding of the traps and tropes?

Choose the Margins

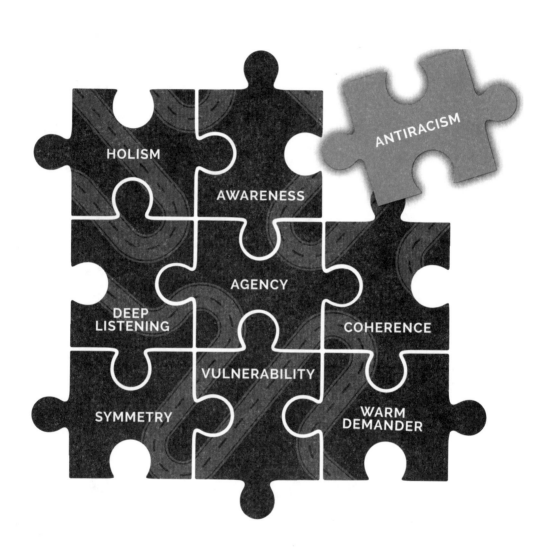

Flip the Dashboard
Street Data Drives Equity

3

Center voices from the margins.

Dashboard Blues

I am sitting around the superintendent's conference table in a diverse, urban school district alongside local parent leaders, teachers, and administrators. The district is a microcosm of California's shifting state demographics: 64 percent of students are Latinx, 70 percent are current or former English language learners (ELs), and twenty-five distinct language groups coexist here. For the past couple of months, I have been helping the superintendent (now in his fourth year and atypical for his staying power) lead a community engagement process to develop a strategic plan.

Tonight, we are serving up Dashboard Data—the state's latest metric system to assess student and school performance—to this group of forty stakeholders. The handouts before us light up in red, orange, yellow, and green.

Arrows jut out to form various angles as community members try to make heads or tails of the graphics. (Later, a parent tells me, "The data is not easy to understand . . . you don't relate to what it means right away. You can compare your own group with other groups, sure, but then you start asking the question: *Why are we at the bottom?*") Blue represents the Dashboard's high-performing hue; notably, the only blue on this page is associated with the marker "No Students." The mood is somber.

A Spanish-speaking mother suddenly speaks up: "Why are our children doing so poorly? Why are the Asian students doing

FIGURE 3.1   Sample Dashboard Data

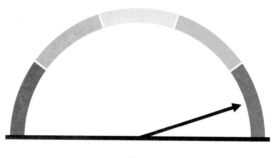

Blue

No Students

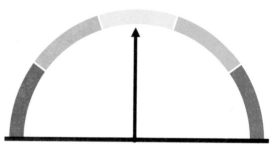

Yellow

American Indian
Hispanic
Socioeconomically Disadvantaged
White

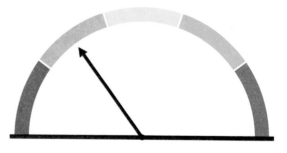

Orange

African American
English Learners
Homeless
Two or More Races
Pacific Islander
Students With Disabilities

better? What can we *do* about this?" An African American mother chimes in: "And what are doing for our homeless students? They are performing among the lowest, and we have nothing in place to support them!" Both women—powerful and engaged parent leaders—are near tears as they pose these questions, and I sense an overwhelming paralysis in the room. Not only is the Dashboard making these parents ask hard questions, it's leaving all of us without solutions or a real direction—only a gloomy sense of Groundhog Day. *Here we go again . . . more confirming data on our most vulnerable students.*

When our small group rejoins the other stakeholders, the teachers in the room are quick to speak up. "I don't trust this data," says a respected veteran and union leader. "It's not accurate, thorough, or helpful." Parents around the room nod their heads in agreement. In a post-mortem conversation, the assistant superintendent of Educational Services acknowledges the weightiness of the Dashboard conversation: "What's happened in public education is that we're told over and over again that there is something wrong, but it never helps us understand *what* is wrong, *why* it's wrong, and what to *do* to fix it."

I leave this meeting feeling like we have failed the community tonight. By offering Dashboard graphics without context, human story, or an explicitly antiracist lens, we have done a disservice to the students and parents in the room. We have contributed to a relentless deficit narrative about the "achievement gap" facing historically marginalized students, and I feel us heading straight for the equity traps and tropes. Isn't there a fuller story to be told? Isn't there another way to understand what is happening for the students of this district?

The Core Stance of Antiracism: Why We Must Flip the Dashboard

> *The heartbeat historically of racism has been denial . . . has been to deny that one's ideas are racist, one's policies are racist, and certainly that one's self and one's nation is racist . . . By contrast, the heartbeat of antiracism is confession, is admission, is acknowledgement, is the willingness to be vulnerable.*
>
> —Ibrahim X. Kendi, *Unlocking Us* podcast, June 3, 2020

In this chapter, we explore the question, *What is street data; how is it antiracist; and how can we collect it?* We consider whose voices are habitually included, tokenized, or silenced as we pursue "improvement" inside a broken model. We also choose the margins, flipping the dashboard upside down to center the experiences of those who matter most: not policymakers and certainly not test makers but the families, students, and educators who breathe life into learning. Māori scholar Linda Tuhiwai Smith writes that the metaphor of the margin has served as a powerful symbol for understanding social inequality, oppression, disadvantage, and power as well as hidden sources of wisdom. Xicana writer Gloria Anzaldua invoked the idea of the *frontera*, or borderland, for this same purpose, while African American author and activist bell hooks wrote of the "radical possibility of 'choosing the margin' as a site of belonging as much as a site of struggle and resistance" (Smith, 2012). Far from places of weakness or impoverishment, the margins are sites of deep cultural wealth and community wisdom.

Flipping the dashboard is an act of antiracism; it requires courage, vulnerability (which we'll revisit in Chapter 8), and an explicitly antiracist stance, defined by scholar Ibrahim X. Kendi as the belief that "racial groups are equals and none needs developing, and . . . supporting policy that reduces racial inequity" (Kendi, 2019). The satellite data testing complex has long promoted the myth that students of color "need developing"—translated: Black, Indigenous, and brown students are broken and schooling will fix them. **To walk the next-generation path of street data, we have to be vulnerable enough to reject this racist lie and stare down the parts of our *own* practice that need to be fixed. We need to confess, admit, acknowledge, and own our racial bias and the racism baked into our institutions.** This means listening deeply to students and families, even (or especially!) when their voices are hard to hear.

Student voices are incontrovertible. We can't dismiss, deny, quantify, or rationalize away the voices and experiences of children at the margins. Allow them to be truthtellers and moral compasses for what you say you believe about equity, but learn to listen deeply without boomeranging into past practice. By choosing the margins as the starting point for our data conversations—those quiet places where the hopes, dreams, and stories of our most disenfranchised students and families live—we invert the pyramid, shift the dynamics of power, and bring children to the center of educational discourse. Street data offers us an operational framework for choosing the margins, as we redefine what it means to work toward equity.

REIMAGINING THE SYSTEM

It's time to repurpose data from a tool for accountability and oppression to a tool for learning and transformation. Let's imagine a new kind of dashboard that lights up with green opportunity zones—classrooms and schools where students of color, LGBTQIA students, and students with diverse abilities experience identity, belonging, and deep learning. This dashboard would be coupled with a professional-learning infrastructure that supports educators to visit, study, and learn from these spaces of equity and opportunity.

Street data will help us pivot from blind compliance with external mandates to cultivating local, human-centered, critical judgment. What if we were to shift our systems change framework from dashboards and ratings toward reflective review processes that are rooted in student and family voices? What if we invested in the observation and analysis skills of trained educators rather than depending on test developers and policymakers to tell us who's successful? What if reflective review teams comprised of educators, parents, and students developed lines of inquiry around a school-based asset or opportunity versus a perceived "gap"?

With this shift in orientation, states and provinces could design and regionalize reflective review models that invert the paradigm and center the expertise of parents, students, and others. Instead of being punitive, school reviews would aim to build local educator capacity by offering recommendations grounded in street data. For example, the review team would interview students and teachers and observe classrooms to capture data on student-teacher interactions, teacher commentary, equitable patterns of student participation, ratios of positive to negative student feedback, and other low-inference data. Teams would gather lots of street data and then sit down to analyze it for growth opportunities.

In such an inverted system, we would

- Create opportunity maps for each state and region, highlighting schools that are centering student voice to imagine new approaches and identify culturally sustaining practices.

- Fund learning visits for educators to get a street-level view of an antiracist school or district that uses student experience, student

(Continued)

(Continued)

work, and other ground-up data to design instruction and adult learning.[1]

- Develop high-quality surveys and focus groups around student belonging and connection, using an explicitly antiracist lens to gain insight into what enables young people to thrive.

- Investigate and measure student agency: What helps a child develop a sense of purpose and efficacy in the world, and what can schools do to cultivate that?

- Start any staff or student-learning process with an inquiry question, such as how do my students learn best, or at the district level, how do families say our students learn best? Identify ways to gather this data, including those highlighted in this chapter.

- Use learning walks to gather street data on our line of inquiry, focusing our notes on close observations of students' responses to various pedagogies (projects, discussions, etc).

- As we gather meaningful information about our students, continuously ask and observe their experiences through ongoing equity transformation cycles (see Chapters 4 and 8).

- When students leave us, do exit interviews with fidelity and an anti-racist lens asking how they experienced agency, connection, and belonging. Use these data to push ourselves to adjust our approaches the following year.

None of this can be uncovered through test scores or other big data.

The Levels of Data

To transform the system, we need a new framework for thinking about data. In my first book, *The Listening Leader: Creating the Conditions for Equitable School Transformation* (Safir, 2017b), I introduced a framework called the Levels of Data that takes center stage in this book. Drawing on the work of assessment expert W. James Popham, I argued that we are using the wrong data to make our most important

---

[1]A word of caution here: Visitors would be asked not to *replicate* what they see in a visit but to take a learning stance in adapting powerful practices to their local context.

FIGURE 3.2 Levels of Data

Levels of Data

Level 1
Satellite Data

Large grain size.

Illuminate patterns of achievement, equity, and teacher quality and retention.

Point us in a general direction for further investigation.

Level 2
Map Data

Medium grain size.

Help us to identify reading, math, and other student skill gaps (e.g., decoding, fluency, fractions), or instructional skill gaps for teachers.

Point us in a slightly more focused direction.

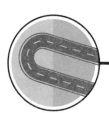

Level 3
Street Data

Fine-grain and ubiquitous.

- Help us to understand student, staff, and parent experience as well specific misconceptions and mindsets.
- Help us to monitor students' internalization of important skills.

- Require focused listening and observation.
- Inform and shape our next moves.

educational decisions and, as a result, further marginalizing the students we claim to serve. Let's take a moment to revisit the levels of data.

Level 1 "satellite data" hover far above the classroom and tell an important but incomplete story of equity. Satellite data encompass broad-brush quantitative measures like test scores, attendance patterns, and graduation rates, as well as adult indicators like teacher retention, principal attrition, and parent participation rates. While satellite data can illuminate trends and point our attention toward underserved groups of students, they have a few fatal flaws. First, they are often lagging, falling into educators' hands long after they have lost their utility to inform instructional and resource decisions. Second, they give policymakers and system leaders the platform and credibility (unwarranted, I would argue) to make sweeping decisions without being close to the locus of learning—the classroom.

Finally and perhaps most problematically, satellite data serve to reinforce implicit biases and deficit thinking about African American, Latinx, Indigenous students, students with diverse abilities, and other historically marginalized learners. They project a single story about "under-performance" rather than illuminating the complexity of learning and the tremendous assets that every child brings. **By attempting to distill the kaleidoscopic process of learning into a metric and promoting a narrow discourse of achievement, satellite data contribute to a long, racist history of insinuating that students of color have lower intellectual capacity rather than differential access to opportunity.**

Satellite data lack context and nuance, failing to account for phenomena like stereotype threat or ground us in the layered, human experiences that young people bring to learning. As Jamila argued in Chapter 2, the pursuit of educational equity is inherently complex, requiring context, texture, and story. Even as we have shifted the national narrative away from accountability, we have clung to a reliance on satellite data. We must turn to map and street level data to uncover student assets, understand root causes, and seek transformative solutions.

Level 2 "map data" hover closer to the ground, providing a GPS of social-emotional, cultural, and learning trends within a school community. Map data include literacy levels gathered through "running records," where teachers listen to and code students reading aloud, rubric scores on common assessments, and surveys that reveal student, parent, or staff perception and satisfaction levels. While Level 2 data paint a slightly richer picture, they still lack the specificity required to transform instructional and leadership decisions and the *humanity* needed to shape an equity-driven change process.

By contrast, **Level 3 "street data"** take us down to the ground to observe, listen to, and gather artifacts from the lived experiences of stakeholders. **Street data are the qualitative and experiential data that emerges at eye level and on lower frequencies when we train our brains to discern it. These data are asset based, building on the tenets of culturally responsive education by helping educators look for what's *right* in our students, schools, and communities instead of seeking out what's *wrong*.** Street data help us reveal what's getting in the way of student or adult learning, illuminate where the learner is in relationship to a holistic set of goals, and determine what might come next. The street data model embodies an ethos and a change methodology that will transform how we engage everything from student learning to district transformation to policy by offering a new way to think about, gather, and deploy data.

It's important to note that street data are not "just stories." They represent systematic information about student learning—how students are *performing* vis-à-vis developmental expectations, *feeling* about their learning environment and themselves, what might be *impeding* a child's ability to thrive, and what *instructional or leadership moves* should come next. They yield systematic information about equity, pulling back the curtain on implicit biases and microaggressions— subtle, everyday slights or insults that convey a hostile or derogatory message to targeted people based on their identity as part of a marginalized group. Only street data can illuminate how these forces influence learner experiences of inclusion and belonging.

What are the benefits of flipping the dashboard to focus on street data? This rich landscape of information will help us uncover stories of hope and harm while revealing students' assets, cultural wealth, and learning needs. Unlike the lagging pace of satellite data, street data provide real-time, leading indicators on the messy work of school transformation. They enable rapid feedback loops that inform our everyday decisions while promoting a bias toward action over stagnation. We don't have to wait for street data; it's right in front of us all the time. We can develop a living toolkit of strategies for gathering street data.

Let's get concrete. Imagine a child is sent out of his teacher's classroom to the principal's office five days in a row. We now have a satellite data point: daily referrals. Now, imagine that this child is a ten-year-old boy who immigrated from Honduras a year ago, was detained traumatically at the border, and has an undiagnosed learning difference. From an intersectionality lens, he faces multiple barriers. As educators, we can ask what factors are contributing to his daily experience of being pushed out of the classroom. Does the teacher have an unconscious bias against the child? Is the instruction too teacher centered, causing the boy's attention to flag and the teacher to become frustrated? Is the boy suffering from PTSD and unable to concentrate without getting therapeutic support? Is there an IEP in place with appropriate accommodations? What does the child tell his caregivers about his schooling experience?

The principal could easily send the child back to class each day without a clear understanding of what's at play. Alternatively, she could interview the teacher, interview the child, call home to ask the family what they are seeing, and observe the child in his teacher's classroom. From that rich constellation of street data, the principal is likely to find an entry point to a solution. Rather than maintain the status quo, he or she has the potential to disrupt a reproductive cycle and design a responsive plan that only the street data can reveal. As an added benefit, by treating this situation as a learning opportunity, the principal may perceive underlying patterns that help her rethink professional learning, referral processes, instructional coaching, and other systems.

Many improvement efforts that claim the equity mantle succumb to Paolo Freire's notion of false generosity (Freire, 1970). We assume we know what's best for struggling families and students and default to savior behaviors like the Great White Hope trope Jamila described in Chapter 2. Dr. Gloria Ladson-Billings, mother of the field of culturally responsive education, describes a *pobrecito* (poor little one) syndrome in which teachers pity their students and therefore fail to appropriately challenge them.

Street data disrupt these dynamics by bringing student voice to the forefront of our discussions and providing more trusted, heartfelt, and personalized information. Equally important, they help us uncover hidden narratives and equity issues. Contributing author Carrie Wilson (Chapter 7) writes in the playbook *Leading by Learning* (Lead by Learning, 2020), "Using data to make students' experience visible is ultimately about equity. When data reveals the student-learning experience rather than just an achievement level, teachers have the opportunity to check their assumptions about student learning against what is actually happening in the data."

THE EMERGING FIELD OF "THICK DATA"

It's worth noting that the concept of street data has recent echoes in other fields. For example, in the corporate world, innovators are beginning to challenge the dogma of "big data" and push for an emphasis on "thick data." Global tech ethnographer Tricia Wang defines thick data as "data brought to light using qualitative, ethnographic research methods that uncover people's emotions, stories, and models of their world. It's the sticky stuff that's difficult to quantify. It comes to us in the form of a small sample size and in return we get an incredible depth of meanings and stories." (Wang, 2016).

She contrasts thick data with big data—"quantitative data at a large scale that involves new technologies around capturing, storing, and analyzing." Sound familiar? Wang sees value in big data, but her critique is sharp: The normalizing and standardizing processes it employs tends to gut the data set of meaning and context—a problem that only thick data, or in our case street data, can rectify.

In a fascinating story about her own research at the cell phone company Nokia in 2009, Wang describes how years of conducting ethnographic work in China helped her uncover an insight that challenged Nokia's entire business model: Low-income consumers were ready to pay for more expensive smartphones. Instead of embracing her findings, the company derided them, arguing that her sample size was too small and thus irrelevant. She responded that their notion of demand was "a fixed quantitative model that didn't map to how demand worked as a cultural model in China" (Wang, 2016). In short, Wang was right, and Nokia met its downfall because it over relied on the numbers and ignored the import of cultural stories and context.

This is the power of street data. It offers us insight into localized cultural models that, if we dig deep, illuminate the root causes of inequities as well as places of opportunity and cultural wealth.

Roots of Street Data

Street data is an equity-centered approach that draws on several fields of study and practice. To be clear, we are not the first writers to say that educators should talk and listen to kids. Many folks speak to the importance of qualitative and action research as methods of school improvement, but it's as if everyone is touching a different part of the elephant and failing to see the whole. What is unique about street data is that it provides a comprehensive model of school transformation, stitching together four often-siloed elements: equity as the fundamental purpose, pedagogy as the fundamental pathway, adult culture as the vehicle, and street data as the GPS system that keeps us on the path of equity-centered transformation.

To understand the power of this framework, let's situate it in relationship to quantitative and qualitative methods. **Quantitative research** attempt to explain patterns through the collection and statistical analysis of numerical data—what I referred to in the introduction as empiricism and its close kin, positivism. This has been the prevailing methodology in education starting in the mid-1800's when formal written tests began to replace oral examinations administered by teachers and schools at the same moment that schools changed their mission from serving the society's elite to educating the masses. It is striking that the birth of modern satellite data coincided with the democratization of public education. Rather than seek to develop a cadre of professional educators with the skills to assess student learning, the field began to batch-process students in tandem with a factory-style approach to assessment.

Qualitative research, on the other hand, seeks to answer questions about why and how people behave in the ways that they do, mining for insight into the messy interplay of human relationships. Qualitative researchers collect and analyze non-numerical data in an effort to gain insight into social conditions and behaviors. **Mixed methods** is a form of research that integrates quantitative and qualitative methods to enact a more holistic approach. **Street data, the topic of this book, is a practitioner-driven, layperson's framework for conducting qualitative research in service of school transformation that drives toward equity and deep learning.**

There are many branches on the tree of qualitative research, all of which emerge from a common process: Identify a research problem, craft a question or set of questions, gather relevant data, analyze and interpret the data, and synthesize findings. While PhD candidates engage in this type of rigorous inquiry, educators—as life-changing as our work is—are robbed of the opportunity. Instead of building our instructional and leadership capacity in this way, we are asked to "improve our practice" by being held hostage to satellite data, sit-and-get professional development, sporadic evaluation, or working on complex problems in painful isolation. Street data offers a way to become ethnographers and researchers in our own classrooms, schools, and districts, in collaboration with colleagues, at no cost.

On the Ground: Ways to Gather Street Data

By now, you have a sense of the purpose and roots of street data. Think of it like a roadmap to an old city filled with hidden alleys and untold routes to explore. In 2011, I took my daughter on a learning visit to the West Bank and Jerusalem for her fifth birthday (my husband and I were teaching high school in Amman, Jordan, at the time—just 155 miles, but cultural and political lightyears, away). I remember wandering the *medina*, or old city, of Jerusalem filled with endless streams of people, foods, sounds, and treasures. We had particular sites we wanted to see, but at some point, we dropped the map and meandered, simply taking in the eruption of rich, multisensory surprises.

When educators embrace the model of street data, we commit to take in the rich cultural microcosms of our classrooms, staffrooms, hallways, and central offices with a new set of eyes and ears. We commit to listen and observe, ask questions rather than offer answers, and seek root causes rather than quick fixes. We also bridge the power of the oral and written word with a focus on **storientation**, a concept introduced in *The Listening Leader* that signifies close attention to the role of stories in school transformation. As we honor the power of story-centered and **oral traditions**, a new constellation of data becomes available, from student identity maps and mini-biographies to educator-developed case studies, oral histories, and listening campaigns.

Street data can be gathered by design, or it can emerge organically. Either way, it has tremendous value in the journey toward equity. Table 3.1 lays out three types of street data for your toolkit.

Here are ten examples of ways to collect street data.

1. **Audio feedback interviews:** Conduct an audio-recorded focus group with students or parents whose voices are typically absent from the decision-making table. Begin by identifying an equity challenge that you want to gain insight around. Invite a small group of stakeholders to engage in thirty to forty-five minutes of

TABLE 3.1 Types of Street Data		
Artifacts	**Stories/Narratives**	**Observations**
Anything created by human beings that yields information or insight into the culture and/or society of its creator and users	*The oral and sometimes written transmission of stories, histories, lessons, and other knowledge to maintain a historical record and sustain cultures and identities*	*The study of human behavior, including micro-interactions, micro-pedagogies, and micro-facilitation moves with a keen focus on nonverbal as well as verbal communication*
• Student work • Video of a performance-based assessment • Audio recording of a student-to-student discussion • Teacher-designed task • Professional-learning agenda • Instructional-coaching conversation plan	• Empathy interviews • Focal student case study • Oral histories • Identity maps • Writing journals • Staff meeting comment cards • Listening-campaign quotes	• Equity participation tracker (tally by race, gender, ELL status, etc.) • Nonverbal observation transcript • Meeting observation notes • Instructional coaching transcript • Sketch of classroom walls

discussion. Prepare and ideally share your questions in advance. Afterward, transcribe and edit the data to highlight key themes and comments (more on this in Chapter 8). With participant permission and/or full anonymity, these data can be used at a staff meeting to ground discussions of the equity challenge.

2. **Listening campaigns:** Listening campaigns involve a set of interviews or focus groups from which the listener assembles and organizes anonymous quotes by theme. The data are usually shared back to the community as an opportunity for growth and reflection. Conduct a series of listening sessions to gain insight and empathy toward a group of people at the margins, for example, LGBTQ students, parents of English language learners, or students with learning differences. Be sure to tap a group of at least five stakeholders so that you are able to get a sense of cross-cutting patterns.

3. **Equity participation tracker:** When visiting a classroom, track who is called on to participate by the teacher, who volunteers to speak, and who is receiving positive versus negative feedback (verbal and nonverbal). Break this data down by race, gender, English-language learner status, gender, learning differences, and other factors. This street data tool will help you study the micro-pedagogies of equity.

4. **Ethnographies:** If you are part of a team that meets on an ongoing basis, consider doing an in-depth ethnography of a group of students. This deep exploration of a campus subculture—for example a group of high-achieving Indigenous students—will entail interviews, observations, and soliciting written reflections from the learners. Begin by articulating an authentic inquiry question that you will investigate through the process. Obviously, get parent and student permission first.

5. **Fishbowls:** Facilitate a fishbowl dialogue to draw out the experiences and perspectives of a group at the margins. The structure is simple: A small group engages in discussion in the middle of the room, while other participants encircle this group and listen intently, jotting down key words and phrases. For example, district staff might facilitate a fishbowl of principals, asking, "What is your daily experience like as school leader? What conditions do you need to be successful? What could we do differently to support you?" Principals can facilitate a fishbowl of teachers, parents, or paraprofessionals. Teachers can facilitate a fishbowl of students. Be sure you have identified a central equity challenge; develop and share the questions beforehand with participants. Panel discussions can serve a similar role. Be willing to listen, even when it's hard to hear.

6. **Home visits:** Home visits are a powerful and underutilized street data tool. Over the years, I have found that many educators are fearful of doing home visits. They're either afraid of high-poverty neighborhoods and communities of color due to unconscious or conscious racism; they're afraid of imposing on families in their private sphere; or both. In the years that led to the founding of June Jordan School for Equity, the school where I was a principal, I had the privilege to do hundreds of home visits as part of a community organizing drive. I always asked the family if they felt comfortable having me in their home or preferred to meet in a community space, like a church hall or café. More often than not, they wanted to host the visit and took pride in welcoming me to their home. I felt deeply honored and, more importantly, gained street-level data on the family and student: their cultural wealth, assets, hopes, dreams, and fears.

7. **Shadow a student:** There is perhaps no better way to empathically understand a student's experience than to put on your tennis shoes and shadow him or her. Put on your comfy shoes and, with permission of course, follow a student through his or her school day. This is particularly impactful if done by a network of leaders and focused on students who are currently outside the

sphere of success. My colleague Jennifer Goldstein, a professor of educational leadership at California State University Fullerton, has principal candidates shadow an English learner for a day, with tremendous impact. A principal can also shadow a teacher throughout his or her day, and a district leader would do well to shadow a principal or assistant principal.

8. **Equity-focused classroom scan:** Do a demographic scan of different types of classes on campus—gifted, remedial, honors, academies, career tech, advanced placement, and so forth. Note the distribution of students by race/ethnicity, gender, ELL status, students with special needs, and so forth. With this data in hand, facilitate a leadership team discussion about the current landscape of equity and access at your site, where to go next for street data, and what your equity imperative is to address this.

9. **Structured meeting observations:** Be a fly on the wall in an upcoming team meeting. Take notes on who speaks and who does not, much like the equity participation tracker. Take notes on how the facilitator responds to different participants and whether the emotional valence of the response (positive, negative, neutral) tracks to race, gender, tenure, or other factors. Capture observation notes on the group dynamic—the energy of the room, including the ways in which people build off each other's ideas, respectfully challenge each other, and ask questions to probe one another's thinking.[2]

10. **Student-led community walks:** I have written about community walks for *Edutopia* (Safir, 2017a) and in *The Listening Leader* (Safir, 2017b). They are an invaluable tool for flipping the dashboard and uplifting the expertise of students and parents. To experiment with this strategy, identify social or cultural groups in your community about whom it would benefit educators to gain deeper knowledge. Invite students from those groups to meet with you to design a professional-learning experience for educators, typically comprised of two afternoons: one to read about the community and listen to student presenters and one to follow students through a guided community walk of their neighborhood. Support and empower students to design this experience with any tools at your disposal—PowerPoint slides, panels of community leaders, a lunch hosted by families in the community, an itinerary that includes important sites (markets, churches, community centers, etc.), and people.

---

[2]Chapter 10 of *The Listening Leader* includes group dynamic thermometers, which are visual metaphors with tips for how to analyze a positive or negative group dynamic.

From Satellite to Street: Uplifting the Voices of Students, Parents, and Teachers

To open this chapter, I shared a story called "Dashboard Blues" where parents and educators in a low-performing district became paralyzed in the face of satellite data as they developed a strategic plan. As we reflected on this meeting, the superintendent and I realized that the satellite story of his district was longstanding and actually quite simple: Enrollment was dropping; test scores and graduation rates were flat; chronic absenteeism and suspensions were up. (He distilled it into a single slide that he shared at the next meeting.) We were spending a lot of time revisiting a narrative that everyone *knew* and yet felt unable to change.

FIGURE 3.3   Profiled District Satellite Data Summary

What is our current state based on the satellite data?

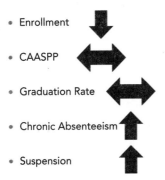

- Enrollment
- CAASPP
- Graduation Rate
- Chronic Absenteeism
- Suspension

But there was so much more to the story of this district—a place rich in cultural and linguistic diversity with a strong union history and parent leadership, dedicated staff, low attrition, and for the first time, a superintendent who was around for the long haul. As we began to plan the next community meeting, the superintendent asked me, "What is *not* told through our satellite data?" before responding to his own question: "Our bright spots and successes, the community and personal stories of our district, and the 'why' behind the data."

We decided to use the next meeting to flip the dashboard and center the voices of the students, parents, and teachers in the room. I proposed a Kiva Panel—a facilitated discussion of an important community issue that aims to bring new perspectives into the public domain.[3] This process

---

[3]Kiva Panels are described in detail in Chapter 10 of *The Listening Leader.* Safir, S. (2017). *The listening leader: Creating the conditions for school transformation* (p. 292). Hoboken, NJ: John Wiley and Sons.

works best when the panel represents distinct but equally strong positions on a topic, so we recruited a diverse cross-section of participants: two high school students (an African American and Japanese American biracial young woman and an Asian American gay young man), two parents (a monolingual Spanish-speaking mother and an African American father), and two veteran teachers and union leaders (both white—reflecting a demographic disconnect common in many urban districts).

During the panel, I posed three questions to each participant in structured "rounds," after which listeners formed small groups to discuss what they had heard:

1. **Share a bright spot in your experience of our district.** *What can we learn from that bright spot?*

2. **Reflect on an experience of inequity or exclusion that you've had in our district.** *How did that experience impact you as a person and a learner?*

3. **Imagine you could wave a magic wand to strengthen equity, relationships, and deep learning in our district.** *What would you change, and why?*

The room was riveted. You could hear a pin drop as the students and parents shared stories of hope and alienation. The Latina mother cried as she talked about visiting her son's school to ask for academic support and being ignored for close to an hour as the staff told her, "No one speaks Spanish here, so you'll just have to wait." The young gay man talked about being bullied and never having a teacher check in with him to see how he was doing. Panelists also shared wonderful stories of project-based and deep-learning experiences—moments where educators had effectively dumped the dashboard to teach content in dynamic and innovative ways.

The Kiva Panel transformed the energy in the room, electrifying a once-paralyzed group charged with charting the district's direction for the next three years. Not a single person stood up and said, "These stories can't be trusted; this data is incomplete," because the stories represented raw, unadulterated data for transformation. Their value could not be quantified. In fact, the same union leader who publicly lambasted the dashboard data at the previous meeting stood up and said, "Wow, this was amazing. It's time for us to put the issues we have behind us and move forward because this is really about the kids. We need to come together."

Reflecting on the cultural shift that happened from the dashboard meeting to the street data panel, the superintendent said:

When people started sharing their stories, everyone listened . . . not with an ear of "who's to blame?" or a need to defend and justify, but really trying to understand the experience of each participant. With the dashboard data, you always feel like you need to justify, defend, or blame. It's not about understanding experience; it's just about "here are the outcomes." And on these metrics, we look like a failure.

Street data offers a new grammar for educational equity. It humanizes the process of gathering data. Rather than positioning students and teachers as objects whose value can be quantified, street data teaches us to engage with people as subjects and agents in an ever-shifting landscape—human beings whose experiences are worthy of careful study and deep listening. It teaches us to be ethnographers rather than statisticians. And the process itself builds trust and relational capital.

The benefits of this approach are beyond measurement. By flipping the dashboard and listening to stakeholder experiences, we interrupt persistent deficit narratives about students, families, and teachers; center the voices of those at the margins; and embrace a bias toward action and experimentation. Next, we take a look at how street data can complement satellite and map data as we move our schools and systems along an equity journey.

GETTING UP CLOSE AND PERSONAL: REFLECTION QUESTIONS

1. Identify an idea or passage from Chapter 3 that stood out to you. Share and reflect on it with a partner or small group: Why did it resonate? What felt challenging or provocative?

2. Where do you have opportunities to develop your practice around the core stance of antiracism? Who will be or *is* your village that helps you stay focused on this work?

3. Identify an equity challenge in your community. What do available satellite and map data tell you (or not tell you) about this challenge? What street data do you need?

4. Which of the street data strategies could you try out in the next two weeks? Make a short plan of who, when, why, and how you'll do this.

5. What might get in the way of you collecting street data, and how will you stay the course?

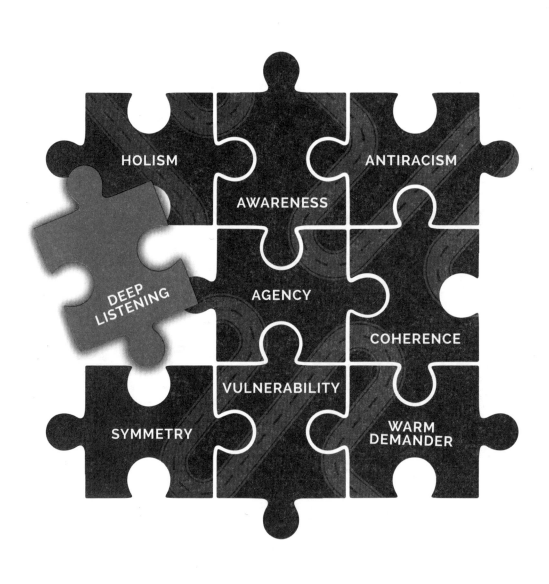

Pound the Pavement

Digging Into the Levels of Data

4

Seek root causes over quick fixes.

We're living in this era of Dashboards, which I want to qualify is insane. This presents the illusion of knowing what's going on. Like everything else electronic, it's hypnotic. This is what globalization has done. We believe that leaders need to know petty information and because we're accountable for it, we get this miniscule look at what's actually going on for children.

—Margaret Wheatley, Keynote at
British Columbia School Superintendents
Association (BCSSA), November 21, 2019

In this chapter, we shift from the *concept* of street data to the *practice*, learning how to facilitate an equity transformation cycle that fundamentally shifts our ways of working together. What would this look like, and how does it differ from current models of improvement? What are the steps? How would you know if you were making a difference for children at the margins? On this leg of our journey, we grapple with the limitations of popular models—like improvement science—to solve complex equity challenges while digging further into the levels of data.

Since No Child Left Behind gave way to murkier reform waters, **improvement science** has gained traction as a problem-solving approach in education. Championed by the Carnegie and Gates Foundations, improvement science encourages practitioners to test new ideas in rapid cycles—often referred to as plan-do-study-act (PDSA)—in which they develop a change idea, test it, collect data on it, and reflect on whether it worked. Employed at various levels to "achieve positive results reliably and at scale" (REL West, 2017), improvement science (and the affiliated term "continuous improvement") has become the dominant improvement model we currently operate under as a field. It's worth noting that continuous improvement is actually a business term drawn from the influence of total quality management (TQM) in the 1980s and that many educators and scholars are reading and writing in opposition to the privatization and commercialization of public schooling.

While its goals sound good at face value, a closer look reveals potential problems. First, you may have noticed that "plan" (develop a change idea) comes two steps before "study" (collect data). When pursuing equity, how can we plan anything responsive without first listening to those at the margins? Where does the voice of the learner—adult or student—fit into this process? Second, the language of "reliability" and "at scale" signals the econometric framework that I wrote about in Chapter 1: a narrow conception of knowledge and data rooted in Western empiricism. Finally, the model itself is equity neutral, without a clear antiracist stance. Presumably, one could develop an idea and set a goal about *anything*, collect whatever sort of data he or she sees fit, and onward.

For our purposes in this book, we are striving to address deep-seated, seemingly intractable equity challenges that have persisted for decades, with roots that burrow down for centuries—issues emerging from systemic racism, implicit bias, and white supremacy culture in schools. We cannot plan-do-study-act our way out of these challenges.

Improvement science has its merits, for sure. But the tendency to oversimplify "improvement" and seek incremental change over deep transformation makes it a mismatch for equity work. Equity challenges are *complex* challenges. They arise from the interplay of systemic oppression—when laws and policies lead to unequal treatment and disadvantaging of a specific group of people based on their identity (gender, race, class, sexual orientation, language, etc.)—with the personal and interpersonal domains of identity, behavior, culture, mental models, and psycho-emotional experiences. They arise through microaggressions and macro-forces that sift children into purportedly "good" and "bad" schools and neighborhoods.

Hold for a moment the idea that the least enfranchised communities—those with "bad test scores" and little access to opportunity—possess vast cultural wealth, despite the deficit narratives used to describe them. Yet our improvement paradigms have us chasing after satellite data gains and quick, external fixes instead of cultivating deep, local knowledge. To transform our schools, we need a nuanced and antiracist way to engage in "improvement" (or perhaps we need to dump that word altogether). We need mechanisms for listening to elders, community leaders, and students and families at the margins who can collaborate *with* us to reimagine outdated approaches. We need to position teachers and principals as change agents rather than consumers of curricula and programs, zigzagging from one intervention to the next.

Deep Listening: A Core Stance for School Transformation

Our guiding principle for Chapter 4 is *seek root causes over quick fixes*. To embody this principle, we have to learn to slow down and engage in deep listening. By inverting our dominant approach to data and listening to the voices, narratives, and perspectives at the margins, we begin to humanize the process of data-gathering. This is a key point because, in the street data framework, the ends do not justify the means: Our approaches to data collection are just as important as any insight, understanding, or actions that emerge. Listening deeply and responsively will help us build relational capital and trust and shift the culture as we gather data.

Street data helps us resist the Great White Hope and Lone Ranger of Color tropes and, instead, take a stance of deep listening and learning. At the root of this shift is a willingness to lean into humility and courage. Rather than fear feedback on our practice, we begin to actively solicit it. Rather than become defensive in the face of hard-to-hear data, we build our muscle at taking it in. This simple pivot in perspective interrupts the tendency toward *solution-itis*—let's fix an ill-defined problem without consulting those most impacted—that upholds white supremacy and maintains unequal power dynamics in schools. When we ground our leadership moves at the street level, we get critical insight into what's working and what's not.

In the street data framework, listening signifies a deep commitment to two things: the technology of skillful listening and an orientation to authentic, present, mindful engagement with stakeholders. Listening tours have become a popular tool of the new leader, and while they seem promising, they carry a risk of becoming a transactional strategy to check off one's to-do list (see Jamila's description of *doing equity* and *superficial equity*, pp. 32–33). The antidote to this is cultivating a practice of deep listening, which is described in Chapter 5 of *The Listening Leader* (Safir, 2017b). Here are a few tips to deepen your listening as you flip the dashboard.

- **Locate the margins of your community.** Whose voices are most unheard and yet potentially most instrumental to solving the equity challenges you face? For example, who are the elders in your community whose wisdom is untapped? Think of paraprofessionals: cafeteria workers, custodians, and security guards who interact with children every day and often come from the same communities as students. When is the last time you invited a paraprofessional to sit and authentically share his or her insights about your school's equity issues?

- **Cultivate awareness of your personal biases.** Whose voices do you tend to gravitate toward and why? What internal scripts are running in your brain about particular students, groups of students, families, or colleagues? Challenge those by stating an explicit intention to yourself: "I commit to listen deeply to students and parents about whom I may carry some judgment. I commit to stay open to new learning and insight."

- **Find a culturally appropriate way to capture listening data.** For some folks, taking notes on a computer as you listen may feel perfectly fine. For others, the computer itself smacks of bureaucracy and power. Know your audience. If uncertain, ask the person, "Do you mind if I take notes once in a while? Would a computer be distracting?" If real-time notes aren't appropriate, practice mindful listening and set aside ten minutes after the session to jot down key data points. I often coach educators to listen for emotional peaks, which may be revealed through upticks in volume or shifts in tone and body language.

- **Pay close attention to nonverbal cues.** Robert Mehrabian's groundbreaking research on nonverbal communication revealed that in any exchange involving emotion, 38 percent of meaning is conveyed through tone, 55 percent through body language, and only 7 percent through words (Mehrabian, 1981). As you gather street data via listening, develop awareness of your own and other people's tone and nonverbal cues as windows into emotional experience. Notice, for example: Are the speaker's arms or legs crossed? Is their face tight and brow furrowed? Or does this expression seem open and relaxed? How are you seated vis-à-vis the speaker, and does your body convey openness and an invitation for authentic sharing?

- **Remember your purpose—healing plus understanding.** Street data is distinct from other forms of data-gathering in that the process itself can be healing. It is an opportunity to build trust and relational capital with people at the margins of your community. Street data is not a technical approach; rather, it is an adaptive, human-centered data dance that unfolds fluidly through caring, inclusive, and culturally sustaining interactions.

If we conduct a listening campaign or observe a group of students in ways that are cold, transactional, or technocratic, we have failed to use the street data methodology with fidelity. Instead, this method demands that we constantly seek to align our means with our ends by modeling curiosity and deep listening in service of equity.

LISTENING DYADS: A STREET DATA STAPLE

Street data can surface intense emotion. As we take in the impact of inequities on our students and begin to examine our own biases and practices, we may drop into a stress response pattern: fight, flight, or freeze. Listening dyads are a powerful tool for emotional reflection and self-regulation that can disrupt our default responses. A dyad is a two-person structure, originally developed by Julian Weissglass at the National Coalition for Equity in Education, with a stated purpose of benefitting the speaker (not the listener) as they reflect and construct meaning. Dyads follow four guidelines:

- Equal time for each speaker (because everyone deserves to be listened to)

- No interruptions or breaking in with personal stories (because people have the capacity to solve their own problems, given time and space)

- Double confidentiality (don't share what you hear or return to your partner later to probe their share because people need to know they can be completely authentic)

- No complaining about mutual colleagues (because this is an opportunity for *self*-reflection and finger-wagging can lead the listener to feel defensive)

A dyad prompt aims to create space for emotional release, reflection, and healing. Sample prompts could be: *What thoughts and feelings does this street data bring up for you? What was the experience of listening deeply to your students like for you? Share a time when you got feedback on your practice that was hard to hear. How did you metabolize and move through that moment?*

FIGURE 4.1 Equity Transformation Cycle

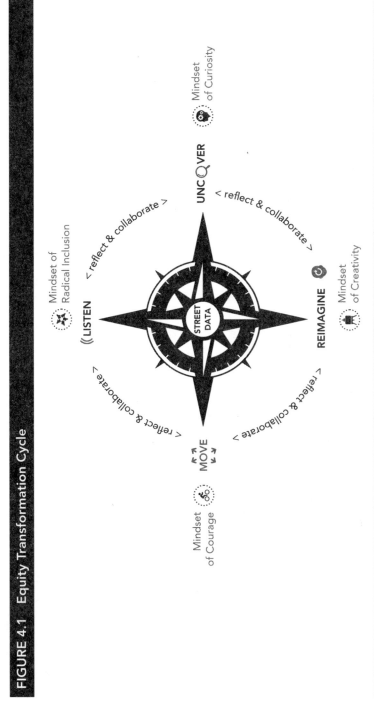

The **equity transformation cycle (ETC)** is the central process tool in this book. The cycle represents a fluid yet structured process that is grounded in core values—radical inclusion, curiosity, creativity, and courage—and centers street-level data. As you move through the cycle, you will learn to listen deeply to voices at the margins, uncover the root causes of inequities, reimagine your current approaches in partnership with key stakeholders, and move a change agenda with courage. In the rest of this chapter, we will unpack what an equity transformation cycle looks, sounds, and feels like. Allow me to point out a few features before we dive in.

First, a note on the word choice of "transformation": It pained me to select a noun here! I agonized over the sound of "inquiry," "improvement," and "change" but ultimately landed on transformation. As I write this, I hear the words of my colleague and dear friend Denise Augustine in my ear. Denise, a leader for Indigenous education with the Ministry of Education in British Columbia, firmly rejects the term "improvement" as connoting incremental change in the face of generational challenges. Improvement feels like we are tinkering around the edges of systemic realities that trace back to slavery, restrictive immigration laws, Native American genocide and dispossession, and centuries of exclusionary policy. **We don't need improvement. We need an approach that fundamentally and radically transforms the experiences of children and families at the margins. This is the purpose of centering street data in a process of transformation.**

Second, you'll notice that the cycle is nonlinear because, guess what, complex change is nonlinear! Linearity, the governing principle of the Western improvement model, seeks simple cause and effect relationships. We seek deep understanding of human stories and root causes of inequity. Notice that the arrows in between cycle phases go both directions to signal that the process is nimble and built for the unpredictable rhythm of complex change. You might think you've moved past the listening stage and are ready to uncover root causes, then realize you haven't listened deeply enough. You might imagine your next move and then realize, wait! I didn't drill down far enough to uncover the underlying root causes. This is the emergent nature of working toward equity.

Third, the model is built for short, six- to eight-week cycles that work at every level of the system—the classroom, the school, the district, or even the region/province/state—though it can be adapted to design spiraling quarterly or semester-long cycles. Like design thinking, the cycle helps us iterate on our ideas and build our collective capacity to respond to changing street-level conditions. The entire process is undergirded by the idea of **emergence**—the theory that simple rules interact with one another in complex ways to shape a change process, *the outcome of which cannot be predicted.* (Think of a chess game. There are basic, universally known rules, but when two players sit down to engage in a strategic game of chess, the result cannot be predicted; it is always emergent.)

The idea of throwing yourself into a change process with no known outcome and just a line of inquiry may feel uncomfortable and revolutionary all at once—a blast of fresh air on the stale econometric framework, which assumes we can data-fy and plan our way into new results. By contrast, emergence calls on us to slow down, listen deeply to those at the margins, bring folks to the table to reimagine the landscape *with* us, and move in partnership to build a new reality. It is a liberatory change model, freeing us from the fantasy of control while pushing us to maximize our influence in service of equity and antiracism.

Finally, you'll note that collaboration and reflection are embedded in every step of the journey. No one ever reached an equity or social transformation goal alone. We need a village. We *belong* to a village, with children at the center. **Who is your village with whom you will build the courage and vision to do this work?**

The equity transformation cycle represents a shift from *evaluating* outcomes to *valuing* well-being (value being the root word of evaluate). Note that Chapter 8 will unpack the cycle in more depth with many concrete examples. At the heart of this process lies the ultimate goal of **well-being**—a state in which educators and students experience healing, agency, joy, and connection as they dismantle oppressive practices and structures and cultivate deep learning for all. If we do not value healthy, thriving communities of adults and children, what really is the point?

LISTEN: The Mindset of Radical Inclusion

Whatever the problem, community is the answer. How we are together in our relationships is the solution. When people are anxious and scared, we withdraw from one another. Listening helps us lean in and hold one another.

—Margaret Wheatley

Equity-centered transformation always, *always*, begins with deep listening. Not with planning an intervention to do, study, and act on, but with the choice to listen deeply to the least heard and most marginalized voices in your community—be that a classroom, school, district, or state. Here, we use the word listening in the broadest sense: as a physical, emotional, cognitive, and even spiritual act rather than a clinical method of "gathering data." Remember: Deep listening is the core stance of this chapter and your superpower as you seek root causes over quick fixes.

FIGURE 4.2   The Chinese Character for Listening

The Chinese character for listening includes five parts: the ear, the eyes, one undivided attention, the heart, and king. When we listen at the margins, we open our hearts to what is *said*, what is *not said*, what is *seen* and expressed nonverbally, what is *perceived* on the level of **neuroception**,[1] and what is *felt* by the listener and speaker alike. Far from a passive act, listening is a dynamic exchange that brings humanity to the process of school transformation. We listen to ensure that the solutions we devise are shaped by voices at the margins rather than our projection of what people might need (the trap of false generosity). As you can imagine, this kind of listening requires great skill and emotional intelligence, areas we will explore throughout the book.

Our guiding mindset at this stage is **radical inclusion**, which scholar Ortiz Guzman describes as "the intentional act of interrupting inequity where it lives . . . Recognizing the multiplicity of stories, truths, their proximities, their intersections, and the people who own the stories, are requisites for equity design work" (Ortiz Guzman, 2017, p. 45). In practicing this mindset, we commit to identify and include the voices of those who may have never had a seat at the decision-making table but whose experiences and perspectives matter. This might be your kindergarteners who "can't sit still," frequently suspended boys, students with attention issues, long-term English learners (LTELs), refugee families, Black mothers, LGBTQ or non-binary students, young staff of color, community leaders, elders, and many others.

---

[1]Neuroception is a scientific term describing how our neural circuits perceive and distinguish, often automatically, whether situations or people are safe, dangerous, or life-threatening.

Whoever we need to listen to, radical inclusion connects us to an internal source of compassion that, as Buddhist nun Pema Chodron writes, is less about "our service of those on the margins, but in our willingness to see ourselves in kinship with them" (Boyle, 2010). It's important to acknowledge that many of us may be grown-up versions of the children we want to better serve. We may carry our own wounds from experiencing exclusion, racism, and other forms of oppression as students, and listening will inevitably surface emotion around those memories. Rather than stuff or sanitize the emotion, we can learn to heal and harness it.

The listening stage invites us to be humble, acknowledging that our best-honed leadership and instructional tools may not hold the solutions we need. It also invites us to stand in solidarity with folks at the margins. In his beautiful article "Note to Educators: Hope Required When Growing Roses in Concrete," Jeff Duncan-Andrade explores the idea of audacious hope, which "demands that we reconnect to the collective by struggling alongside one another, sharing in the victories and the pain. This solidarity is the essential ingredient for 'radical healing' (Ginwright, 2009)" (Duncan-Andrade, 2009).

Just like the equity traps and tropes Jamila described in Chapter 2, each phase of the cycle contains micro-traps that we have to train ourselves to resist. First and foremost, our *approach* to listening is at least as important as the time we set aside to do it. If we listen to a student or parent in transactional ways, for example, we run the risk of alienating and further marginalizing the person. Transactional listening can look like

- Forgetting to frame the listening with a clear "why" ("My purpose in this listening session is to . . .") and close with authentic appreciation ("Thank you/I want to honor you for . . .")

- Taking notes so diligently that you never look up, make eye contact, and take in nonverbal cues as critical street data

- Conveying a lack of warmth and care through aloof facial expressions or body language

- Allowing ego to inflect our listening and becoming defensive in the face of hard feedback (we will explore this further in a Chapter 8 discussion of white supremacy culture)

Another pitfall we must guard against is listening with unchecked implicit biases or a narrow cultural frame. Listening provides an opportunity to practice self-awareness. Before engaging in this stage, ask yourself: *What assumptions, stereotypes, or deficit-based scripts am I holding right now? How can I press pause and open up new ways of thinking and understanding? What are the limitations of my own cultural frame, and how can I listen for the assets and cultural wealth that the speaker possesses? This takes practice, and it won't be perfect, but cultivating a practice of mindful listening will help a lot.*[2]

The listening phase of the cycle may emerge from satellite or map data, or it may erupt from an inciting incident—for example, a racist event that has rocked your classroom, school, or district. However you begin, ask these three questions:

1. What is the equity challenge we need to address right now, and why does it matter?

2. Who is most impacted by this challenge?

3. How will we listen deeply to their voices and experiences?

STREET-LEVEL INCIDENTS

An equity transformation cycles often begins with a crisis event, like the three below, all based on actual events. Think about who you would need to listen to in each scenario and how you would model the stance of deep listening.

A group of teachers in a predominantly white town with an increasing Latinx population dress up as Mexican caricatures for Halloween, with ponchos, sombreros, and fake mustaches. Four of them pose as panels of the proposed border wall, on which they have plastered "Make America Great Again." Rather than go underground, they post public pictures on Facebook. Latinx and other local families are enraged and start a petition.

A district reels as Black and Asian students come forward with multiple stories of racist taunts by peers that went unchecked by adults or peers.

A transgender male high school student stops attending school because his history teacher refuses to call him by male pronouns and his chosen name, despite the fact that it is listed on the attendance rolls.

---

[2] I discuss mindful listening in Chapters 1 and 5 of *The Listening Leader* (Safir, S. [2017]. *The listening leader: Creating the conditions for equitable school transformation.* San Francisco: John Wiley & Sons).

In addition to listening campaigns and shadow days (both described in Chapter 3), you can organize focus groups, audio or video interviews (recorded with permission, of course), and/or empathy interviews (see Chapter 8). You can also bring student and other stakeholder voices into the public arena by facilitating a panel or fishbowl discussion, as depicted at the end of Chapter 3. Here are sample questions you can adapt for listening to students, parents, and colleagues.

SAMPLE QUESTIONS: STUDENT LISTENING SESSION	SAMPLE QUESTIONS: PARENT LISTENING SESSION	SAMPLE QUESTIONS: ADULT LISTENING SESSION
• What is going well for you in school right now? What is something you feel proud of? • What is your biggest challenge or frustration? • (If an inciting event has happened) How did the incident affect you? What feelings came up? • What do you want or need to heal? • What changes would you like to see (in our classroom or school), and why do they matter to you? • What feedback do you have for me to make our school or classroom more equitable and inclusive?	• What is going well for your child right now? What is something you feel proud of? • What is your biggest challenge or frustration about their school experience? • What should we know about your beliefs, values, and/or culture to best support your family and child? • What changes would you like to see in our classroom or school, and why? • What feedback do you have for me to improve your child's experience or the school in general?	• What is something in your practice that you're feeling good about/proud of right now? • What's frustrating you/ keeping you up at night? • (If an inciting event has happened) How did the incident affect you? What feelings came up? • What do you want or need to heal? What do you think our *community* needs to heal? • What is one critical change you'd like to see in our school culture, systems, or structures? • What feedback do you have for me as a leader/colleague to support equity and inclusion?

VOICES FROM THE STREET

Students and Caregivers

According to the most recent U.S. Department of Education Office for Civil Rights data, from kindergarten to twelfth grade, Black girls are seven times more likely than white girls to be suspended from school and four times more likely to be arrested at school. (For more on this, read Monique W. Morris's book *Pushout: The Criminalization of Black Girls*, 2016.) Latinx girls are more than 1.5 times as likely as white girls to receive an out of school suspension, and Native American girls are suspended at three times the rate of white girls. These are the satellite data.

The story of Alyssa, a bright, socially conscious eighth-grade Black girl overcoming learning and mental health challenges exemplifies the impact of systemic racism, implicit bias, white supremacy culture, and intersecting systems of oppression. After an altercation with a classmate involving a verbal threat but no physical harm, Alyssa was suspended for nearly three weeks despite the fact that *physical* incidents by non-Black peers had been met with minimal punishment. When she returned, Alyssa was made to jump through multiple hoops, switch her entire course schedule, and barred from extracurricular activities, including her beloved Black Student Union (BSU). Rather than listen to Alyssa and her family, engage her and the peer in restorative processes, or dig for root causes leading to the argument, the school responded in transactional ways that left Alyssa feeling hurt, disenfranchised, and marginalized.

I had the opportunity to listen deeply to Alyssa and her mom Jackie (both pseudonyms) and want to share with you the type of rich, meaningful street data that comes from orienting ourselves to this stance. I asked them both what happened, how Alyssa's identities shaped her experience, how the school's response impacted her social, emotional, and academic well-being as well as her sense of belonging and efficacy, and finally, what both women *wished* the school would have done differently. Below are some of the responses I heard from Alyssa and her mom. When you finish reading, use the Reflect and Collaborate questions that follow to make meaning of the data. Then, imagine that you are beginning an equity transformation cycle in which you will next analyze the data to uncover root causes, reimagine your school's response in partnership with Alyssa and her family, and move forward in a courageous, antiracist manner.

Alyssa's Words (student)

It was a really stressful situation. I had no idea what was going to happen; I thought I was going to be expelled. . . . I knew that they were doing an investigation of sorts, but I didn't really know what was

(Continued)

(Continued)

going on with that. One time I was like, "Mom, why am I not in the conversation? I was in the incident, so why am I not in conversation?"

They pulled me out of my old class, which ironically had most of the Black girls in the grade in it. They pulled me out of the yearbook club and the band. . . . It was really hard, especially the first few weeks . . . it was actually so bad that I literally wouldn't even go to class because I didn't know the kids in my class that well and, well, because I have social anxiety.

I used to hide in the bathrooms and wait until the teacher came out and yelled at me for skipping class. Then I'd go to class and obviously I didn't have good grades because I wasn't participating in class. Yes, at that point it was pretty low, and the school still didn't seem like they were going to put me back in my old class. The BSU progressed and did their thing, and they (the administration) asked me not to be a part of it.

The argument was because of a race issue . . . That was the issue at heart. I thought if the school could understand that, then maybe they could understand why I was that mad and why it was that big of a deal, but to isolate me from essentially all other students that look like me only made it a worse experience for me.

Well, this incident wouldn't really have happened if I was not Black. It's hard to say, but it did feel like they, as a school, didn't really care about having a safe space for the Black students at the school as much as they cared about saying, "Hey, we have a Black Student Union and we're a diverse school." . . . They know who I am, they really know me. . . . This is not the first time that I've discussed racial issues. They should have included me in that because I'm more than capable of discussing it, like a normal person.

I've always considered myself a smart person, not in a cocky way, but there's been a lot of instances where I'm trying to explain a concept to a kid my age and they just don't understand it. I know that I'm very conscious of the world and this society and stuff and the way that things work in America. . . . I just really wanted to graduate, maybe not with perfect grades but with maybe higher grades or with some fun experience that I got to do at the school. . . . It felt like that was taken away.

(Here, I asked Alyssa what she wished the school had done differently.)
I don't know why I have to say this, but I wish they would've actually

talked to me and listened to what I'm saying and understand that I have feelings too. In a way, I ended up being a victim of the situation in the end, even though I was not seen that way . . . Just look at both sides of the story I guess.

I think they let me speak, but it felt after I spoke, they just didn't care what I said. Just take into account all different perspectives and also understand that as a Black kid in America, a lot of people don't really look like you, and a lot of people don't really like you just because of the way that you look. That's why you actually might want a space at school where you can meet up with other kids that do look like you and do know what you're experiencing and just understand each other and have a safe space like that.

Jackie's Words (mother)

I think the way in which the school responded was in this way that didn't, one, look at what the impetus was leading to the pain that Alyssa was experiencing and what they could do about that. . . . The result was a lot of changing of course. One thing that was so striking from the start is that when they initially called us, they didn't just frame it as a conflict between the two girls, but they made it sound as if she was dangerous, and they framed it that way for the other family as well. That immediately set this on a course that was hard to recover from. And, having been on the other side of the equation when my child was injured by another child, I had never heard that characterization before. At first they were like, "She did something bad; she's going to be out of school for a day." Then it was, "No, she's going to be out of school for three days." Then it was like, "Oh no, we're not sure, we're doing another investigation. We'll let you know when you can come in. You can come in on this day—Oh, actually, we don't want to have you come in. We just want to talk with any other professionals that happened to be talking with her."

I kept asking these questions like, "What is happening?" They were like, "We're just doing our investigation." Alyssa kept asking us, "What is happening?" I said, "They're doing their investigation." She said, in a really mature way, "How are they doing an investigation when they're not talking to me?" We're like, "Good point." My spouse calls them up and says, "If you're doing your investigation, I think you should talk to my daughter. She would like to share what happened from her

(Continued)

(Continued)

perspective." He took her in to be able to share, but it never occurred to the school to even speak with her.

She was at a place where she didn't have very many friends, and so removing her from one group both had the effect of impacting her academics and impacting her social and emotional state. We kept underscoring to the school, "This may not seem evident to you, but this is really devastating for this child in this moment, and here's why." They refused to hear any of it. I requested that there be a restorative justice process. They said, "Yes, that sounds great. We will do that." When she finally went back to school, the restorative justice process was supposed to start. We had started working on it . . . We met with the restorative justice consultant over Thanksgiving. The other family was also supposed to meet with the person over Thanksgiving but decided they didn't want to do the restorative justice process.

I think that was a critical moment, because in my mind, that was the moment where the school (by virtue of a set of values and policies informed by those values) should have said, "To be a part of our school community, when we have issues we need to resolve between young people, we ask them to participate. This is what you sign up for when you sign up for this school, so you can't opt out," especially when the restorative justice office was a gatekeeper to resolution so that Alyssa would be able to go back to her former life.

She had to drop out of all of her clubs and activities because of the experience. She was switched from the classroom because of this experience. There was no schoolwork being done. It had a deleterious effect on her academics; it had a deleterious effect on her personal relationships, on her social life; trying to go back to school and be with her friends was really difficult. It was just really difficult all around. She felt socially isolated because of this experience. This is a kid who fell into a very deep depression, requiring meds, a kid who has really struggled. . . .

I think, in a lot of ways, it has made her question her trust in adults, made her question her trust in white adults, made her question her trust in authority figures, and made her really skeptical about who she can trust to actually take care of her and what people's fundamental motives are when they are engaging with you. . . . I think for her it underscored that actually when you're Black, you're treated differently. When you're female, you're treated differently. When you're young, you're treated differently.

(Here, I asked Jackie what she wished the school had done differently.) *Well, let me just say that all of this could have been avoided in my utopian world. What would have happened is that there would have been a space for Black students to have, in these predominantly white schools, a place of solace because then all of this would have been avoided.*

The reason all of this came up is because Alyssa was advocating for that kind of space, and the school was not active in actually trying to support that in happening. This conflict emerged between these two girls about it, which the school, because of their own racial position and uncertainty about what to do, didn't know how to resolve. I think that's a really important part of the story, of where the school owns some responsibility to get clear about how they want to deal with issues of race and justice, because they had no view on that and were afraid to do something that would offend people, as opposed to looking at what are the needs of their students, and why, and how could they get some clarity around how to support the needs of those students.

They actually elevate this idea that every situation is different, and so we take it on a case by case basis . . . taking it on a case by case basis, you leave yourself open to bias because there are no consistent practices or values or policies that undergird how you address issues. "Well, we can't really compare this to that. It's very individualized." Well, yes. Individualization has been used to lock people out of opportunity for centuries.

REFLECT AND COLLABORATE: GUIDING QUESTIONS

- What stands out from the listening data? What are the patterns and themes?

- What is most painful to hear? *Sit with and acknowledge your own emotions and where you feel them in your body.*

- What new questions emerge from this data?

- What additional listening might we need to do and with whom?

- How does what I heard help me understand the satellite and map data?

UNCOVER: The Mindset of Curiosity

 In the next phase, we probe all the available street data to uncover the root causes of our equity challenge. It is critical to do this in a collaborative fashion by studying the data with a team. By listening deeply to voices at the margins, we have disrupted the improvement habit of diving into planning before gathering street data. Even at this stage, however, it's easy to jump into a solution space before we have thoroughly explored the data. Uncovering helps us slow down, reflect, and *value* the street data by making it the centerpiece of team conversations. A good team meeting will help us stretch our thinking and assumptions.

At this stage, we can also bring forward complementary forms of street data to comb through: artifacts, observation notes, video clips, and more. Say, for example, we are a group of seventh-grade teachers who have identified fluent writing as an equity challenge for our English learners. We just completed empathy interviews with eight students to understand their self-perception around writing. We asked the students to share their best and worst writing experiences, how they feel about themselves as writers, a piece of writing they feel proud of, and a writing role model. For today's team meeting, we have assembled short writing samples for each student (artifacts). In addition, each of us has captured observation notes over the past week on the two students we interviewed, focusing on behaviors they exhibit when we assign writing tasks (engagement, avoidance, stop-and-start, etc.). We now have a rich array of street data to examine for root causes.

The critical mindset at this stage is **curiosity**: setting aside our preconceived notions, checking our confirmation biases, and thinking hard before coming to any conclusions. As we study the data, we try to uncover patterns, hidden stories, and misconceptions while maintaining a stance of wonder: *What does the street data reveal and not reveal? What underlying patterns are becoming visible? What more is there to this story?* Uncovering root causes and hidden truths is such hard work. How do we retain what educational justice organizer Jitu Brown calls "ferocious humility" (Brown, 2019), recognizing how much we *don't* know? We stay curious. Curiosity helps us sharpen our brains to analyze street data with cognitive discipline—to look and listen for deeper meaning.

The biggest pitfall at the uncover stage is a failure to slow down and engage in the messy meaning-making required to dig up root causes. It is so easy to defend our current ways of doing things—to boomerang back, as Jamila said, from the edge of what it might mean to transform our practices. It's much easier to continue with business-as-usual than to push and pull and probe with our colleagues to figure out what is *really* going on underneath the surface. Here, collaborative discussion protocols are our friends, helping us stay focused and disciplined as we build our capacity to have rigorous street data conversations.

Two protocols will serve you well at this stage: the **iceberg** and **peeling the onion**. Designed by systems theorist Peter Senge, the iceberg helps us move from an event we might typically *react* to into the deeper waters of patterns, trends, systemic structures, and mental models that shape our thinking (Senge, Kleiner, & Roberts 1994). When we encounter an iceberg, only a small portion (that which surfaces above sea level) is visible from a distance. In our iceberg metaphor, this surface level corresponds to *events*—what just happened? Beneath the water lie deeper levels of inquiry—the *patterns*, *trends*, and *systemic structures* forming barriers to equity—what has *been* happening? Have we been here or somewhere similar before? What forces are at play that contribute to these patterns? Finally, at the ocean's base, we encounter **mental models**—personal, internal representations of reality that people use to interact with the world around them, constructed by individuals based on their unique life experiences, perceptions, and understandings of the world (Jones et al., 2011). Here, we might ask, How does our thinking allow this situation to persist?

Moving through the iceberg never fails to yield insight into root causes. Give your team sufficient time to work through this tool, at least forty-five minutes to an hour. To see one depiction of the iceberg model, visit http://www.ascd.org/ASCD/pdf/journals/ed_lead/el200910_kohm_iceberg.pdf.

Peeling the Onion also provides a structured way to look at a problem without immediately trying to solve it. It includes a series of timed steps that help you get to the heart of an issue. You can find a detailed version of this protocol at http://schoolreforminitiative.org/doc/peeling_onion.pdf.

REFLECT AND COLLABORATE: GUIDING QUESTIONS

- What were our assumptions going in, and how does the street data challenge them?

- What is most surprising in the street data?

- What root causes are revealing themselves as we analyze the array of street data?

- What invisible mental models may be shaping the outcomes we currently have?

- What entry points are emerging for disrupting business-as-usual and trying something really different?

REIMAGINE: The Mindset of Creativity

As I wrote in Chapter 1, the test-and-punish era incarcerated the imagination in many school communities, driven by a top-down accountability system that marginalized student and educator expertise. The third phase of equity-centered transformation invites us to reimagine our current reality with a mindset of creativity. When we engage in this phase, we aspire to knock down the psychic walls that keep us boomeranging back to the same responses and strategies we've been using. Now that we have centered voices from the margins and begun to uncover root causes, we have an opportunity to radically reshape our pedagogy, leadership, and school culture. We can't do this in an echo chamber, however; transformational, antiracist thinking will emerge from convening a range of perspectives around the table or even flipping the table altogether!

How do we push ourselves beyond the usual solutions and the curse of knowledge—that phenomenon where technical expertise becomes a barrier to innovation? We bring the stakeholders we initially listened to into the conversation as co-designers and co-dreamers. (And yes, I mean the kindergarteners you did listening sessions with! I mean the LGBTQIA students who shared their stories and insights on what needs to change. I mean younger BIPOC staff who perhaps weren't nominated to the leadership team but have a vision of how to move forward.)

For example, imagine sitting in a circle with five of your adorable kindergarteners who have had a hard time sitting still during whole-class instruction. You have done listening sessions with students and parents as well as captured video (with parental permission) to observe how the students engage during guided instruction. You have uncovered their assets as learners as well as some initial root causes: The students describe feeling "wiggly" in their bodies when they have to sit for carpet time. In circle, you ask the students to co-design some new approaches with you:

- When you feel wiggly in your body, what kinds of movements do you want to make? (Students could draw or write their response before sharing verbally.)

- What's great about feeling wiggly, and what's difficult about it for you?

- If you had a magic wand to change one thing about carpet time, what would it be?

- Where and how could we make movements in class so that we don't accidentally hurt others?

- What do you want me to say or do to help you when you feel wiggly?

The reimagine phase is about inquiry *with* those at the margins, not inquiry *for*, which can default into a dangerous type of paternalism or white saviorism. The powerful approach of participatory action research (PAR) can support our efforts here by empowering marginalized community members to learn and apply research techniques in order to uncover innovative solutions to community challenges. The branch of youth participatory action research (YPAR) brings youth and adults together in partnership to improve the conditions of young people's lives and communities. YPAR is anchored in the belief that students are valuable experts with potential to become changemakers and connected to the notion of creating "third spaces" in which students develop hybrid identities that lead to greater engagement and achievement (Gutiérrez, 2008). In Chapter 5, we will return to this theme.

To reimagine, we must convey to everyone assembled that no idea is too "out there" and we are seeking to use all means at our disposal to create new ways of being and learning together. We can stimulate creativity in the physical materials we offer people (markers, pipe cleaners, paint, chalk, three-dimensional papers, etc.), in the design of the meeting space (circles and small groups, chart paper, lots of wall or whiteboard space for visualizing and mapping ideas, etc.), and in the agenda (movement, music, art, meditation, and other non-traditional learning modalities to foster healing and stimulate the group's creative juices).

PROCESS TIPS FOR THE REIMAGINE STAGE

Begin by setting up conscious agreements for the data conversation. A few that Jamila and I employ in our workshops include: *make space, take space; listen and speak with heart and integrity; assume positive intent but think about your impact; notice your discomfort and stay curious; keep our most marginalized students at the center.* Once you have established agreements, you can

- Review street data trends, patterns, and any root causes that have been revealed

- Ask participants to explore their thoughts and feelings about the data through a journal reflection, a listening dyad, or a walk and talk activity (A sample prompt might be, *What emotions does this data raise for you?*)

- Engage the group in a visioning activity, either all together or in small pods (See Reflect and Collaborate questions following.)

- Continue to pose questions to stimulate dreaming (See following questions.)

- Have each group share their ideas, asking others to reflect back what resonates

- Facilitate a dialogue about cross-cutting themes and exciting ideas

- Set clear next steps that might include further street data-gathering

The biggest pitfall at this stage is reverting to the same strategies you've been using because they're familiar, comfortable, or don't shake the table. At the reimagine phase, the rubber meets the road as you move from analyzing street data toward action; it can be incredibly seductive to stay the course with past practices, even dysfunctional ones. Doing something really different may be terrifying enough to elicit resistant responses like "Why not retain our one hundred-point scale grading system? You want me to eliminate the zero and shift to criteria-based rubric grading? No way!" This is why we need additional stakeholders at the table—parents, students, paraprofessionals, teachers who aren't usually consulted—to hold our feet to the fire. With openness and the right set of voices in the mix, we can reimagine the current landscape.

REFLECT AND COLLABORATE: GUIDING QUESTIONS

- What are the people we listened to telling us they want and need?

- In what new directions do the root causes begin to point us?

- What creative ideas and approaches are naturally emerging from the data and dialogue?

- What would success look like if we moved in these directions?

- What do you feel excited to do or try next?

MOVE: The Mindset of Courage

We all know what it's like to set an intention to transform a habit or pattern but then default into old ways of being. Change is *hard*. Just because we've reimagined the landscape of possibility doesn't mean we

have fortified ourselves to act. The final stage of equity-centered transformation, therefore, is to move on your emerging ideas with a mindset of courage. That's right. Strap on your bike helmet, climb onto your bicycle (or into your mobile wheelchair), and pound the pavement. To move signifies the need to act without complete information or the perfect design and is captured in a team agreement developed by my colleague John Watkins for the Deeper Learning Dozen, a project he runs: "Accept non-closure . . . but not non-action" (Watkins, n.d.).

When we commit to move, no matter what the outcome, we commit to be courageous in the face of inequity. We *will* meet with resistance, recalcitrance, defensiveness—all of those things that stymie progress. But as Frederick Douglass wrote, "If there is no struggle, there is no progress" (Douglass, 1857). It's time to be bold and try something new. Remember that the solution to an equity challenge is unknown and emergent. It can only be revealed by continuing to gather street data, uncover root causes, and reimagine our systems, structures, and ways of being together.

REFLECT AND COLLABORATE: GUIDING QUESTIONS

- What is the team's call to action now, emerging from the data?

- What will you try and do together in the next four to six weeks?

- How will you know it has succeeded or failed as an experiment? What additional data will you gather?

- What will help you be courageous together and stay the course?

If Love Were to Guide Us

As you think about how to flip the dashboard, pound the pavement, and center street data in your efforts to pursue equity—consider these wise words by author adrienne maree brown who reminds us that love is the center of the work:

> *If love were the central practice of a new generation of organizers and spiritual leaders . . . we would see that there is no such thing as a blank canvas, an empty land or a new idea—but everywhere there is complex, ancient, fertile ground full of potential. We would organize with the perspective that there is wisdom and experience and amazing story in the communities we love . . . we would want to listen, support, and grow . . . we would understand that the strength of our movement is the strength of our relationships, which could only be measured in their depth. Scaling up would mean going deeper, being more vulnerable and more empathetic.* (a. m. brown, 2017, pp. 9–10)

GETTING UP CLOSE AND PERSONAL: REFLECTION QUESTIONS

1. Share your reactions to the equity transformation cycle (listen, uncover, reimagine, move). Which phase feels most intuitive to you? Which feels like a stretch, and why?

2. What do you see as the key differences between improvement science (plan-do-study-act) and the street data model?

3. Reflect on a time when you tried to plan-do-study-act. What might have gone differently if you had used the equity transformation cycle instead?

4. How will you develop your practice around the core stance of deep listening? When does it get hard for you to listen deeply, and how can you stay grounded in this stance?

5. Set ONE next step in your journey as a street data educator.

Deepen the Learning

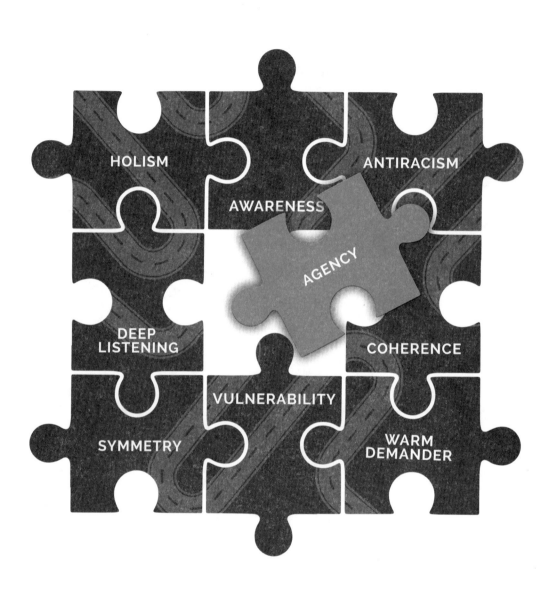

Redefine "Success"

Street Data and the Pedagogy of Voice

5

The BALMA Project (Balboa High School and Marin Academy): In 1998, four years before No Child Left Behind transformed the American educational landscape, Shane was a young teacher launching the Law Academy program at a diverse urban public high school. At a summer workshop on project-based learning, she met a phenomenal woman educator of Afro-Cuban descent from Marin Academy, a nearby private school serving affluent, predominantly white students. Together, they hatched the BALMA project, inviting their students from vastly different worlds to meet, connect, and investigate equity in education. The project unfolded over several months and included reciprocal site visits, an overnight retreat at Marin Academy, shared readings and discussions, and a final multimedia presentation of learning to over two hundred people from both communities. Through this story, which was made into an Emmy-nominated PBS documentary called *Making the Grade* (Bay Window, 1999), Chapter 5 redefines student success and examines the transformative impact of deep-learning experiences that are shaped by a pedagogy of voice.

Equity work is first and foremost pedagogical.

You teachers were like, "I'm not going to sit up here and just talk about my life and tell you that my path is your path. I'm going to listen to you and you're going to tell me your narrative." That showed me that it's *not just about educating. It's not just about academia, right? There's academics, and there's educators . . . the difference is that educators, they give the power to <u>you</u>. They don't just teach you and expect you to follow that path with no questions asked.*

—Krishtine de Leon (aka Rocky Rivera),
BALMA graduate, hip-hop journalist and MC;
winner of a contributing editor position on
MTV's docu-series *I'm From Rolling Stone*

When we did this project, affirmative action had just been dismantled. The question hanging in the air was, "If you had access [as a low-income student of color], will you be able to be on par?" Not only were our students on par, but they <u>outperformed</u>, and not only outperformed, but made changes to the system, to the institution, and played a significant role while they were there.

—Rex de Guia, BALMA project teacher

I was lucky to become a teacher in 1997, before the test-and-punish era dawned and stripped so many educators of a sense of agency and possibility. I was lucky to have professors in my teacher preparation who pushed me to define my pedagogical philosophy—to say what I believed about teaching and learning and stand firmly in those beliefs. I remember being asked to write a paper on what social justice teaching meant to me: Was it convincing students to take up a cause, or building a classroom environment in which they discovered their *own* voices and causes? I struggled with this question at first, but as I read the research and saturated myself in seminal work like Cherry A. McGee Banks and James Banks's "Equity Pedagogy" (1995), I knew. My job was to help young people find their voices, not stamp them with mine. This was before the standardized testing movement had convinced us that learning could be captured, like a Polaroid snapshot, in a number. This was before terms like "teacher-proofing" and "pacing guides" and "scripted curricula" had entered the popular educational lexicon.

As a young teacher in the late 1990s and early 2000s, I was standing on the shoulders of giants—part of a long legacy of educators who sought to disrupt the social order by emancipating the brilliance of students the world said weren't good enough, smart enough, or worthy of an intellectual life.

I was standing on the shoulders of Paolo Freire, the Brazilian educator who popularized the theory of critical pedagogy and whose *Pedagogy of the Oppressed* (Freire, 1970) radicalized how I understood my role in the classroom.

I was standing on the shoulders of John Dewey, Deborah Meier, and a century of educators who argued that democracy *depends* on giving students the chance to grapple with ideas and construct knowledge through hands-on learning experiences.

I was standing on the shoulders of more than a century of Black educators and scholars—from Mary Jane Patterson and Fanny Jackson Coppin to Edmund Gordon, Jacqueline Irving, Geneva Gay, and Gloria Ladson-Billings—who, despite a racist academy, radical *exclusion*, and relentlessly hostile environments, insisted their students were brilliant and had the right to learn.

This powerful legacy reminds me of our chapter principle: Equity work is first and foremost pedagogical. I believe we have lost something intangible since testing overtook the educational psyche: our collective imagination. The ability to dream and manifest a different way of teaching, learning, and *being* together persists and chafes against the status quo in classrooms everywhere; yet it is often a lonely pursuit—going against the grain of state, district, and school policies that functionally incarcerate our imagination. If we don't seize this moment to transform our fundamental approaches to teaching and learning, we will navel-gaze and boomerang ourselves into the same played-out approaches and results: a pedagogy of compliance for children at the margins and "success" for the privileged.

If we accept that success can be defined by a metric—if we hold true that a child's test scores or grade point average are determinants of her future—we will find ourselves forever suspended in a hamster wheel, chasing external solutions, curricula, and validation. But if we believe that every student is more than a number (or a "trauma" story)—is in fact a complex, layered human being with endless potential, brilliance, and access to community cultural wealth—we can choose a pedagogy of voice that transforms everything from our classrooms to our adult cultures to our policies. **Such a pedagogy says, "I see you. I believe in you. You are safe to grow and thrive here. I want to hear your voice."**

Measuring What Matters: The Core Stance of Agency

For me, growing up in San Francisco, I feel like so many of us hadn't left our own community. So many of us hadn't seen the resources and what other people were experiencing in other parts of California, and many of them not far away. The BALMA Project was empowering. It helped me take ownership of my own education. Even though you had to look at structural inequalities and systemic injustice, you felt empowered knowing that you didn't have to sit silently with it. It riled you up to have a sense of activism, a sense of purpose, and a sense of feeling empowered.

—Taina Gomez, BALMA graduate, deputy public
defender at Solano County Public Defender's Office

Agency is the core stance of this chapter. Our equity efforts truly begin when we redefine success as the cultivation of student agency and realign our *measures* of success to this goal. This requires an explicit shift from satellite data to street data. To make such a shift, we must grapple with why voice and agency matter, particularly for historically marginalized students, and how to reshape our curriculum and pedagogy to these ends. Let's look at the BALMA project for insight.

The BALMA project was a social experiment where three teachers— one white (myself), one Afro-Cuban (Lisa), and one Filipino (my teaching partner, Rex de Guia)—linked arms to pull back the curtain on educational inequity and empower our students as changemakers. Through this experience, our students developed college literacy and critical thinking skills; wrote incisive essays about the opportunity gaps they were witnessing, drawing on the work of James Baldwin, Paolo Freire, and bell hooks; and created reflective art pieces about who society was molding them to be versus who they wanted to become. As they developed collective efficacy, they designed and led a community forum with over two hundred people from San Francisco and Marin counties to share their findings and attended school board meetings to demand structural change.

In short, they developed a profound sense of agency by connecting to each other and to something larger than themselves. Each of the examples above—essays, reflections, public speaking, community advocacy—provided us, their teachers, with rich street data on learning. None of them could have been captured in a "metric."

FIGURE 5.1 Agency Framework

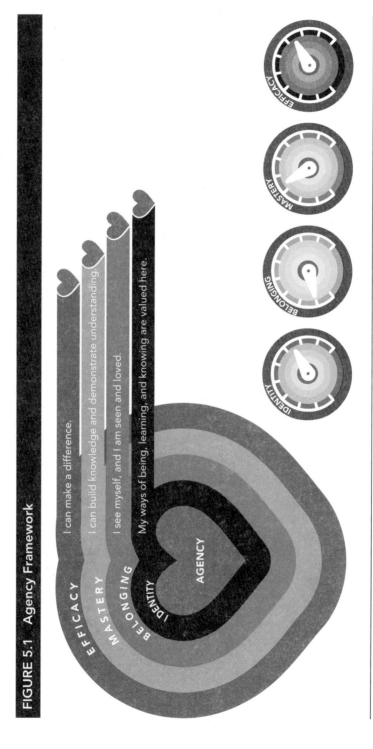

EFFICACY — I can make a difference.

MASTERY — I can build knowledge and demonstrate understanding.

BELONGING — I see myself, and I am seen and loved.

IDENTITY — My ways of being, learning, and knowing are valued here.

AGENCY

IDENTITY BELONGING MASTERY EFFICACY

If we are serious about creating equitable school systems, we need to stop measuring children on norm-referenced tests and start measuring what matters: student agency. **Agency** is the idea that people have the capacity to take action, craft and carry out plans, and make informed decisions based on a growing base of knowledge. In the social ecology of the classroom, agency is about connection to self, peers, adults, the community beyond the classroom, and ultimately the world. Agency doesn't emerge in a vacuum, nor does it flourish in a traditional classroom where the teacher is positioned as a content expert dishing out knowledge. It emerges in a learning space where power is distributed, knowledge is democratized, diverse perspectives are welcomed, and children are intellectually and emotionally nourished.

Let's think about agency in relationship to four domains: identity, mastery, belonging, and efficacy. To experience agency, you must first feel that your core **identity**—your ways of being, learning, and knowing in the world—is valued. Tunison (2007) notes that "lack of identity, lack of voice, and low self-esteem" can damage the **learning spirit**—an Indigenous concept that spirits travel with individuals and guide their learning, providing inspiration and the unrealized potential to be who we are. Author and founder of the abolitionist teaching movement Bettina Love defines **spirit murdering** in schools as "the denial of inclusion, protection, safety, nurturance, and acceptance because of fixed, yet fluid and moldable, structures of racism" (Love, 2013).

The second component of agency is **mastery**, framed as the ability to build knowledge and demonstrate understanding as a learner. To experience mastery, students must be able to show what they know in nontraditional ways. Pencil-and-paper tests not only trigger acute anxiety for many learners, they also lack the nuance and texture of street data. In reality, they are micro-versions of standardized tests that function like satellite data inside the classroom. *Why did the student solve the problem the way they did? How were they feeling when they took the test? What happened earlier that day or morning that may have impacted their performance?* With traditional assessments, we are left guessing. Project-based learning, performance assessment, and discussion-based classrooms, on the other hand, create an infrastructure for students to explore, construct, reflect on, and publicly demonstrate knowledge. Students become agents in their own learning rather than consumers of curriculum. For example, when our BALMA students presented their findings to a community forum of two hundred people, they enjoyed an authentic audience to share their learning with. This held them accountable and raised the stakes on their work in the best possible way.

At my second teaching job in Oakland, California, I was asked to create a graduate capstone project for seniors. I was teaching ninth and twelfth graders, almost exclusively Black, Latinx, Southeast Asian, and first generation to college students. My seniors would be the first class to present and defend their capstones to a committee of teachers, peers, and community members. I vividly recall Alberto—a young man who had left behind a life of stealing, stripping, and reselling Honda vehicles to become a budding scholar—presenting his capstone in a beautiful *guayabera* shirt, translating each part into Spanish for his proud mamá. I was Alberto's advisor and English teacher, so I had the privilege to coach him through the process. He had meticulously prepared, did a fantastic job, and when the committee announced that he had passed his capstone, he broke down in tears. Why? He felt an overwhelming sense of agency in having shared his knowledge publicly in ways that honored his family, heritage, and language. What test could possibly capture that?

The third component of mastery is **belonging**, which is encapsulated in the statement, "I see myself, and I am seen and loved here." Belonging emerges in a classroom characterized by deep and caring relationships. Author Zaretta Hammond frames relationships as the onramp to learning, particularly for marginalized students who may have little reason to trust their educators (Hammond, 2014). Herb Kohl describes the phenomenon of "willed *not* learning," whereby students resist being intellectually vulnerable in the face of teachers who don't authentically care about them (Kohl, 1995). Deep learning can only happen in a classroom where a child feels a sense of belonging.

Despite piles of research on the importance of relationships and connectedness to the neuroscience of learning, many Black and brown students experience an acute *lack* of belonging when they enter their school buildings. According to Californians for Justice, a youth organizing group, one out of every three California students cannot identify a single caring adult on campus. I have worked with districts where that number rose to 50 percent. Meanwhile, 30 percent of African American students and 22 percent of Latinx students in California enter high school only to drop out before graduating, a data point replicated in high-poverty regions across the nation. We have a crisis of alienation in our schools, driven at the highest levels by the insidious messages of satellite data, in effect: "You are not achieving on these measures; therefore, we have to fix you with interventions. By extension, you don't really *belong* to this academic community. You are a problem to be solved, a gap to be filled." It hurts my heart to write those words because I know that so many young people experience school this way.

Fostering a sense of belonging does not mean plastering our classrooms and school walls with ethnically diverse posters and inspirational sayings or celebrating "diversity days"—the so-called Heroes and Holidays approach (Lee, Menkart, & Okazawa-Rey, 1998). Rather, it demands rigorous attention to systemic racism, school and classroom cultures, and the micro-interactions that characterize a student's passage through the school day. This is why shadowing a student delivers such powerful street data: It gives us a ground-level view of the ways in which children are included, excluded, marginalized, or just plain invisible in their learning environments.

Finally, agency is about nourishing students' sense of efficacy—a feeling that "I can make a difference here." Collective *teacher* efficacy, the shared belief among teachers in their ability to positively affect students, has emerged in John Hattie's research as the number one influence on student learning (Hattie, 2008). For our purposes of assessing student agency, efficacy means the learner's ability to set an intention and produce a desired result, and it is absolutely critical to healing from and transforming oppression. Scholar Shawn Ginwright describes the importance of helping young people take "loving action, by collectively responding to political decisions and practices that can exacerbate trauma" (Ginwright, 2018). Taking action via project-based learning, peer surveys, organizing a walkout, or building a resource for your community vests students with a sense of power and control over their lives, which research has shown is one of the most significant factors in restoring well-being for marginalized groups.

HOW CAN WE MEASURE AGENCY? THREE IDEAS

1. **Administer a ten-question pre- and post-survey on 1–4 Likert scale, from strongly disagree to strongly agree.**

   - My culture, identities, and ways of being are valued here.

   - My ways of learning are valued here.

   - My ways of knowing and understanding the world are valued here.

   - I have opportunities to build and construct my own knowledge.

   - I have opportunities to demonstrate understanding to peers and teachers.

- I have opportunities to demonstrate understanding to the community or groups of people beyond my classroom.
- I see myself represented in the staff, curriculum, and school culture.
- I feel seen and loved by my teachers.
- I feel seen and loved by my peers.
- I feel like I can make a difference here.

Elementary Version: 5 Questions

- I feel important here.
- Everybody knows my cultural identity and how to pronounce my name.
- I get a lot of chances to show what I know here.
- I feel like my teacher cares about me.
- I feel like my classmates care about me.

2. **Conduct agency interviews with a sample of students, asking the following:**

- To what extent do you feel your ways of being and learning are valued here?
- How often do you have opportunities to construct your own knowledge (versus taking notes or digesting information provided by the teacher)?
- How often do you have opportunities to demonstrate your understanding in a way that's different from a test or quiz? What is that experience like?
- To what extent do you feel like you belong here? Why or why not?
- To what extent do you feel seen and loved here? Why or why not?
- When is the last time you felt that you could make a difference here about something that matters to you? What was that like?
- What ideas do you have to make our school a place where you feel a greater sense of power and agency?

Elementary Version

- Does this class help you feel smart? Why or why not?
- When is the last time you came up with your own idea in this class, and how did it feel?

(Continued)

(Continued)

- What's your favorite way to show what you know?
- Do you like coming to this class? Why or why not?
- Do you feel loved by your teacher and peers? Why or why not?
- If you could wave a magic wand to make something different here, what would it be?

3. **Have students regularly complete a single-point rubric[1] reflection on agency:**

ROSES	AGENCY AREAS/ DOMAINS	THORNS
WHAT IS SOMETHING THAT WENT WELL IN THIS AREA?		*WHAT GOT IN THE WAY OR WAS HARD FOR YOU IN THIS AREA?*
	Identity "This week, I felt like my culture, identity, or ways of being, learning, and knowing were valued here."	
	Mastery "This week, I had opportunities to build my own knowledge and/or demonstrate my understanding of key ideas."	
	Belonging "This week, I felt like I belonged here. I felt seen and loved in this classroom."	
	Efficacy "This week, I had an opportunity to make a difference in this (classroom or school)."	

---

[1]According to blogger Jennifer Gonzalez, a single-point rubric breaks down the components of an assignment into different criteria but only describes the criteria for proficiency; it does not attempt to list all the ways a student could fall short, nor does it specify how a student could exceed expectations (Gonzalez, 2014).

Toward a Pedagogy of Voice

Reorienting ourselves from test scores to student *agency* requires a pedagogical reorientation that transforms power in the classroom and ignites the natural curiosity and intellect of young people. **Critical pedagogy**, a teaching approach popularized by Paolo Freire, helps students question and challenge the status quo, develop habits of mind that go beneath surface meaning, uncover root causes of oppression, engage in deep thinking, and create counternarratives about their lived experiences. It is a practice that cultivates critical consciousness in students whose voices and ideas have been marginalized. **Culturally responsive education** invokes a pedagogy that recognizes the importance of including students' cultural references in all aspects of instruction and calls for deep cognitive engagement of learners whose culture and experiences have been relegated to the margins (Ladson-Billings, 1994).

A **pedagogy of voice** emerges at the intersection of critical pedagogy and culturally responsive education, offering an instructional technology and way of being that shifts the locus of learning and power to the student. A pedagogy of voice transcends numbers and metrics to create street-level learning experiences that foster healing, cognitive growth, and agency. **It centers street data through dynamic student dialogue and rich student work, and it *de*centers compliance, grading, the quest for "answers," competition, and all the other features of dominant classroom culture that uphold the testing-industrial complex.**

To cultivate student voice, we must first feel a sense of agency as educators. We have to free our minds from the persistent narrative that test scores and even grades tell a legitimate story about our students' success. We have to free our *own* learning spirits to be bold and experimental—to try pedagogical approaches that feel new, edgy, and perhaps uncomfortable. We have to be willing to flip our pedagogy and instructional leadership to center student and teacher voices, just as we flipped the dashboard to center street data. This requires that we recognize the features of a pedagogy of compliance that still operate inside many classrooms and professional-learning spaces.

A **pedagogy of compliance** continues to dominate the majority of American classrooms, particularly at a secondary level, characterized by lecture-style instruction, students in rows looking toward the teacher as knowledge expert, and teachers carrying the cognitive load. This model minimizes instructional conversation between teacher and student and among students. According to a Gallup poll, only 53 percent of our nation's students report they are engaged in their formal learning, as measured by three factors: enthusiasm for school, whether they feel well known, and how often they get to do what they do best. Latinx and African American teens are especially disconnected (Gallup, 2014; Annie E. Casey Foundation, 2012). Compliance-driven pedagogy leads to student disengagement.

Freire described the compliance approach as a **banking model of education**, which positions the teacher as subject and active participant and the students as passive objects. Education is viewed as a process of depositing knowledge into students' brains, with little to no attention to students' preexisting knowledge and cultural schema. The purpose of the banking model is to develop students into "adaptable, manageable beings. . . . The more completely they accept the passive role imposed on them, the more they tend simply to adapt to the world as it is and to the fragmented view of reality deposited in them" (Freire, 1970). Compliance is the end game. Table 5.1 frames the shift from a pedagogy of compliance to a pedagogy of voice.

What if shedding the pedagogy of compliance and embracing a pedagogy of voice were easier than it appears? What if we could subscribe to a few simple rules that, if held with fidelity, would produce the kinds of dynamic, holistic, and equitable classrooms we dream of and long for? I am a big believer in **simplexity**, a term coined by global thought leader Michael Fullan as a way to navigate complex realities with simple rules. Fullan's advice is to identify a small number of core factors (6 or so) that constitute your focus (the *simple* part), recognizing that the challenge is how to make them coalesce in actual learning spaces (the *complex* part) (Fullan, 2009).

Six simple rules guide a pedagogy of voice that will release you from the shackles of compliance:

- Talk less, smile more

- Questions over answers

- Ritualize reflection and revision

- Make learning public

- Circle up

- Feedback over grades

TABLE 5.1	Shifting From a Pedagogy of Compliance to a Pedagogy of Voice	
	FROM A PEDAGOGY OF COMPLIANCE . . .	. . . TO A PEDAGOGY OF VOICE
Primary Form of Data	Tests and quizzes (traditional assessments)	Street data (formative assessments, performance-based assessments)
Core Belief	Hierarchy of power: teacher wields expertise and distributes "content"	Democratization of power: teacher and students build knowledge together
Core Instructional Approach	Lecture-style dissemination of information	Active learning through inquiry, dialogue, projects, simulations, etc.
Roots in Critical Pedagogy	Freire's banking model of education	Freire's problem-posing model of education
Roots in Culturally Responsive Education	Rests on invisible norms of dominant culture (quiet, compliant, task oriented, individualistic) Views marginalized students through a deficit lens: *What gaps can I fill?*	Rests on foundation of collectivist cultures (collaborative, interdependent, relational) and includes students' cultural references in all aspects of learning Views marginalized students through an asset lens: *What gifts do you bring?*
Views Students as . . .	Vessels to fill with information	Culturally grounded critical learners

If you are a teacher struggling to break free from traditional methods, breathe these ideas in and let them settle in your mind. If you are already living inside the pedagogy of voice and want to bring your colleagues along with you, use these ideas as an invitation to conversation. If you are an administrator working to transform instruction, adapt these ideas into an instructional vision, use them to structure coaching and adult learning, and shape them into a public narrative about where you want your school to go. Let's dig in.

Simple Rule 1: Talk Less, Smile More

In Lin Manuel Miranda's musical *Hamilton*, politician Aaron Burr is mentoring the young Hamilton, in a bar no less. His main piece of advice is to talk less, smile more, and not let people know what his beliefs and views are. If I could write the perfect lyric to capture the pedagogy of voice, this would be it! Colleagues, if you can change one thing tomorrow—whether you're a classroom teacher, teacher leader, coach, or administrator—try to talk less, smile more, and design lessons and professional learning that allow learners to discover what *they* think and feel.

Why does this matter? As long as we do the talking and make knowledge deposits into the learner's brain, we are carrying the cognitive load. We are doing the thinking. We retain power and inhibit the growth of agency. Shift the thinking and cognitive load to the learner by designing curriculum (and adult learning) around probing, reflective questions with ample time for discussion. My personal rules of thumb are as follows:

- Never talk more than ten to fifteen minutes without pausing for information processing and/or reflection.

- Design lessons and adult learning so that learners are engaged in conversation with *each other* at least 75 percent of the time.

- During that time, circulate, coach, and ask *more* questions. Model a culture of inquiry.

What about the "smile more" part of Aaron Burr's advice, you might be wondering? Here, we turn to the power of nonverbal communication to foster or shatter a child's experience of belonging. When we smile and use tone and other nonverbal cues to convey warmth, we signal to students that they are safe, welcome, and able to take risks. (Note: This doesn't mean we never model *gravitas* or firmness in our demeanor.) For students who have been personally and educationally marginalized, this is crucial. Think about a classroom in which students have experienced trauma, including microaggressions by peers and/or teachers. The teacher's emotional tenor will be at least as important as the content they share. Talking less and smiling more helps us communicate to every child, "You are seen and loved here."

Simple Rule 2: Questions Over Answers

Children are naturally inquisitive. A recent study led by British child psychologist Dr. Sam Wass found that children ask an average of seventy-three questions per day (Steingold, 2017)! Good questions are important, interesting, and don't have a clear answer. Unfortunately, far too many students are still required to sit quietly and absorb information from their teachers. Those children who dare to ask questions risk being pathologized as "disruptive" and "off-task." This is especially true for many Black students whose brilliance and curiosity is filtered through a lens of racism and bias.

In order to shift the cognitive load, we have to create a culture of inquiry in our classrooms and professional-learning spaces. This means that we begin to prioritize questions over answers. I remember watching Danfeng Koon, a founding math teacher at the school I led, circulate around her ninth grade algebra classroom as students labored in small groups. When stumped by a new concept, a student would pop his hand in the air, sending out an SOS to Danfeng, who would slowly and calmly approach the table. The student would pitch a question, and Danfeng—without fail!—would respond with another question. *What do you think? Who else could you ask? What are different ways to approach that problem?* She held a firm belief: Never tell students something they can figure out on their own. A simple rule.

In the BALMA project that opened this chapter, we spiraled students through many layers of questions. On the project level, we asked, *What can we learn about equity in education through a private-public school collaboration?* As students from the two schools came together and witnessed extreme opportunity gaps in their respective experiences, we asked, *What are you learning and discovering? What thoughts and feelings are emerging for you? And what do want to do about it?* We also had them apply the learning inside their own school buildings, exploring the question, *What types of pedagogy are happening down the hall, and how are students impacted?* As students learned about Freire's banking and problem-posing models of education, I arranged for them to observe other classrooms and take copious notes on what they saw (street data!). When they came back to my class, I drew a Freirean spectrum on the board and had each student ethnographer locate the pedagogies they had observed, justifying their responses with evidence.[2]

I think about questions through the lens of fractals—those never-ending patterns that replicate across different scales. When you embrace a pedagogy of voice, you commit to investing your energy in

---

[2]To state what I hope is clear, do this activity with full transparency and permission from your colleagues.

developing sharp, intriguing, rich questions at every level of the learning experience. Table 5.2 outlines different ways to think about this.

The best learning is driven by students' authentic questions—the kinds of wonderings that keep them up at night and light their cognitive fires. As an educator and instructional leader, you have the power to model relentless curiosity and the power of inquiry. Design learning experiences that allow students to begin to discover their own

TABLE 5.2   Questions as a Fractal Pedagogy

UNIT OF INQUIRY	EXAMPLE(S)
Students pose their own questions.	• Journaling: *What questions are coming up for you as we begin this unit study?* • KWL: *Jot down what you k(now) and w(ant) to know about our new area of study. At the end, we will write down what we l(earned).*
Students ask each other questions.	• Small group or fishbowl discussions, centered around students' questions (have them jot down questions on sticky notes first and take turns asking them). • Reciprocal teaching model: A scaffolded discussion technique that incorporates four main strategies—predicting, questioning, clarifying, summarizing. • Give one, get one: Have students develop questions, then stand, pair-share, and trade. Encourage them to find answers on their own or by engaging with peers.
Students ask you questions.	• Cognitive apprenticeship/teacher-as-coach: Instead of answering student questions, respond with questions. • Conferencing: Organize mini-conferences with students on a significant piece of work in which they come with their own questions.
Teacher poses questions to the class.	• Socratic discussion: Pose open-ended questions with no clear answer. Over time, have students lead the discussion.
Teacher structures an assessment, task, project, or unit around an essential question.	• Initiate a unit around an essential question that students revisit each week and do a final assessment around. • Organize project-based learning or performance-based assessments around provocative open-ended questions.

ideas. Stay tethered to our goal of student *agency* by ritually asking the following questions:

- "What matters to you about this content/project, and why?" (identity)

- "What is getting in the way of your learning/engagement, and how can I best support you?" (belonging)

- "What is the evidence for the claim you're making?" (mastery)

- "What ideas do you want to contribute to this discussion/project? What action do you want to take?" (efficacy)

Simple Rule 3: Ritualize Reflection and Revision

Centering student voice doesn't mean we stop giving feedback, but it does mean we shift our role from expert lecturer to expert *coach*, charged with the cognitive apprenticeship of students. Reflection and revision are two of our strongest tools in this regard and help students at the margins accelerate their skills over time. Scholar Linda Darling-Hammond has written about a culture of revision and redemption that characterizes equitable classrooms:

> Another important characteristic of schools with an adaptive pedagogy is a learning environment where teachers are aware of what students are thinking, and where the curriculum does not move on when students do not learn immediately. Unlike the traditional "teach, test, and hope for the best" approach, . . . adaptive teachers don't say, "You got a C-" on this assignment and then move on to the next unit without looking back. Instead, they give students the opportunity to tackle difficult tasks without fear of failure by promoting a culture of revision and redemption that encourages students to attempt challenging work, provides continual opportunities for practice and revision, and supports students in developing the courage and confidence to work continuously to improve in their successive efforts. (Darling-Hammond, 2002, p. 28–29)

Reflection and revision can take place daily, weekly, and throughout a unit of instruction. Here are a few ways to operationalize this simple rule:

- Teach reflection and revision as explicit skills and processes. Consider this core content and model it in your instruction. Be vulnerable in sharing times when you have had to revise a piece of work to make it better. Reflect publicly on instructional mistakes you make.

- Begin a class period with time for students to reflect in writing and/or a turn and talk: *What did you learn yesterday that stuck with you? What's a concept that still feels confusing?*

- Use the traffic light strategy for students to signal how well they understand the current content. Give each student a red, yellow, and green square of paper or mini-plastic cups. Have them put the color on top that indicates where they're at: green for "I'm good," yellow for "I sort of get it, but have some questions," red for "I'm lost! SOS!"

- End each week with a reflection protocol: *What did I learn this week? What's one thing I feel proud about? What's one thing I'm still struggling with?* Have them share their responses in small, ongoing peer groups and close with each student giving the peer to their left or right an appreciation.

- Provide students with graphic organizers and structured protocols for giving each other feedback on their work. Teach them to sandwich feedback! *"What I loved about this piece of work was . . . One question I had was . . . One suggestion I have is . . ."*

- Whenever possible, make time for one-on-one conferencing with students around their work. Conferences can provide the most impactful learning moments.

Simple Rule 4: Make Learning Public

> *You were courageous to take some kids that were very city-oriented to other areas, trusting us. You trusted us to run a classroom of juniors as mentor seniors, right? You said, "Here's your parameters; now create your lesson plan."*
>
> —Damien Padilla, BALMA graduate, union organizer, and grassroots safety lead, Pacific Gas & Electric

One of the quickest ways to embrace a pedagogy of voice is to put students in the driver's seat by having them design and teach lessons. On a macro-pedagogy level, you can build units and projects around culminating exhibitions and/or performance-based assessments. To cultivate agency, we have to stop being the only audience for student work. We must create authentic ways for students (and adult learners) to *share* the knowledge they are building. Student work is the yin to the yang of student voice. Public learning, which contributing author Carrie Wilson will apply to an adult-learning context in Chapter 7, is most impactful when situated in a holistic performance assessment *system* that is based on common, school-wide standards and integrated into daily instructional decisions. Such a system shows students what they need to do by providing models, demonstrations, simulations, and exhibitions of the kind of high-quality academic work they need to produce. More on this in Chapter 6 when we discuss coherence!

Here are a few features of public learning that you can begin to experiment with in your classroom, grade-level team, department, school, or district:

- Portfolios of student work that showcase in-depth study via research papers, original science experiments, literary analyses, artistic performances or exhibitions, mathematical models, and more

- Rubrics that represent explicit, shared standards against which to assess student work and performance

- Oral defenses by students to a committee of teachers, peers, and, potentially, community members that allow educators to listen for in-depth understanding

- Multiple opportunities for students to revise their work, redeem their academic status, and grow their skills in order to demonstrate learning (Adapted from Darling-Hammond, 2002, p. 16)

Simple Rule 5: Circle Up

The structure of compliant classrooms is painfully predictable: students in rows, plugged into individual desks like widgets, taking notes from a sage-on-stage up front. This scene implicitly communicates to students that their voices don't matter, their cultural schema and knowledge are tangential at best, and their job is to get "filled up" by the expert at the helm. By contrast, reshaping our classrooms and adult-learning spaces into circles communicates equality of voice and membership in the community. Circles represent the village coming together for dialogue and signal to the learner: "You belong here, just as everyone around you belongs here. I want to see your face and hear your voice."

My colleague Perry Smith, an education leader in British Columbia, notes that circles are an Indigenous structure used for thousands of years across North America and the world. Rooted in Indigenous ways of knowing, circles surface in ceremony, gatherings, events, the cyclicality of verses in songs, and even the shape of the drum. In Perry's words, "All the power in the world comes from the circle. When we sit in a circle, there is no head. Everyone is equal" (P. Smith, 2020). Disrupt the pedagogy of compliance by reshaping your classroom around the circle. Use circles to design the following:

- Socratic seminars

- Concentric circle activities: An inner group of learners faces outward, and an outer group faces inward, forming discussion pairs. One circle rotates each time the teacher offers a new prompt or question for dialogue.

- Science lab experiments or mathematical modeling where students huddle around a table

- Design-build projects where students huddle around materials and a design challenge

- Literature circles where students engage over time in academic discussion of a shared text, with their questions driving discussion

Circles are an adaptable shape and the signature structure of a democratic classroom. They transform power, allowing each student to find their voice and including the teacher in a non-hierarchical community of learning and practice.

Simple Rule 6: Feedback Over Grades

Finally, a pedagogy of voice requires us to break the stranglehold that grading has over classrooms across the country. As a parent and educator, I see teachers lost in algorithms, equations, and formulas that strip critical judgment out of teaching and learning. Grading echoes the econometric framework of testing, presuming that we can encapsulate learning in a number or a letter. Street data reminds us that our primary task as educators is to provide regular feedback to students so they can grow, not to evaluate them in order to anoint them academically capable or not.

Feedback can be its own equity trap and trope, contributing to distrust or diminished confidence for BIPOC students if not delivered with care. Claude Steele and his colleagues coined the term wise feedback to describe a way of providing students of color with structured, empowering explanations that mitigate stereotype threat and reduce the possibility that feedback is experienced as biased (Cohen, Steele, & Ross, 1999). This process includes three instructional elements: Describe the nature of the feedback being offered; emphasize and explain the high standards used to evaluate the student work, and organize the feedback; explicitly state a belief that the student has the skills needed to meet those standards.

Feedback helps us remember that learning is messy, in the best possible way! Every moment in the classroom is an opportunity to gather street data on the cognitive complexities of learning—the aha moments, the stumbling blocks, the bursts of creativity, the spirals of self-doubt and shame, the neurological effects of stress and trauma. Rather than contribute to our understanding of what's getting in the way for students, grades often create added stress and emotional pressure, particularly for children with learning differences and those struggling to catch up to grade level.

My colleague Joe Feldman's masterful book *Grading for Equity* (Feldman, 2018) takes up this topic in-depth (I highly recommend it), but I'll offer a few tips in the spirit of simple rules:

- Stop grading homework. Homework should be framed as low-stakes practice on new skills, not a hammer to promote compliance or punish children who struggle to get it done.

- Stop measuring participation. Participation grades are rife with bias, inviting unconscious discrimination against students with attention challenges or cultural/communication styles that don't mirror the teacher's. Participation is notoriously hard to measure, so just don't. As a footnote, reimagine all behavior charts. They are often punitive, shaming, and biased.

- Allow late work. One principal I know established a three-day grace period for every student for every assignment. He explained it like this: "The penalty for not doing the assignment is *doing* the assignment!"

- Allow redos and retakes. Any student should be able to retake a major assessment for a full new grade as long as they are coming to school and putting in basic effort. This tacks to the culture of revision and redemption we discussed earlier.

- Use descriptive, criterion-based rubrics instead of points. Points promote a culture of bean-counting and competition, whereas rubrics, when well-crafted, promote reflection.

- Use grades to summarize student achievement over time, after the child has had ample opportunities to redo and revisit, not to punish or change student behavior.

- Eliminate the zero. It severely disadvantages learners who are struggling for a variety of reasons and breeds hopelessness.

- Make time for narrative feedback and student conferencing, whenever possible. If your student load is too high, teach students to do this with each other in structured peer conferences.

The six simple rules cut across micro- and macro-pedagogies, from small moves at the interpersonal level to big moves in curriculum and assessment design. Put together, they will help you shape a pedagogy of voice that generates rich street data and cultivates the most important measure of all, student agency.

The BALMA Project, Revisited

In this chapter, we connected the concept of street data to the instructional core, positing that equity work is first and foremost pedagogical. We reframed success through the lens of student agency, imagining what it would be like to measure identity, mastery, belonging, and efficacy rather than test scores. And we explored six simple rules of a pedagogy of voice that will help us break free from the compliance mindset sewn by the testing era. The implications of these shifts are monumental. Access to a pedagogy of voice and agency can change a student's life trajectory.

I recently had the opportunity to sit down with five BALMA project students who are now adults with careers, families, and lives of their own. Taina Gomez (2019), now a public defender, shared this:

> *Our teachers inspired us to believe that we could do anything. They inspired us to believe that we were worthy and smart and capable. I think they saw something wonderful in us. . . . [The BALMA project] helped us see beyond our own communities, that there is this huge big world out there and despite the obstacles that we faced, some of which we had no control over, we could overcome. . . .*

I was able to be the first one in my family to go on to college. I obtained a full tuition ride to UC Berkeley, and I was able to go on to law school afterwards.

The BALMA project was simply one project that allowed students to find their voices, become agents of change, and develop critical consciousness around culturally and personally relevant issues. Our day-to-day lessons emerged from the micro-pedagogies of relationship, belonging, inquiry, feedback, discussion, field research, and taking action. Teachers across the country and globe build learning experiences like this every week. As I look back, a thought arises in me: This felt like the practice of freedom.

GETTING UP CLOSE AND PERSONAL: REFLECTION QUESTIONS

1. Share a passage that struck you. Reflect on the feelings it brought up and its implications for your practice.

2. What are your reactions to the idea of measuring student agency in the areas of identity, belonging, mastery, and efficacy? What would this look like in your role and context?

3. Which of the six simple rules for a pedagogy of voice most resonate with you and why?

4. Set a practice goal for yourself, either around moving toward student agency as a core stance and metric or around a pedagogy of voice. Write your goal below, alongside one concrete next step you'll take.

MY PRACTICE GOAL WITH RESPECT TO AGENCY/PEDAGOGY OF VOICE IS . . .	ONE NEXT STEP I'LL TAKE IS TO . . .

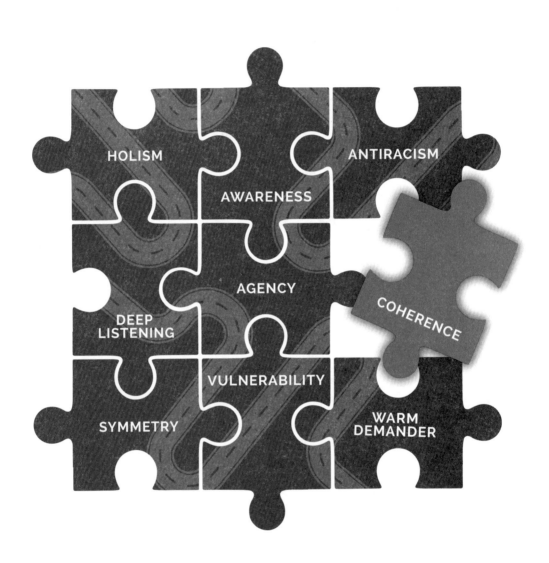

Build Coherence

Focus, Holism, and Well-Being

6

Less is more; focus is everything.

We are combating the narrative of the system. The system was created to keep our voices down, and so in all shape or form, when we're doing something that is flipping the script, we still have to speak louder in more persuasive ways. . . . We flipped the script on an age-old institution that really thought that learning started with just adults. That whole idea of sage on the stage and students as an empty sieve.

—Han Phung, assistant superintendent,
large urban school district

In Chapter 5, we laid out a pedagogy of voice, grounded in six simple rules and oriented toward a measurement that truly matters: student agency. In this chapter, we explore an essential question: *How do you bring an entire school or system toward a pedagogy of voice?* Put differently, how do you get past the **outlier syndrome**, where a few exceptional teachers work their magic in a handful of classrooms—those proverbial "pockets of excellence"? Showcasing outliers is not a sustainable change strategy nor one that will increase equity for students at the margins. We need a change strategy that deepens learning and transforms instruction across the system . . . but how?

To explore this question, we will examine a missing link in many transformation efforts: what Fullan and Quinn call a "focusing direction"

(Fullan & Quinn, 2015). You will begin to invite colleagues into critical conversations around

- **What really matters to us *here*, in *this* community, *right now*?**

- **What is our equity imperative—our call to action that courageously names the racism and inequity inside our own buildings?**

- **What is a vision and set of assessment principles we can stand behind?**

What if your community took the time to build a graduate profile (no matter what level of the system you're working at) and authentic assessment approach that offered a counternarrative to the pedagogy of compliance and a systematic way to gather street data? Imagine what is possible for our students if we liberate ourselves from the dominant satellite paradigm. Those of us who teach children at the margins have been sold a bill of goods about the need to fill, fix, intervene, script, pace, and instruct our students into "proficiency." As a result, many children have become what Zaretta Hammond calls "dependent learners" (Hammond, 2014) rather than the creators, thinkers, dreamers, designers, and intellectuals they were born to be. Many educators have internalized mindsets and biases that are hard to shake, from compliance pedagogy to punitive discipline to a focus on control over connection. We may police the bodies of Black and brown students in tacit consent with systemic oppression. Think of Grace, a fifteen-year-old Black girl with ADHD who was literally sent to juvenile detention for not doing her online homework (Cohen, 2020).

What gives me hope is that it *is* possible to transform our ways of thinking, teaching, and being with students. We are made for rebirth and renewal, constantly changing and growing. As author Glennon Doyle writes, "We can do hard things" (Doyle, 2020). So take a deep breath and walk the path with us as we share stories of schools and districts moving toward agency and pedagogy of voice. Find quiet moments to lean into your imagination. Dream of classrooms that don't exist yet or that only exist in pockets. Believe in the impossible.

The Core Stance of Coherence

Our leadership stance for Chapter 6 is coherence. **Coherence** comes from a Latin word meaning "to stick together." *Co* signifies *with*, and *coherence* literally translates into *the act or state of binding one thing with another.* In education, I think of coherence as the need to slice right through the old paradigm—testing, benchmarks, grades, seat time—to allow something much deeper to emerge and bind people: shared vision. Fullan and Quinn define coherence as "a shared depth of understanding about the purpose and nature of the work . . . in the minds and actions, individually and especially collectively" (2015, pp. 1–2). They assert that coherence is *not* the same as structure, alignment, or strategy. We won't arrive at coherence just by rearranging the deck chairs of our organizational charts or writing a new strategic plan.

In a phenomenal article, "Making the Complex Work of Teaching Visible," scholar Pam Grossman argues that to restore teaching as a profession, we need common language around the work teachers do as well as vision. She describes the lack of shared language for teaching as an existential dilemma for the profession:

> The problem, though, is that teachers have never had much consensus around matters of teaching practice. All too often, teachers have been portrayed and even valorized as isolated artisans, each doing their own thing in the classroom . . . we must redouble our efforts to develop a language of teaching that captures the specifics of teaching's intellectual and relational work . . . In particular, we need better ways to capture how teachers create trusting relationships with students—both when teachers and students share racial or linguistic identities and when they do not . . . Similarly, as we try to prepare teachers to address inequity in their classrooms and schools, we need richer ways to describe what the complex work of addressing inequality in learning opportunities in the classroom look like." (Grossman, 2020, para. 12)

Coherence is foundational to both systems change and social-emotional well-being. In its absence, educators lack a sense of direction and struggle to develop agency. There are simply too many things coming at them at once—all with a stated urgency—and it becomes overwhelming and, in turn, paralyzing. The same holds true for students who receive competing messages about what matters. What does it mean to do well in math? What does it mean to write well, to be a good citizen, to "participate" in class? What does it mean to earn an A? If those messages vary from classroom to classroom—and I would argue that they do in most schools—students experience fragmentation, diminished well-being, and a loss of agency.

Coherence, engendered over time through broad stakeholder engagement, offers an antidote to **program-itis**, that phenomenon whereby layer upon layer of underfunded mandates are piled on teachers as demands to personalize learning for an increasingly diverse student body mount (Berry, 2020). By investing in rich human conversation around the purpose and nature of the work, we accomplish a few crucial things:

> **Focus:** The ability to know where we are going as a community and reinforce it consistently through our messages. (Less is more; focus is everything.)
>
> **Holism:** A tenet of Indigenous epistemology discussed in Chapter 1, holism helps us account for the whole of the system and the individual learner—the emotional, spiritual, physical, intellectual, and cultural dimensions—rather than fragment people into parts.
>
> **Well-being:** An *experience* of holism as integration of mind, body, spirit, and identity. We can't transform instruction if we are cognitively and emotionally overloaded by competing initiatives, nor can students develop agency and thrive in such a context. Our primitive brains kick into high gear to protect against stress.

To achieve coherence, we need a shared vision. We need to imagine a world that may not exist yet and set forth to manifest it. I invite you to consider three questions:

- What is the truest, most beautiful and holistic portrait of a graduate you can imagine?

- What is the truest, most beautiful way for students to demonstrate their knowledge you can imagine?

- What is the truest, most beautiful antiracist classroom you can imagine?

Building a Graduate Profile

A **graduate profile** is an accessible, succinct description of what every graduate must know, understand, and be able to do. While typically articulated with seniors in mind, you can create a graduate profile at any level of the system: fifth grade, eighth grade, even kindergarten! Some people call this 21st century skills. Some call it Habits of Mind or Habits of Mind, Work, and Heart (shout-out to Deborah Meier, my mentor, friend, and the founder of Central Park East and Central Park East Secondary School whose groundbreaking work in this arena transformed the field!). Some call it Profile of a Learner. It doesn't matter what you call it. It matters that you *create* it, in partnership with colleagues and ideally students, so that you can tell a story about what matters in your community. This story serves to cultivate student and adult agency by reorienting everyone toward a powerful set of localized indicators.

Ideally, a graduate profile exemplifies holism, speaking to cognitive, emotional, spiritual, and even physical domains. This signals to students that you value every part of their development and view them as interrelated. Holism requires practice, so that we begin to integrate these new ways of knowing, learning, and being until we can ultimately embody them as deep knowledge. When you adopt a graduate profile, the implication is that people at every level of the system are practicing these core skills and competencies—students and adults alike. A graduate profile, along with an authentic assessment system, forms the central storyline of transformation and guides the collection of street data.

Han Phung is the assistant superintendent of middle schools in the San Francisco Unified School District (SFUSD), a large, rapidly changing metropolitan system. SFUSD has built a six-part graduate profile that tells a story about what it means to graduate from this school district (see Figure 6.1). Han, in turn, chose to focus her middle school network on *one aspect* of the graduate profile: sense of purpose, **sense of self** (think of the spiritual and emotional domains of holism) (see Figure 6.2). She made this choice for developmental reasons: Middle schoolers live and breathe in that awkward transitional space between childhood and adolescence. They desperately need to think about their sense of purpose and self! She also made it for coherence: Schools need a less-is-more approach, and she wanted to start somewhere instead of *everywhere*.

FIGURE 6.1 SFUSD Graduate Profile

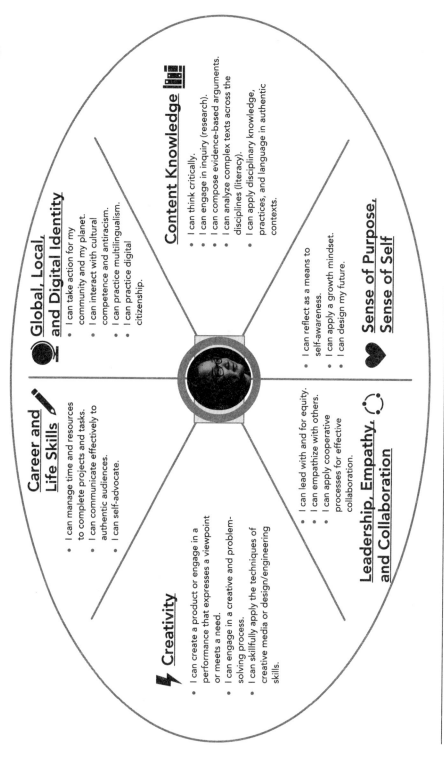

Career and Life Skills
- I can manage time and resources to complete projects and tasks.
- I can communicate effectively to authentic audiences.
- I can self-advocate.

Global, Local, and Digital Identity
- I can take action for my community and my planet.
- I can interact with cultural competence and antiracism.
- I can practice multilingualism.
- I can practice digital citizenship.

Content Knowledge
- I can think critically.
- I can engage in inquiry (research).
- I can compose evidence-based arguments.
- I can analyze complex texts across the disciplines (literacy).
- I can apply disciplinary knowledge, practices, and language in authentic contexts.

Creativity
- I can create a product or engage in a performance that expresses a viewpoint or meets a need.
- I can engage in a creative and problem-solving process.
- I can skillfully apply the techniques of creative media or design/engineering skills.

Leadership, Empathy, and Collaboration
- I can lead with and for equity.
- I can empathize with others.
- I can apply cooperative processes for effective collaboration.

Sense of Purpose, Sense of Self
- I can reflect as a means to self-awareness.
- I can apply a growth mindset.
- I can design my future.

Student Photo by Alexandre Debiève at https://unsplash.com/@alexkixa

FIGURE 6.2   SFUSD Middle School Network Focal Domain of Graduate Profile

Sense of Purpose, Sense of Self

Reflect as a Means to Self-Awareness

- Identify cultural and personal identities, and leverage as strengths
- Analyze my learning journey to identify strengths and areas of expertise

Apply a Growth Mindset

- Demonstrate how to increase knowledge and skills through effort, practice, feedback, and so forth
- Identify challenging learning situations; generate multiple solutions; and continue to implement solutions until goal is accomplished or task complete
- Persist through productive struggle, and use mistakes and failures as learning opportunities

Design My Future

- Identify academic and personal goals; identify and apply a range of strategies to meet goals; and monitor progress toward accomplishing goal
- Analyze setbacks, celebrate successes, and adapt approach as needed to successfully reach academic and personal goals

If you are interested in an elementary-level example of a graduate profile, see Appendix 6.1.

It is possible that you already have a graduate profile in place, either district or schoolwide. If so, that's great! Think for a moment about the degree to which this document *actively* guides curriculum, instruction, assessment, and adult learning. We hope the questions below will help you strengthen implementation of this tool. When developing a graduate profile, here are a few considerations, adapted from the work of Envision Learning Partners (ELP).[1]

---

[1]Envision Learning Partners is an organization that has been supporting schools, districts, and states around performance assessment for ten years.

CONSIDERATIONS	QUESTIONS
• Keep it simple	*Is the profile comprised of six or fewer categories?* *Does it fit on one page?*
• Keep it visual	*Is the grad profile displayed in a form that all stakeholders can understand?* *Are there icons to represent each area? (Consider enrolling student artists to design visuals, graphics, and icons!)*
• Keep it inclusive	*Does the profile use inclusive language that is accessible to students as well as families who are not proficient in English?* *If there is imagery, does it represent the diversity of your community?*
• Keep it student centered	*Does each area describe what the <u>student</u> should know, understand, or be able to do?* *Are there clear definitions for each area of the profile that a student reader would grasp?*
• Keep it authentic	*Are the skills in the profile relevant beyond the walls of school? Do they reflect core competencies of real-world disciplines and jobs?*
• Keep it equitable	*Is there room for a student to demonstrate mastery in some skill areas and struggle in others?* *Does the profile offer a counternarrative to the pedagogy of compliance? Does it point toward student voice and agency?*
• Keep it actionable	*Is the profile actively employed as a tool for curriculum and assessment design?* *Does the profile guide the design of professional learning, with adults having frequent opportunities to practice the core competencies as well as teach them?*

Building a graduate profile takes time, but it is time worth spending. Ultimately, it will point the community toward a pedagogy of voice, providing a local framework for deep learning. Think of this as an iterative process, and engage as many stakeholders as possible (including students!) at every stage. Figure out how you will seek and gather feedback in the form of map and street data (surveys, focus groups, student panels, etc.). Surface questions throughout to mobilize a process of wonder and learning, not just produce a document.

STREET DATA CHECK

Graduate Profile

How is the graduate profile driving the system toward coherence? Here are some ways to monitor the living, breathing street-level impact of a graduate profile.

- **Hallway/classroom walls artifact scan:** Walk and visually scan the hallways with a notebook or phone camera in hand to capture street data. What evidence do you see (or not see) of the graduate profile and student work linked to the profile domains?

- **Classroom observations:** Listen in on student-to-student dialogue in the classroom and take notes. To what extent are students using the language of the graduate profile? (e.g. "My purpose in this project is to . . ." "I am using a growth mindset to . . .")

- **Quick student interviews:** During learning walks, sit with individual students for a few minutes to ask, *How is this lesson connected to the graduate profile? Which of the core competencies are you learning through this unit or project? For elementary students: What are you learning today, and why does it matter?*

- **Project exhibitions:** Invite families and caregivers in once or twice a year for an evening exhibition. Ask visitors to explore how each project demonstrates the student's movement toward the graduate profile.

VOICES FROM THE STREET

Students

Danielle "Dani" Martin is a twelfth-grade student at Impact Academy in Hayward, California, who participated in a collaborative process to revise her school's graduate profile. As part of the process, Dani did listening sessions with seven peers to gather street data on their

(Continued)

(Continued)

perspectives and then presented her findings to adults and peers. Here are her words:

> I reached out to my friends who don't want to do work, who I myself have to push them to do the work. I also reached out to people who just don't do anything—no parents around, no nothing, don't have the motivation to do anything.

> I reached out to two 11th graders, four 12th graders, and two alumni. I decided to ask them, "Do you know what the mission and vision is for Impact?" . . . Also, I asked them a few questions about, "What do you want to take away from Impact after you graduate?" Some people said public speaking skills, good study habits, social skills, collaborating with coworkers, knowing what credit cards are, debit cards, communication. One of my closest friends, who loves to walk into class very late, told me that he wants to take away social skills so he could talk to more people.

> One of my classmates sent me another long essay saying what she thought we should focus more on "adulting" so she doesn't have to lean on her parents after all of the hard work that they have done for her. She wants to prove to her parents that, "I can do this now. I can help you now instead of you helping me" . . . showing a little bit of independence.

> Also, I reached out to the alumni and I asked, "How do you know how to do these things, like bills and taxes? How do you pay for your school?" He (one alumnus) was like, "Oh, not by myself." I asked, "Do you wish that Impact taught that (financial skills)?" "Yes," he said. Sometimes people, when I bring out the fire and ask, "Do you think after high school . . . you're prepared for the real world?" [they] say, "Kind of, but I would like there to be more financial skills."

> We've sent out surveys, plenty of surveys, and they're just one-word answers like, "I don't know what to do with my future. I don't know what I want to do." If students like us here use our own power: knowing your own friendships, knowing

the people around you, knowing your environment . . . That is
what I did. I knew that I'm actually here for a reason to make
something better.

What I did was I contacted people who are different than me
and who we want to change the different generations going
to Impact . . . So then the next generation, we have to prepare
them. They prepare the other generations. We have our
own power to connect to people that we have relationships
with. Teachers, you may have good bonds with some of the
students, but they might not open up as much as they would
with other students.

A note on this story: You may be wondering, If students collect
this type of powerful street data, what comes next? How can these
data inform future actions on the part of the school community?
We will explore these questions in Chapter 8, but for now, the
lesson is this: Have students gather street-level data from other
students. They may hear and learn things that we would not hear
and learn as adults. To practice the mindset of radical inclusion, as
the organization in which Dani's school sits did, be sure to invite
students to share, present, and make meaning around the data they
collect, alongside their educators.

Building a Performance-Based Assessment System

Once you have prototyped a graduate profile, the question becomes,
how will students demonstrate evidence of the holistic competencies and
their growing sense of agency: identity, belonging, mastery, and efficacy?
This is the moment when we give ourselves permission to shed everything we have been taught about assessment for the last twenty years
and embrace some of the most promising, research-based work in the
field. Scholar and policy leader Linda Darling-Hammond has long
championed **performance assessment**—the demonstration and evaluation of applied skills in authentic settings—as a strategy for equity
and deep learning. In a recent report, Darling-Hammond and her
colleagues at the Learning Policy Institute described how performance

assessments, coupled with rich curriculum and quality instruction, drive improvements in teaching and learning.

> As states, districts, and schools are expanding instruction to include the competencies associated with college, career, and civic readiness, they are also developing ways to measure mastery of these deeper learning and higher-order thinking skills. These measures include performance assessments, such as portfolios, capstone projects, and senior defenses, alongside classroom performance. Meanwhile, more than nine hundred colleges have made standardized tests optional in their admissions processes and are looking for more effective ways to recognize an array of student accomplishments. As a result of these converging trends, a growing number of colleges are seeking more ways to include these broader portfolios of student work in their admission processes. (Guha et al., 2018)

In performance assessments, students use higher-order thinking skills to create a product, complete a real-world process, and publicly demonstrate their learning. Tasks range from in-class constructed responses (e.g., a reflective writing prompt on a *New York Times* article) to complex design challenges (e.g., create a policy framework to combat homelessness, make COVID-19 predictive models). Students can demonstrate their learning through multiple modalities, including the option of using multiple languages to make their learning/thinking visible. When I taught *Macbeth* to mostly Arabic-speaking high school students in Amman, Jordan, I had my students select, stage, costume, and perform scenes to an audience of about sixty peers and educators. I encouraged them to include Arabic phrases if they wanted to as well as local cultural referents, and the result was a set of incredibly dynamic, engaging, and sometimes-funny scenes!

As curriculum designers with an eye toward student voice, we can develop tasks like this that reflect the mindsets and habits of professionals in the field: scientists, performers, engineers, authors, nurses, mental health experts, historians, mathematicians, and others. **This shift from students as consumers of information to practitioners of field knowledge is especially significant for Black, brown, and Indigenous students, signaling that they *belong* to a larger intellectual community from which many have been excluded by white supremacy.**

Performance assessment reorients us from a pedagogy of compliance toward a pedagogy of voice. At full maturity, these assessments move beyond *presentation* of learning to **defense** of learning. A defense involves a student revising and preparing over weeks or even months to share polished pieces of academic work before a committee or "panel." Panels typically include peers, teachers, a significant adult, and a community member. At June Jordan School for Equity, the school I helped to found and lead, students did a low-stakes defense at the end of tenth grade to transition from "Junior Institute" (ninth and tenth grade) to "Senior Institute" (eleventh and twelfth grade) and a higher-stakes defense at the end of twelfth grade in order to graduate. If they didn't pass the assessment, they had to further prepare and come back to try again. Failure was not an option. Should failure ever be an option?

Our graduate profile at the time was rooted in six Habits of Mind, captured in the acronym PROPEL: perspectives, relevance, originality, precision, evidence, and logical reasoning.[2] Teachers used the PROPEL habits to develop shared rubrics across all grade levels, customized by content area, that helped students self-assess and revise their work. This included the schoolwide defense rubric in Figure 6.3, which shows the 5-point longitudinal scale we used to describe growth over time from ninth through twelfth grade. As technical as all of this sounds, live defenses can be profoundly emotional experiences, as they manifest transformational moments of student agency. Watching a student discover the power of their own voice while publicly defending their ideas is magical. I recall dozens of times I witnessed students and family members in tears at the accomplishment of passing a defense.

Like any pedagogical approach, performance-based assessment can be implemented poorly or in ways that feel transactional rather than transformational. To distinguish *high-quality* performance assessment, Envision Learning Partners articulates the four criteria in Table 6.1. Notice that the descriptions offer a rich roadmap to gathering street data, from tasks that ask students to demonstrate real-world skills to exemplars of student work to moments of teacher and student reflection. The macro-pedagogical shifts embedded in a move to performance assessment will pave the way toward the micro-pedagogical shifts embedded in a pedagogy of voice.

---

[2]You might notice that our Habits of Mind sat largely in the cognitive domain of holism. It's worth noting that the school later developed a companion set of core values called RICH—respect, integrity, courage, and humility—which integrated the emotional and spiritual domains as well.

FIGURE 6.3 Portfolio Defense PROPEL Rubric

Student's Name: _____ Date: _____

Grader's Name: _____

Total: [   ]

HABITS OF MIND: WHEN PRESENTING HIS/HER WORK . . .	FAR BELOW STANDARD (1)	APPROACHES STANDARDS (2)	JUNIOR INSTITUTE STANDARDS (3)	SENIOR INSTITUTE STANDARDS (4)	COLLEGIATE STANDARDS (5)	ACADEMIC PRESENTATION	GRAD PLAN PRESENTATION (SI ONLY)	AVERAGE
Perspectives: *Does the student take a clear and strong stand and demonstrate a sophisticated understanding of the topic?*	No, not really	Yes, at times	Yes, most of the time	Yes, almost always	Yes, throughout the presentation			
Relevance: *Does the student effectively demonstrate the importance of what they are talking about to themself and to the world?*	No, not really	Yes, at times	Yes, most of the time	Yes, almost always	Yes, throughout the presentation			
Originality: *Does the student demonstrate original thinking, individual style, and creative problem solving?*	No, not really	Yes, at times	Yes, most of the time	Yes, almost always	Yes, throughout the presentation			
Precision of Expression: **Visuals:** *Is the student's visual work beautiful, creative, and neatly presented?* **Verbal:** *Does the student speak clearly and use appropriate voice projection?* **Body:** *Does the student demonstrate good body language and eye contact?*	No, not really	Yes, at times	Yes, most of the time	Yes, almost always	Yes, throughout the presentation			
Evidence: *Does the student provide compelling, and accurate evidence in the form of facts, quotes, or data to support their perspectives?*	No, not really	Yes, at times	Yes, most of the time	Yes, almost always	Yes, throughout the presentation			
Logical Reasoning: *Does the student support their perspectives in a well-organized, logical and convincing way?*	No, not really	Yes, at times	Yes, most of the time	Yes, almost always	Yes, throughout the presentation			

TABLE 6.1 Four Criteria for High Quality Performance Assessment	
CRITERIA	**LOOKS LIKE . . .**
1. **Elicits evidence of skills and knowledge that matter**	Design tasks that ask students to demonstrate their ability to apply transferable, real-world skills including the following: • Solve challenges involving authentic problems • Form cross-curricular connections • Apply higher-order thinking processes • Make social-emotional learning visible
2. **Is tight on quality criteria while open to different approaches**	Explicitly communicate a sharp focus on what's being measured and provide descriptive criteria for evaluating student work: • Provide clear performance outcomes articulated in a rubric or similar assessment tool • Offer exemplars (i.e., student work samples) of what quality looks like • Allow the learner to exercise a significant amount of choice in terms of the learning process and product
3. **Is authentic**	Prioritize real work, real results, and real examples, asking students to engage in the real work that adults do in the world: • Shape tasks around a real purpose such that students are solving actual problems, contributing to a real need, or pitching an idea to a real audience • Expose students to the work of adult experts in the field as models
4. **Offers a learning experience in and of itself**	Present opportunities to learn for both students and their teachers: • Incorporate moments to reflect, gather feedback, and revise • Reject the idea of a "one and done" assessment • Push all parties to identify how the task has revealed growth or gaps and how that might inform next steps

Source: Envision Learning Partners.

In addition to building coherence, performance assessment provides a dynamic vehicle for street data cycles, which we will revisit in Chapter 8. When a student stands up to present their academic work, we have an incredible opportunity to listen deeply, uncover the students' strengths and struggles, reimagine our curriculum and pedagogy, and move with an antiracist and student-centered lens. The fact that caregivers, peers, and community members sit in on student panels to offer feedback and pose questions exemplifies the mindset of radical inclusion. Can you imagine a parent sitting in to engage with their student on a standardized test?

When it comes to cognition, performance assessments epitomize high-quality street data. Each task offers its own rich landscape of insight into a learner's cognitive processes, values, misconceptions, academic identity, and more. To give you a taste of how exciting this approach can be, I want to bring in the voice of Abby Benedetto, one of the smartest educators I know, to share her perspective on portfolio defenses.

VOICES FROM THE FIELD

Educator Abby Benedetto

Yvonne, what is the battle you are fighting with the slingshot? As a young Latinx woman, first in her family to graduate from high school and attend college, Yvonne had chosen the metaphor of an Aztec warrior's slingshot as the frame for her high school journey. Now a senior presenting her portfolio defense to a panel of her teachers and peers, she paused. With emotion heavy in her voice, she explained that it was the battle she had been fighting all of her life—trying to shoot down the stereotypes attached to her as an immigrant, a child in a single-parent household living in poverty, and a woman of color. For Yvonne, completing her defense was proof enough to vanquish those stereotypes for the moment. The slingshot metaphor was culturally meaningful for her, and even now . . . seven years later, I still remember how she wove it through her defense masterfully.

I think I can accurately say that I have never heard of someone being moved to tears by the power, the personal meaning, and the transformation they experienced while completing a standardized test. Over the past fourteen years, witnessing hundreds of student defenses, tears happen more often than not—both on the part of the presenting student as well as the audience. Defenses challenge students to bring their whole selves into the room in deeply rigorous and reflective ways. Yvonne, who is now twenty-five, still remembers exactly what she wore on the day of her defense and where each adult in the room was sitting as we listened to her showing us what she knew and who she was because of that knowledge. Find me any twenty-something who could do the same for the day they bubbled in answers for a state standardized test.

For students from the most marginalized populations, Portfolio Defense infuses equity into the most high-stakes assessment within a system by providing a container for self-authorship: Students choose how they want to portray themselves and what evidence they want to use to support that portrayal. This honoring of voice and story is deeply powerful and offers a different way to think about the type of data we can gather from assessment—data that represents the lived student experience as they move through their learning journey.

Yvonne is now thriving at a San Francisco-based media company that promotes health and wellness. She graduated from UC Berkeley, paving the way for her younger siblings to pursue higher education as well. She has been asked to speak to educators across the country about her experience of doing a portfolio defense. What she says again and again is that the process prepared her for college and life beyond K–12 schooling. In Yvonne's words, *"There was no better preparation for who I have become."*

> Teaching Channel original video featuring Yvonne: https://www .youtube.com/watch?v=PufMWeaHfaM

> Follow up video from Hewlett when she was finishing Cal: https:// hewlett.org/students-journey-self-regulation-paved-way-success/

STREET DATA CHECK

Performance-Based Assessment

How are performance assessments driving the system toward coherence? Here are ways to gather street data on the impact of performance assessment on equity and learning.

- **Performance Task Artifact Probe:** Review a collection of performance tasks from different content areas. To what extent are students being asked to demonstrate the skills of the graduate profile in every discipline? Is the profile living more in some areas than others?

- **Rubric Artifact Probe:** Schedule time with each grade-level team or department to review the assessment tools they are using to evaluate students on the skills of the graduate profile. Are there shared rubrics across content areas or at least common language? If not, what is a next step in this direction?

(Continued)

(Continued)

- **Student Reflection Survey:** Conduct a survey and follow-up interviews with students about the extent to which reflection, key to a pedagogy of voice, is a ritualized component of their assessments. *How often are teachers asking you to reflect on what you're learning in connection with the graduate profile? For elementary students: How often do you get to think and talk about what you're learning and why it matters?*

- **Student Exit and Alumni Interviews:** Schedule interviews with students who have just completed a performance assessment as well as with alumni. *How do you feel your experience of completing a performance assessment (e.g., portfolio defense) prepared you for college and/or life beyond high school? How did it impact your identity as a learner? In what ways did or didn't it foster a sense of agency? What could we do to better prepare you?*

- **Teacher Agency Focus Groups:** Pull together a diverse group of teachers to hear their authentic perspectives on the move toward performance assessment. Ask, *What excites you about the move toward performance assessment? What feels scary or daunting? What support do you need to move in this direction?*

Making a Pedagogy of Voice Come Alive in Your Community

The work of developing a graduate profile and performance assessment system builds momentum toward a pedagogy of voice. It's hard to teach lecture-style in rows if students are publicly accountable for demonstrating their learning on shared school or districtwide criteria! If you are a teacher, use the power of shared vision to begin to shift your practice toward the six simple rules in Chapter 5. If you are a coach, principal, or other administrator, begin to align coaching conversations and professional learning to the graduate profile, the design of and reflection on performance assessments and related curricula (projects, unit assessments, etc), and the constant opportunities for teachers to collaboratively plan, share, and refine lessons that promote voice and agency.

While I hope the pedagogy of voice resonates with you, I also want you to feel empowered to make those ideas your own. Taking time to prototype a local, community-responsive instructional vision can be a powerful exercise in and of itself. Let me tell you a story about that. . . . When I left the principalship of June Jordan School for Equity, the school was beginning to launch what they called a Pedagogy Project to capture video clips of strong instruction. This seed germinated over several years to eventually blossom into the Art of Social Justice Teaching (AOSJT), a framework describing JJSE's unique pedagogy. The staff worked hard over time to develop shared language for teaching and learning through staff retreats, small working group meetings, peer observations, student observations, and more. Ultimately, both the process and the product led to greater coherence across the school. The AOSJT framework came to anchor classroom walk-throughs, teacher evaluation, and collaborative lesson-planning, becoming a touchstone for the ongoing work of transformation. Figures 6.4 and 6.5 show AOSJT juxtaposed with detailed descriptors of each element. Visit Appendix 6.2 to see student-created descriptors of the Art of Social Justice Teaching that came from student-led classroom observations.

FIGURE 6.4   Six Key Aspects of Social Justice Pedagogy

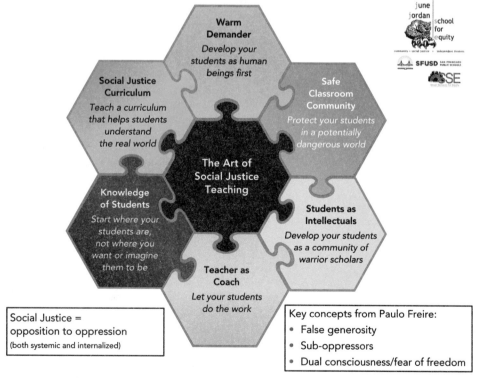

Source: June Jordan School for Equity.

FIGURE 6.5 Six Aspects of Social Justice Pedagogy

WARM DEMANDER

Develop your students as human beings first.

Family & Culture: Understand and honor the strengths of the community

Authenticity: Model vulnerability and humility; be an ally; respect your students

Clear Boundaries: Show strength, listen and affirm, challenge and offer a choice

Growth Mindset: Believe in the "impossible," embrace failure

KNOWLEDGE OF STUDENTS

Start where your students are, not where you want/imagine them to be.

Prior Knowledge: What do students know? What are their experiences, preconceptions?

Student Voice: What do students care about? What do they think? (examples of activities like sort, chalk talk, dot voting, etc.)

Individual Needs: Differentiation without tracking, adjusting instruction based on formative assessment

Choice: Students have real choices about how and what they learn

STUDENTS AS INTELLECTUALS

Develop your students as a community of warrior-scholars.

Inquiry: There is no "right answer;" questioning, evidence, students as sources of knowledge

Collective Accountability: Classroom as intellectual community

Code Switching: Academic language and discussion formats

Intellectual Challenge: High-level multicultural texts, complex problems, big ideas, less is more

SOCIAL JUSTICE CURRICULUM

Teach a curriculum that helps students understand the real world.

Clear Purpose: Students know what they are doing and why it matters

Relevance: Curriculum helps explain the real world and oppression (including multicultural curriculum, community connections, and cross-curricular connections)

Encourage Dissenting Opinions: Critical thinking is the goal

Human Values: Curriculum grounded in justice, fairness, dignity, and cultural strengths

SAFE CLASSROOM COMMUNITY

Protect your students in a potentially dangerous world.

Prevention: Clear expectations; talk about values, teacher voice, one mic

Rituals: Mindfulness, talking circle, strong start, strong finish

Jedi Awareness and Control the Mood: Be aware of the class culture and respond proactively

Intervention: Assume positive intent; keep it in perspective; deliberate escalation, when to stop the curriculum, and when/how to remove students

TEACHER AS COACH

Let your students do the work.

Metacognition: Students should know how they learn and how to self-assess

Academic Skills: Binders, annotations, note-taking skills, etc.

Culture of Revision and Practice: Models of excellent work, multiple revisions, guided practice

Team Work: Heterogeneous groups, clear roles, focus on the process, address status

Source: June Jordan School for Equity.

I want you to hear directly from Matt Alexander, the former JJSE principal who drove this process after I left. Pay attention to:

- How the staff came together to articulate which teaching and learning practices they wanted to focus on and why

- How the staff engaged in public learning (a subject that is covered in depth in the following chapter), inquiring: *When I use these practices, what's actually happening for kids? What street data do I need to determine that?*

- How the process itself was iterative and at least as important as the product

- How Matt naturally incorporates the pedagogy of voice

VOICES FROM THE STREET

Former Principal Matt Alexander

Me: You helped lead the creation of the Art of Social Justice Teaching framework. What was your purpose?

Matt: Good teachers everywhere are already doing this work. We need common language and a forum to talk about it. Both new and veteran teachers will benefit from making the invisible visible, and making teaching public creates real accountability.

Me: How did you make the process meaningful for new teachers *and* veteran teachers?

Matt: It was for both! To the extent that teaching is really complex and an art form, even veteran teachers are constantly screwing up. I think sometimes there's this narrative about teaching, that it's all or nothing or that a teacher is good or bad. Even great teachers have crappy lessons, a lot of the time, or they handle a situation badly. The issue is trying to get more consistent. It's not good or bad. It's like, "How do we make our practice more consistent on a daily basis?"

Me: Why is this process of creating a local instructional vision important?

(Continued)

(Continued)

Matt: Although we've moved away from No Child Left Behind, those values have become embedded. I feel like the teacher ed programs have bought into that. I mean, look—just even one thing is that they're always talking about learning objectives for every single lesson. Learning objectives are fine; that's great. You should have an idea of what you want students to learn, but it starts to produce this whole mentality that you can pour knowledge into someone's head and measure it. If you have thirty different people in a classroom—thirty different humans—why would they all learn the exact same thing from a lesson? Why would you even expect them or want them to? It's just much more complicated than that.

Me: The AOSJT framework was just germinating when I left June Jordan in 2008. Tell me about the process you used as an instructional leader to get the staff to construct this vision.

Matt: We really spent four years working on this, and the process was in many ways more important than the product. We started with a summer all-staff retreat that we called "Vision of Teaching and Learning." We had teachers brainstorm high-leverage instructional practices that would meet our equity challenges: In groups of three, they had to come to consensus on the top five practices.

After the retreat, a smaller group looked at all these lists and started to consolidate so that by the fall, we had the essential elements of JJSE teaching and learning. For the next few years, it was a constant iterative process. We were constantly asking, "What are the elements of good teaching and learning?" We began the Pedagogy Project, capturing video clips of classrooms where the elements felt alive. We started to do peer observations and think about evidence to find specific examples of these practices. By 2014, we had really refined the framework, and we had video examples of each of the six elements.

Me: What are your biggest takeaways from this process?

Matt: I think we have to move past the place where the instructional vision is "whatever it takes to get students to do better on these tests." For some school leaders, there is no instructional vision yet. It's not about *re*-imagining; it's imagining it for the first time. But that's cool! You have to have something that you're all working toward. Once you have that, then you can do the street data cycles you are writing about. Then come back around to reimagining again. This might mean making sure your instructional vision has a strong enough lens of equity.

Me: What were some of the key leadership moves you used in this process? Can you isolate two or three or them?

Matt: I think three key leadership moves were (1) I did not try to impose an instructional vision on staff but rather expected them to develop and articulate a common vision that was student centered and justice oriented. My job was to hold the frame and provide support for the process, not to tell them what good teaching looks like, since they were the ones doing the work every day in the classroom. (2) I asked that classrooms be public spaces, where staff, students, and parents were welcome as observers at any time (exceptions were made for sensitive discussions). This allowed us as a school community to talk openly about instructional practice and created authentic relational accountability. (3) I focused on the positive and building on teachers' strengths, including highlighting everyone's successes in all-staff emails. Feedback from classroom visits focused on how to do more of what was working rather than dwelling on failures or missed opportunities. Because of this approach, teachers were more able to be vulnerable about their practice and, when they needed help seeing an important growth area, to receive critical feedback with humility.

From Many to Few: Walking the Path of Transformation

Common Core State Standards, Next Generation Science Standards, college entrance requirements, SATs, APs, standardized testing . . . the list is dizzying. It's hard enough for adults to keep all of these things in our brains; there's no way students should have to. Luckily, there is another path—building coherence by embracing focus, holism, and well-being over scattered initiatives, fragmentation, and distress. Like equity, coherence is not a destination to be measured; it's a complex, adaptive process of collaboration, dialogue, and alignment. To build instructional coherence and transcend pockets of excellence, we have to do the slow, steady work of charting a vision and reorienting our assessment and pedagogy. Like Jamila taught us in Chapter 2, there are no shortcuts. It's about the process. It's about the conversations. It's about the adult-learning culture.

A good graduate profile captures the important cognitive, social, and emotional competencies that every learner needs to develop in a simple list: "This is what you need to focus on. You just need to get good at these things. And if you do, we believe you will develop the foundational skills that allow you to thrive and begin to create the life that you want after high school."

A strong performance-based assessment system shifts our lens from breadth—or content coverage—to depth. It empowers students at the margins as agents of learning, gives them a public platform to reflect and show growth, and exemplifies radical inclusion by engaging parents, peers, and community members in the process. Finally, all of this is designed to move you closer and closer to a pedagogy of voice—antiracist classrooms where children feel increasingly liberated to think, feel, and dream.

Here is my advice: Start anywhere, but do it together. Engage *every* educator on campus—custodians, paraprofessionals, security, and others have a role to play as well. Engage students in the coherence-building process as I have tried to model in this chapter. Engage parents and caregivers as much as possible. Be willing to learn, fail, motivate each other, and stay the course.

GETTING UP CLOSE AND PERSONAL: REFLECTION QUESTIONS

1. On a scale of 1 to 10 (10 is high), how would you assess the current level of coherence in your school, district, or organization?

2. Which of the pathways to coherence—developing a graduate profile or a performance-based assessment system—do you feel compelled to work on next and why?

3. What were your key takeaways from the story of June Jordan School for Equity's design of the Art of Social Justice Teaching framework as a local approach to pedagogy of voice?

4. What type of courage will it take for you and your community to move in this direction, and how will you strengthen your resolve and moral imperative to do so?

5. Set a clear next step for your work to build coherence. Reflect in writing on the courage it will take for you to move forward on this journey.

MY NEXT STEP TO BUILDING COHERENCE IN MY CONTEXT WILL BE . . .	SUPPORT I'LL NEED/ PEOPLE I NEED TO COLLABORATE WITH INCLUDE . . .

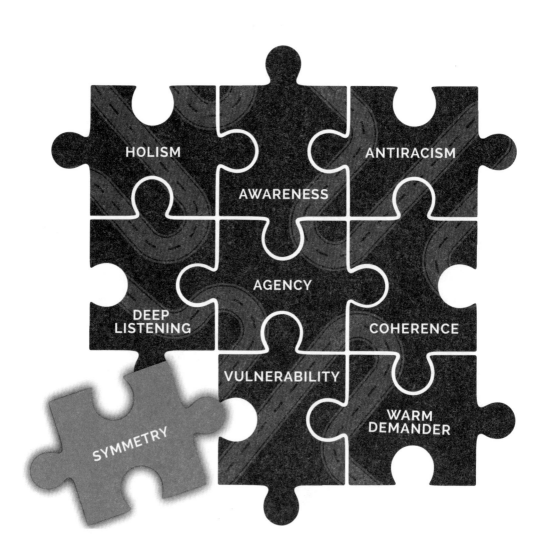

Make Learning Public
Valuing Teacher Voices

By Carrie Wilson

7

For the past decade, Lead by Learning (formerly Mills Teacher Scholars), a community-facing program of the Mills College School of Education in Oakland, California, has built a network of partner schools and districts that seek to foster a pedagogy of voice among educators as a method to provide more equitable learning experiences for students. Carrie participated in the program as a high school English teacher and now leads the program's development efforts. The Aspen Institute's report *How Learning Happens* called out the work of Lead by Learning as a promising practice in supporting adults' social and emotional capacity building in service of students' learning. This chapter shares Lead by Learning's central practice of public learning.

Mobilize a pedagogy of voice for educators.

Cheryl, the principal at Brookmont High, perceived the staff culture at her school as a "bulletin-board culture." Teachers were great at presenting their best work, but when it came to sharing the uncertainties they faced in the classroom, few stepped up. Cheryl realized that this mirrored the student experience: Teachers tended to emphasize students' polished end-of-year exhibitions and focused less on the vulnerability and complexity of learning. In both settings, the classroom and the adult learning space, Cheryl saw a reluctance to ask questions and voice uncertainties, so she decided *to dedicate fifteen minutes of each staff meeting to practicing **public learning**—an opportunity to shine a light on a dilemma or challenge and think it through collaboratively with the benefit of street data.*

One of the most powerful public-learning experiences of the year was when Maria, a ninth-grade teacher, shared classroom data and a dilemma with colleagues. In order to figure out how to strengthen her students' writing, Maria captured audio recordings of several writing conferences. She wanted to listen closely to what her students had to say about writing but was surprised to discover her own biases emerging in the conferences. With students she considered "less capable" writers, she did a lot more of the talking. With students she considered "skilled" writers, she gave them more space to find their voices and articulate their ideas. Through looking at the data with colleagues, Maria realized the equity issue before her: Her unconscious biases were stripping emerging writers of their voice and agency as learners. "They didn't judge me," Maria says of her colleagues. "They listened and then asked what would help me to create more equitable writing conferences."

(Lead by Learning, 2020 p. 31)

In the story above, Maria's colleagues conveyed what Shane described in Chapter 5 as a teacher practicing the pedagogy of voice with their students: "I see you. I believe in you. You are safe to grow and thrive here. I want to hear your voice." These core values and beliefs are fundamental to antiracist work and uncovering implicit biases. These beliefs give Maria the opportunity to grow professionally in service of her most marginalized students.

Such values do not just happen. They are intentionally created by leaders and teachers working together to create better learning opportunities for their students. Like the equity work that Jamila describes in Chapter 2, enacting these values is a continuous journey and requires that we mobilize a pedagogy of voice for educators, with many of the same principles Shane outlined for students in Chapter 5. The practice of public learning provides a street-level way forward to center our attention on our learners, adult and student. It anchors adult conversation in student experience and deepens teachers' capacity to more clearly envision their goals around abstract ideas—like agency, academic discussion, and evidenced-based writing—and to connect those goals to concrete instructional moves.

The purpose of this chapter is to explain how the practice of public learning builds adaptive expertise and facilitates a pedagogy of voice for *educators* so that they, in turn, can enact this shift for their students. I unpack the practice of public learning as an antiracist practice—a backbone tool for street data—including the theory behind the practice, the elements of the practice, and some ways to get started with the practice. Additionally, I will include examples that illustrate how communities of educators go beyond monitoring satellite data proficiency to activate street data in order to better understand the needs of students. I use the term "educator" broadly to include after-school staff, coaches, teachers, and leaders.

The Why of Public Learning: Symmetry, Agency, and Adaptive Expertise

As long as we "teach" educators through a pedagogy of compliance, we will reproduce a pattern of passivity that leads to privatization of practice and stymies our equity work from the start. Recall Jamila's Superficial Equity trap in Chapter 2: When we fail to take into account complexity and local context and build deep equity fluency, we generate behavioral shifts in the absence of mindset shifts. Lacking a space for public learning and reflection, we get superficial instructional shifts at best that fail to produce the intended outcomes. How do we create a culture of curiosity, agency, vulnerability, and exploration for educators so that they, in turn, can provide that to their students?

The design principle of symmetry (Mehta & Fine, 2019) dictates that what we want for our students, we must provide for our educators. Symmetry has proved challenging for public education systems. Although neuroscience has established the importance of curiosity and engagement for students and adults (Immordino-Yang, 2016), education systems continue to struggle with how to activate this science in their designs for educator professional learning. Many districts' professional-learning plans remain tethered to distant satellite dashboards instead of rooted in the real-time dynamic experiences of learners in the classrooms—what we call street data. **Educators are asked to prepare for and track progress on districtwide assessments as opposed to cultivating awareness of what's happening for**

students inside moments of instruction. As a result, we lose access to the complex human experience of learning, and our definitions of improvement and learning are severely constrained.

Pedagogy of Voice Requires Agency and Adaptive Expertise

Agency, or as Jim Knight calls it, "autonomy" (Knight, 2015), is as critical to the transformational learning for adults as it is for students. Agency is particularly crucial in creating change agents within systems of oppression who are willing and ready to address systemic racism. When professional-learning spaces model the domains of agency described in Chapter 5—identity, mastery, belonging, and efficacy— our adult-learning conversations move from the abstract to the contextual, from the general to the specific, from the content standard to the student's daily lived experience. And when this activation is public and routine, it establishes a new way for colleagues to work together so that they can facilitate a pedagogy of voice for their students.

Public-Learning Practice: A Pedagogy of Voice for Educators

The practice of public learning creates a routine structure for educators to share their uncertainties, analyze street data, and invite colleagues to challenge their ideas and interpretations.

Public learning mobilizes a pedagogy of voice in two important ways:

1. **As a process for acknowledging complexity by giving voice to educator uncertainty and understanding.** Public learning provides a space for teachers to clarify their goals for students and adapt their instruction in response to the current reality of student experience (Senge, 2009). Public learning serves as a vehicle for creating the conditions for adults to deeply learn in service of their students. Deep learning emerges in parallel form at the classroom and adult collaboration levels.

2. **As a catalyst for professional-culture change.** Public learning positions both student voice and educator curiosity about the student experience at the heart of professional learning. The practice normalizes a new way of working together across a school or organization. Dedicating your team to the routine of public learning creates the opportunity for symmetry and lasting change. As public-learning practices ripple through the system, a culture of public learning emerges.

Too many leaders and teachers have stagnated inside a system that does not acknowledge the complexity of teaching and learning, valuing instead only a routine expertise knowing the best practices, staying on the pacing guide, and fixating on standardized test scores and other satellite data as the primary indicators of learning. Leaders with the desire to build a culture of adult learning are often stuck in ways of working together that prevent them from addressing implicit biases and transforming their practice.

VOICES FROM THE STREET

Educators

Following are some examples of narrative street data that suggest stagnant cultures of routine expertise:

- "We have a culture of nice—we politely agree with each other. We cannot challenge each other's ideas."

- "Everyone's teaching practice is privatized. We're not permitted to comment on each other's instruction."

- "Our teachers talk about their plans but no one really talks about what they're unsure about, so nothing is up for discussion."

- "There is really never any discussion of implicit bias and how it operates in our school."

- "We aren't using classroom data to figure out how we can improve; we just keep planning together."

- "Our collaboration time is spent discussing events and the bathroom policy, not the learners' experience in their classrooms."

- "The teachers just won't change their plan regardless of whether it's working for their students are not."

- "We don't have time to learn."

Now read back over this list and consider how the culture in these schools might undermine deep equity work. Leaders and teachers with a desire to transcend this way of interacting consistently ask, "What can I do to change the conversation and have people work together in ways

(Continued)

(Continued)

that will transform their instruction?" This question itself reveals part of the problem. The question should be, "What do I need to *believe* and *value* to have people work together in a way that deepens their understanding and changes their instruction?" The shift from "doing" to "believing and valuing" is monumental. As Jamila discussed in Chapter 2, we cannot "do equity" any longer; we need to transform our fundamental ways of being. And to enact what Jamila describes as an "unwavering commitment to a journey" of equity, we need practices that inspire and guide educators into new ways of being. We need practices that help us recognize and move beyond the traps and tropes that stymie our efforts to create excellent learning opportunities for our Black and brown students. Public learning is a key mobilizing practice for addressing implicit bias and oppressive structures.

A Window Into Public Learning

The practice of public learning elevates the curiosity, awareness, and care needed to build effective adult learning. It explicitly and continuously shines a light on the adult social-emotional capacities and ways of interacting required to support deep adult learning. It assumes that adults, like students, must continuously learn about *themselves* and systematically reflect on their growth and evolution. This is especially true for white teachers who must continually work to understand their privilege, which is largely invisible if left unexamined.

Public learning can happen in dyads (groups of 2) or in triads (groups of 3). It can happen fishbowl style, with a small group discussing an instructional dilemma in the middle of a room full of listening educators, and it can happen in a grade-level team. It could happen at a district office or a county office. Most importantly, the practice of public learning is *intentional* and *public,* and it deepens over time. Whereas it often begins as a fishbowl activity, over time it frames a new way of being and learning together.

Experiencing Public Learning

The best way to understand public learning is to experience it. Take this public learning example of Sam, Kendrick, and Cheryl, who are computer science teachers at a large public urban high school. Imagine that you are sitting around the fishbowl listening to their conversation. Notice the implicit mindsets that allow this conversation to lead to moments of learning. What evidence do you see that Sam's colleagues value and support his learning?

Scenario: Sam is curious about how to better support his students' problem-solving. He has brought street data to his computer science team collaboration: a video recording of himself helping students engage in problem-solving, a core competency in computer science. The colleagues watch two short clips from Sam's conversations with his "focal students,"[1] Myleah and Alex, before entering into a discussion.

Kendrick: One thing I noticed in the videos is Alex had a longer session with Sam than Myleah.

Sam: Well, Myleah described the problem so well; I knew she knew how to fix it. So I turned the recording off and just said, "Go fix it."

Cheryl: What about with Alex?

Sam: With Alex, I've been confused about his process, what he does to try to solve a problem. So I helped him understand the problem.

Kendrick: Did you think you ended up helping him understand the problem?

Notice that Sam feels comfortable saying "I've been confused." This vulnerability is essential in a learning culture. Also notice that the statement itself reflects Sam's perception that it is his professional *responsibility* to understand Alex's process. Here, Kendrick opens up a public thinking and learning opportunity for Sam, connected to Sam's stated goal of "helping students understand the problem." If you had heard Kendrick ask this question in person, you would note his tone of sincerity and openness. Rather than lead Sam to a predetermined conclusion, he gives Sam a chance to understand his *own* goals for students.

---

[1]A focal student approach is a practice that allows teachers to see individual learners and their individual approaches to learning. It supports a deep dive, an asset-based stance, an opportunity to ground abstract goals in a student's lived experience.

Next, notice how Sam arrives at a sharper understanding of what he is doing and connects that to his goals for his students—in this case, student agency:

Sam: [Pause] I think so. I mean . . . I, well I can see I talked a lot more with him than with Myleah. I didn't really understand what he was trying to do, so I just gave him that suggestion of what to move where. [pause] I guess I just gave him part of the answer, so he could move on.

Cheryl: What do you ultimately want Alex to do when he gets stuck?

Sam again admits his confusion, and Cheryl creates the opportunity for Sam to get clear and visualize success for Alex. This is a pivotal moment in how public learning creates a pedagogy of voice for educators in service of students. Note that Alex's ability to access deeper learning in Sam's classroom depends on Sam's clarity around what success would look like. Through articulating his vision for Alex, Sam establishes a professional commitment to meeting Alex's learning needs and begins to explore what instructional moves will support Alex's growth.

Sam: I want him to have some strategies for moving forward on his own. Now I'm thinking I talked too much in response to him having a hard time. [pause] OK, now I'm thinking I need to figure out what strategies would help the students who are having a hard time move[ing] forward on their own without me giving them an answer or telling them how to move forward and robbing them of their thinking. (Lead by Learning, 2020)

Notice how Sam freely acknowledges a misstep in his teaching! This is the essence of public learning and requires real vulnerability and courage, which only exist in a context of trusting relationships. This awareness will allow him to better support Alex and other students in the future. Cheryl and Kendrick's questions helped reveal a blind spot for Sam; Sam hadn't realized that he was preventing his struggling students from learning to solve the problems on their own.

In *Culturally Responsive Teaching & the Brain*, Zaretta Hammond distinguishes between dependent and independent learners (Hammond,

2014). She explains that culturally responsive teaching requires us to allow students the opportunity to productively struggle in order to become independent learners. The symmetry in this example is striking; Sam is able to learn how to support his students to become more independent learners because his colleagues afford him the opportunity to engage in productive struggle. At the end of this interaction, Sam arrives at a question that will propel him through his next phase of learning. Sam's ability to feel energized as he clarifies his vision and develops a deeper understanding of what is happening for students is critical to building an adult-learning culture.

In this street data story, I unpacked for you the implicit mindsets and explicit moves that allowed this learning experience to unfold for Sam. Imagine yourself sitting on the outside of the fishbowl: how would you answer these questions:

- What struck you about this interaction?

- What did Sam seem to believe and do that made this a learning experience? What social and emotional competencies did he demonstrate?

- What did the listeners, Kendrick and Cheryl, do that made this a learning conversation? What social and emotional competencies did they demonstrate?

- What role did the street data play in making this a learning conversation?

This meta-moment cultivates awareness and intentionality, building the capacity for you to engage in such conversations on your own.

Cultivating Curiosity and Building Adaptive Expertise

Enacting a pedagogy of voice for adults and students depends upon our ability to foster the curiosity of learners like Sam. Sadly, professional learning in many systems is synonymous with telling people to "do" things, and "supporting learning" means making sure they did it. Helen Timperley, a New Zealand scholar-practitioner urges us to recognize the kind of professional learning that is aligned with the complex work of teaching. Her work resurfaces the concept of adaptive expertise versus routine expertise (LeFevre et al., 2019). With this distinction, Timperley makes the widely accepted point that effective teaching is not solely routine and technical work; it is complex, adaptive work demanding constant attunement and responsiveness (2018). Yet, too many designs for educator learning reflect a sole focus on routine expertise. While building routine expertise is essential to good teaching, it is only one part of the equation. Table 7.1 illustrates the two approaches.

TABLE 7.1 Routine Expertise and Adaptive Expertise	
ROUTINE EXPERTISE	**ADAPTIVE EXPERTISE**
Apply a set of skills with increasing fluency and efficiency	Ability to flexibly retrieve, organize, and apply professional knowledge
Own beliefs taken for granted and not open to scrutiny	Aware of own beliefs underpinning practice and when they get in the way
Based on notions of novice to expert—practice makes perfect	Recognize when old problems persist or new problems arise and seek expert knowledge

Source: Adapted from Timperley, 2018.

In the United States, we have long had an educational system that solely values routine expertise. The bar for what qualifies for educator learning reflects a singular focus on building routine expertise—follow the program manual, implement the best practices, stay on the pacing calendar, and track proficiency levels. Though called "professional learning communities," these common collaborative learning structures tend to be monitoring and planning structures (supporting routine expertise) as opposed to spaces that hold the complexity of teaching by supporting meaning-making.

Public learning helps us move from solely supporting routine expertise to cultivating adaptive expertise. I cannot overstress the role of intentionality and awareness in realizing the possibility of public learning. New ways of being and working do not simply happen. They are intentional and practiced. In the *Power of Transformative Practice*, Maina and Haines (2008) distinguish between default and intentional practices. **Default practices** are what we automatically do. **Intentional practices** are "those that we choose to do in order to transform the way we show up in the world" and are an essential element of antiracist work. Intentional practices give us the opportunity to "increase choice and alignment with values" (Maina & Haines, 2008). Routine expertise is a default way of approaching learning for many teachers and leaders. The practice of public learning presents an opportunity to normalize a new way of working with each other, shaking off the default practices that currently define and limit the way colleagues collaborate.

While it seems obvious to say that intentional practices require intentionality, it is necessary to emphasize that mobilizing a pedagogy of voice for educators requires us to pay attention to what we don't normally pay attention to. When observing a public-learning conversation, the practitioners on the outside of the fishbowl tend to get swept up in the content of the conversation—the reading strategies, the student work—and struggle to notice ways their colleagues are interacting or the architecture the conversation. When participants are asked to take a "meta-moment" to consider the implicit mindsets, language, and even body language that allow the conversation to promote learning, they realize that they hadn't thought so much about these things as the content of the conversation. It is precisely that level of intentionality—asking, "What just happened? What made this a learning conversation?" And, "How did that feel?"—that helps build our awareness and breaks us out of our default practices.

Elements of Public Learning

There are five core elements of the practice of public learning, which animate the work of the street data cycle (see diagram at the end of this chapter).

- **Begin with curiosity:** shines a light on the experience of learning and promotes a listening stance by openly inviting the presence of uncertainty, complexity, curiosity, vulnerability and wonder

- **Uncover student experience:** centers the voice of the adult learner on understanding students' learning experience through relevant street data

- **Build space for sense-making and challenging bias:** acknowledges (1) the messiness of making sense of what success looks like and where the students are in relation to the goal, and (2) the unavoidable presence of implicit bias, which is made visible through inviting multiple perspectives

- **Acknowledge that learning is social and emotional:** insists upon collective, explicit reflection on the social and emotional aspects of adult learning to continually deepen and strengthen the learning practice

- **Value the learning at a systems level:** sits inside of a system that values practitioner learning and knowledge-building. This value is an essential part of fueling the motivation to continually learn while carrying out the challenging work of teaching

Let's unpack how these elements show up in a public-learning moment.

Scenario: First-grade social and emotional learning (SEL) teacher leader Jaymie and her district coach Ajia sit in the middle of a fishbowl surrounded by other elementary teachers. The teachers have been brought together by the district's SEL department for a professional-learning day. The SEL department is interested in learning how teachers are thinking about SEL competencies within the instructional routines they are using. This, in itself, exemplifies that teacher learning is valued at a systems level.

Prior to this exchange, everyone in the room watched a two-minute clip of Jaymie's English learner focal students in their partner-reading conversations. The clip uncovered the learners' experience in Jaymie's classroom. Jaymie has been focused on how to make reading partnerships more meaningful and address the social and emotional competencies that are required in the partnership.

Jaymie:	An end goal would be that when students are reading, and they think of something, they're able to pause and share with their partner whatever they're thinking. But, I don't know how I'm going to get there yet.
Aija:	If you could envision what came right after the "Did you know ____?" sentence stem, what would you like to see?
Jaymie:	I guess just back and forth about the statement that that person made.
Aija:	[pause] And how might you model that?
Jaymie:	[long pause] That's a good question . . . I'm not sure. Because it seems like whenever I see it, it's just happening on its own, and I don't know how they're doing it.
Aija:	It sounds like a next step for you is thinking about the back and forth that you want to see and how to design a mini-lesson or instruction showing students the back and forth after the sentence stem (Lead by Learning, 2020, p. 31).

At the end of this public-learning session, the facilitator asks participants on the inside and outside of the fishbowl to step back for a moment and consider a series of reflection questions. The reflection questions are intended to build awareness of the intersection of social and emotional competencies and learning. This pause activates intentionality and is a critical part of shifting from our default practice of solving each other's problems to a more intentional practice of supporting our colleagues' knowledge-building.

Applying the lens of the elements, let's unpack that interaction:

TABLE 7.2   Elements of Public Learning

ELEMENT	EVIDENCE
Begin with curiosity	Jaymie is curious about her students' experience in the reading partnership, so she records them to find out what's happening.
Uncover student experience	The video data reveal the experience of the learners in the classroom.
Build space for sense-making and challenging bias	Aija asks Jaymie to "envision," and Jaymie admits to not knowing how to model her vision. Aija's questions helped reveal a gap for Jaymie, who didn't realize she hadn't fully visualized all of the steps involved in the process she wanted her students to engage in. Jaymie's admission of "not knowing" opens the possibility for new learning. The space illuminates what is known and unknown.
Acknowledge that learning is social and emotional	After the interaction, Jaymie and Aija reflect on the social and emotional competencies that they employed in the conversation.
Value the learning at a systems level	The purpose of the gathering is for the SEL department to learn from their teacher leaders. The teachers' learning is the driving force of the department's strategy.

VOICES FROM THE STREET

Principals

Here is a window into the practice of public learning in an urban elementary school principal community of practice:

Julie is the principal of an elementary school in East Oakland. She is in her first year as principal after teaching for many years. As the public learner, she shares a copy of the mid-year

(Continued)

(Continued)

> survey (map data) from her staff that provides insight into how
> they feel about her leadership across a series of topics. While
> the scores are quite high, they are all lower than the same
> time in the previous year when there was a veteran leader.
> Jen, a facilitator, asks Julie, "Where do you want to take this?
> What area can we dig into?" Julie decides that she wants to
> talk about how to improve in the area of communication. She
> says she feels like a good communicator, so she can't see the
> weakness. Jen follows up with, "Is there a teacher that you
> trust who can help you see what you can't see on your own?
> Do you feel safe enough to talk about this with her? She could
> be an amazing partner in supporting your learning."

In this example, Julie starts with Level 2 map data in the form of a
survey. Through public learning and Jen's skillful facilitation, Julie arrives
at a key next step: gathering street data in the form of an interview with
a teacher she trusts who can provide critical friendship and feedback.

Getting Started With Public Learning

How can leaders begin to shift from a **culture of compliance**, focused
solely on satellite data, to a **culture of public learning**, which centers
student voice, cultivates curiosity, and moves professional learning
beyond the low bar of implementing "best practices" to a high bar
of cultivating practitioner knowledge about how their students learn?

I want to offer a few ways you can get started with public learning that
leverage the power of street data.

Do a Collaborative Time Audit

A great way to get started is to gather street data on how collaborative
time is currently spent in your system. Everyone claims to want a
learning culture; yet when we ask people to inventory the way they
spend their time (e.g., learning versus planning, tracking proficiency,
and doing), the learning tends to get the smallest slice. In fact, when
we ask this question, leaders and educators often realize they are
spending all of their time planning, sharing, tracking proficiency, and
doing and *no* time deepening their understanding of their learners or
making sense of their collective vision.

Provide Teachers a Model of What Public Learning Looks Like

One of the best ways to begin practicing public learning is to provide teachers with a model of what it looks like to engage in public learning. Prepare and gather street data ahead of the exercise. Grab a quick video clip of students working collaboratively, copy a student's writing assignment—anything that will provide information. The fishbowl-style conversation that I discussed earlier provides a common experience for the group to think about public learning together. It also builds trust and community. Here are a few tips from our playbook, *Leading by Learning: A Playbook for Creating the Conditions for Adult Learning*:

- In advance of the public-learning session, invite a teacher to be the "public learner" and share a student learning dilemma. Consider choosing a colleague who is open to sharing uncertainties.

- Help prepare your public learner:
  o Ask them to collect street data artifacts from two to three focal students that shed light on the dilemma.
  o Ask them if there is anything that they feel worried about in discussing their uncertainty and data with colleagues.

- Open the session by framing the purpose of public learning as valuing the complex process of figuring out how to best serve our students and seeing our students from an asset-based lens.

- Invite the public learner to share their student-learning dilemma and street data. Ask them to think aloud about what the data reveals about student understanding.

- Assume the role of the listener in the conversation, asking the public learner questions to support their learning:
  o *What is your learning goal for students?*
  o *What would success look like if students were meeting this goal? What would students be feeling, thinking, doing?*
  o *What do you notice in your data?*
  o *What does your data tell you about your students' progress toward your goal?*

(Continued)

(Continued)

- Ask the group to discuss what they notice about the data, speaking from an asset-based stance.

- Return to the public learner and ask them what they're thinking now.

- Express gratitude to the public learner and acknowledge that it isn't easy to share uncertainty in front of colleagues.

- Provide time for teachers to try on the process in pairs or trios, giving everyone a chance to be the public learner.

- Invite all teachers to think about the public-learning experience in small groups:
  - *What was it like to be the public learner?*
  - *What was it like to be in the role of the listener?*
  - *How did the public learner's thinking change during the conversation? What social and emotional competencies did you observe?*

As a Leader, "Go Public" With Your Own Learning

Going first and trying it out yourself signals to teachers that you're learning alongside them, fosters symmetry of practice, and allows you to develop empathy as you experience first-hand what you want teachers to experience. Consider these tips (Lead by Learning, 2020):

- Be honest with teachers about a professional dilemma you are facing.

- Model a learning stance by wondering aloud about your uncertainties related to the dilemma.

- Discuss what information might better help you understand what's happening for your learners.

- Model looking closely at that information to see what it reveals about learning.

- Invite teachers to share their perspectives on your thinking and data. Encourage them to ask clarifying and/or probing questions to help you move forward.

This experience, in addition to modeling vulnerability, will provide you with rich street data on teacher perspectives.

Pursuing the Spirit of Public Learning

Oftentimes when schools implement new practices, leaders focus on following the instructions rather than pursuing the spirit of the vision. I want to close with some important pitfalls to avoid along with some guiding ideas to keep in mind as you embark on your public-learning journey.

The Magic Is in the Mindset

In our years of leading colleagues through public learning, we always begin by saying that "the magic is not in any protocol or plan that we hand out; rather the magic is in the mindset of the people who are sitting down to engage in that protocol." While the practice of public learning is a concrete method for transforming the adult-learning culture, this tangible practice relies on a set of mindsets that arises from the belief that learning is the heart of strong teaching.

Be Careful Not to Make This One More Thing

One of the mistakes we made early on in our partnerships with schools was that we didn't put enough emphasis on the principal's ability to message the work of public learning. Trying out the practice should be communicated in a way that illustrates its alignment with the school's vision of equity for student learning and professional growth for teachers. Be cautious that teachers don't experience this as (yet another) disembodied activity they are being asked to do.

This Is a Learning Practice, Not an Accountability Tool

While public learning can foster professional responsibility through understanding and shared learning, it will not hold that power if used as an accountability tool. A principal once remarked to me after a teacher shared her uncertainty, "Well, she should have already known that." In order to build an adult-learning culture, the principal will need to shift her mindset to reflect, "Figuring out what you don't know is an important first step forward."

Safety in Public Learning Is Not Equally Accessible to All People

There are adult equity issues in public learning. It is far less risky for some people because of position, gender, or race to name what they don't know. I was in a public-learning session where we were debriefing the experience and a district coach who is a woman of color said, "I cannot be the public learner. At my job, I cannot yet share what I am uncertain about. It doesn't feel safe for me." She had tears in her eyes as she told me this and shared that she defaulted to hiding what she wasn't certain about. I told her that most of us were doing this, as evidenced by the way we accept talking about complex issues as if they are straightforward and easy to solve. I asked her if she knew one person with whom she could practice public learning and if that ally could help her begin to normalize the practice at her site. It is important for leaders to acknowledge and name the reality of this inequity.

Continue to Bring Attention to the Mindsets, Process, and Feelings

There is resistance to repeatedly slowing down inside of an overworked system of doers. Busy people don't want to pause and consider how something felt emotionally or how implicit bias could be at play. Our feedback surveys are often full of suggestions for "spending less time on the public learner portion of the session" and "more time for individual work." Adults often feel the same way as students about practice: "I don't like to practice. I already know how to talk to my colleagues." We have learned over the years to balance time spent on cultivating intentionality and metacognition around the practice with time spent *doing* the practice.

The practice of public learning embodies the belief that an educator's agency and voice are essential to professional learning and therefore invaluable to the system's quest for educational excellence and equity. My mentor and the original designer of the practice of public learning, Dr. Anna Richert, was an incredible advocate for honoring the learning of practitioners. As a high school teacher who engaged in Dr. Richert's early inquiry group at Mills College, I would bemoan that my learning about my particular students felt small and insignificant. She would reply, "But how can you say that? No one else can know these things about your students in your classroom. It's so important that you seek the answers to these questions, that you build this highly contextualized knowledge. It will be life-changing for the students that you teach."

GETTING UP CLOSE AND PERSONAL: REFLECTION QUESTIONS

1. Which of the ideas from Chapter 7 stood out to you?

2. When you reflect on your professional-learning opportunities, to what extent do they go beyond routine expertise to also build adaptive expertise?

3. In what spaces could you imagine introducing and using public learning? What would it take to get this started?

4. How might public learning support you and your colleagues to address your site or district equity goals?

5. What might get in the way of starting the practice of public learning and why?

Transform the Culture

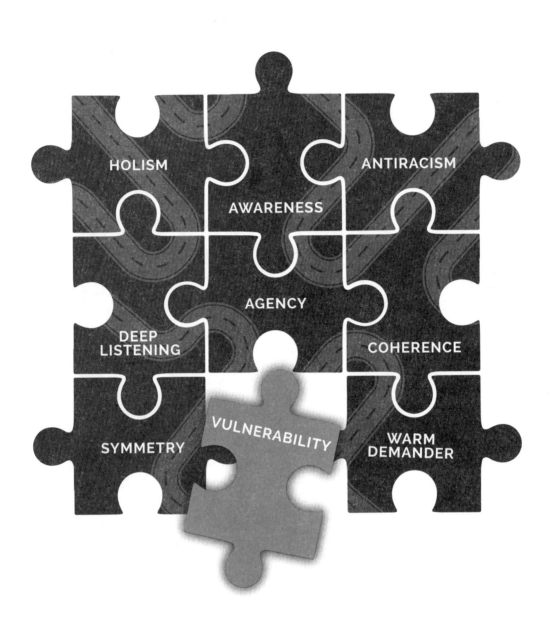

Embrace Vulnerability

Moving Through Street Data Cycles

8

Break the cycle of shame.

We were given the freedom to be transformational and the permission to do anything. If we're working to solve for increasing opportunity and access for African American students, that means we're trying to disrupt the discourse and the legacy of our entire society so we can do almost anything. . . . We have the permission to be transformational. We have the permission to do something different. We have the permission to listen to our kids and respond to them.

—Emma Dunbar, principal

In working with oppressed and marginalized students, you feel like you can't make any mistakes and like there's no time to waste. "All eyes on me like 2pac." I used to transfer that dehumanizing stress to my staff. It used to be terrifying to make a mistake. But then I started letting go of the pressure to be right all the time, or to have all the answers. I allowed myself and my staff to innovate, to liberate, and we started getting somewhere. That begins with vulnerability.

—Joe Truss, principal and racial equity coach

We are almost there, folks! The last few chapters introduced you to a *pedagogy of voice* (Chapter 5), a framework for building instructional *coherence* (Chapter 6), and Carrie's *public learning model* for educators

(Chapter 7). In this chapter, we revisit the equity transformation cycle (see Figure 8.1), exploring how this process can help us embrace vulnerability and progress over perfection as we strive to transform our school and organizational cultures. We get down on the street level to see how leaders at all levels move in ways that restore trust and dismantle racism and other forms of oppression by collecting street-level data, centering voices from the margins, and reimagining current reality *with* stakeholders.

While school transformation requires coherence, coherence alone won't transform a pedagogy of compliance into a pedagogy of voice or an oppressive culture into an antiracist one. We need to shift our core mindsets and ways of working together so that we are constantly, relentlessly, *purposefully* gathering data at the margins. We must continue to prioritize the least heard voices while learning to listen deeply and in culturally affirming ways that convey, "I am here to learn from and alongside you. I am a partner, not an expert. I see you as the singular individual you are, and I want to hear your story and your song." **Gathering street data is a practice of humanization and liberation, not a technical act done by "data-driven" educators.**

What if you engaged in the equity transformation cycle—listen, uncover, reimagine, move—gathering street data at every step to see if your vision is translating into practice? What if you leveraged instructional leadership at all levels to slowly reorient the entire system around student voice and choice? This is the messy, dynamic process of transformation—the good stuff that cannot be leapfrogged by grasping for test scores, incremental goals, or external vision statements.

In the culture you are building, educators must feel safe to try new things and even to fail. In a way, safety is the wrong word, making failure seem like a quiet, closeted pursuit—a pedagogical "don't ask, don't tell." More pointedly, we need to break the cycle of shame associated with failure. Shame has a fractal bent to it: When teachers feel ashamed of their inability to "meet standards," "hit targets," or implement a new practice, this trickles down to students who begin to privatize *their* learning challenges. This dynamic can have a spirit-crushing effect on students of color, students with learning differences, and other historically marginalized groups who may have internalized messages of inferiority from the dominant culture. Feeling isolated in their struggles, they may disengage in class, stop coming to school, or even drop out.

In Chapter 2, Jamila defined white supremacy as a system of beliefs and structures that can infiltrate the ideologies and actions of educators,

FIGURE 8.1 Equity Transformation Cycle

BUILDING
COHERENCE THROUGH
STREET DATA

including BIPOC staff. Shame is a key tool in the playbook of **white supremacy culture (WSC)**, which manifests in our schools and organizations in myriad ways: from racialized tracking of students into remedial classes to discipline policies that disproportionately punish Black and brown students to grading systems that sort students of color down the achievement ladder, and teacher-student micro-interactions that convey racist, colorist, sexist, xenophobic, homophobic, and ableist messages. If we are unaware of its tenacious presence, white supremacy culture will sink our equity efforts.

In their powerful article, Jones and Okun identified thirteen characteristics of white supremacy culture that act as *implicit* standards without being named *explicitly* inside an organization (Jones & Okun, 2001). To break the cycle of shame and liberate a pedagogy of student voice, we have to pay close attention to the four features outlined in Table 8.1: perfectionism, either/or thinking, power hoarding, and defensiveness. Recognizing how these elements play out will deepen our equity work and help us amplify the voices of students and educators of color.

For teachers of color, the pervasiveness of white supremacy culture can activate **stereotype threat** (Steele & Aronson, 1995). As leaders of all backgrounds, we have to create adult cultures characterized by public learning, public failure, and radical inclusion—where struggles and mistakes are not just tolerated, they are embraced. To resist the grip of white supremacy culture, we must deprivatize our practice and break the cycle of shame. This begins with vulnerability.

The Core Stance of Vulnerability

> *Vulnerability is the birthplace of love, belonging, joy, courage, empathy, and creativity. It is the source of hope, empathy, accountability, and authenticity. If we want greater clarity in our purpose or deeper and more meaningful spiritual lives, vulnerability is the path.*

—Brené Brown

The core stance of this chapter is vulnerability. Resisting white supremacy culture means resisting perfectionism, either/or thinking, defensiveness, and power hoarding and *choosing* imperfection, multiple ways of knowing, openness and reflection, and power sharing. At the center of this path lies **vulnerability**, defined by qualitative researcher and author Brené Brown as an unstable feeling of uncertainty, risk, and emotional

TABLE 8.1   White Supremacy Culture: Four Characteristics That Promote Shame and Their Antidotes

PERFECTIONISM

Looks like	Antidotes
• Little appreciation expressed among people for the work that others are doing • Pointing out either how the person or work is inadequate or personalizing mistakes • Little time, energy, or money put into reflection or identifying lessons learned	• Develop a culture of appreciation and a learning organization, where we expect to make and learn from mistakes • When offering feedback, always speak to the what went well before offering criticism • Ask people to offer specific suggestions for how to do things differently

EITHER/OR THINKING

Looks like	Antidotes
• Things are either/or, good/bad, right/wrong, with us/against us • Closely linked to perfectionism in making it difficult to learn from mistakes or conflict • Results in trying to simplify complex things—for example believing that poverty is simply a result of lack of education	• Notice when people use either/or language or oversimplify complex issues • Push to come up with more than two alternatives • Slow it down and encourage people to do a deeper analysis

POWER HOARDING

Looks like	Antidotes
• Little, if any, value around sharing power • Power seen as a limited quantity • Those with power feel threatened when anyone suggests organizational changes	• Include power sharing in your organization's values statement • Calibrate what good leadership looks like and include the notion of sharing power • Understand that challenges to your leadership can be healthy and productive

DEFENSIVENESS

Looks like	Antidotes
• The organization is structured to protect power as it exists, creating an oppressive culture • People respond to new or challenging ideas with defensiveness, making it very difficult to raise these ideas • A lot of energy in the organization is spent trying to make sure that people's feelings aren't getting hurt (white fragility)	• Understand the link between defensiveness and fear (of losing power, losing face, losing comfort, losing privilege) • Work on your own defensiveness; name defensiveness as a problem when it is one • Discuss the ways in which defensiveness or resistance to new ideas impedes the mission

Table adapted from Okun and Jones, 2001.

exposure that we get when we step out of our comfort zone or do something that forces us to loosen control (B. Brown, 2015). When we embrace vulnerability, we allow ourselves to sit with other people's pain and struggle as well as our own. We learn to tolerate our mistakes and failures rather than anesthetize ourselves to them. This is key to embracing the path of street data.

I want to acknowledge that being vulnerable is harder than it may sound. "Just be vulnerable! Open your classroom (or school) to regular observation; ask your students what they think of your teaching (or staff of your leadership); share your worst moments with colleagues. Admit that you uphold white supremacy in subtle ways." Notice what you feel in your body when you hear these suggestions. Do you tense up? Freeze? Want to run out the back door, close this book, or shout, "Hell, no!" These classic stress responses signal the depth of fear, shame, and denial inculcated through the one-two punch of white supremacy culture and the test-and-punish era. Educators have been blamed for society's woes and ridiculed for having an easy job where one can just "phone it in." BIPOC teachers have been isolated or denigrated for speaking out about inequities. All of us have been called upon to uphold the cloak of purportedly color-blind policies and rhetoric. It's going to take time to rebuild the resilience needed to be vulnerable with each other. You may need to cry, scream, journal, meditate, and more to heal. Know this: Healing is a critical element of the street data paradigm.

In the rest of this chapter, we revisit the street data cycle (or more formally, equity transformation cycle) as a dynamic process that enables vulnerability and moves us toward a pedagogy of voice. I will share concrete strategies you can use to collect data, unearth root causes, and monitor progress. While many of these approaches can be applied to parents and families, we will keep our focus here on internal stakeholders: staff and students. I hope you feel empowered to try, fail, learn, adapt, thrive, heal, and grow together.

VOICES FROM THE STREET

Principal Joe Truss

I was in my third year as principal of an urban middle school. This was the first year we were rolling out project-based learning (PBL), to the whole school. Folks were worried, skeptical, and somewhat resistant. There were a lot of challenges to the idea of doing PBL and some conversation about whether it was against the union contract. I felt like I was trying to move a boulder all by myself. Folks thought they were going to be evaluated on the quality of their teaching, relative to expert-level PBL. Teachers thought they were going to "be in trouble" if they failed. This is where the perfectionism of white supremacy culture took over, and I realized that the best counter is compassion.

I remember saying directly to the staff, "Thank you for being up for this challenge, for overhauling your curriculum, team-teaching, or jumping in to plan cross-curricularly." I added, "You aren't going to be evaluated on how good of a PBL teacher you are. We are all learning; the point is to learn, to try, to reflect." I could feel the tension release, like someone opened the front door of your house after baking all day. I added, "Of course I will give you feedback and I want to see movement, but I want to see movement on experimentation, movement on trying deeper learning practices. You have to try; you don't have to be an expert yet." I even eliminated evaluations for the previous year, since we were experimenting with PBL, and I didn't want evaluations to hinder creativity and risk-taking. Finally, I remember sharing that I too was in a learner stance: attending conferences, reading books, and talking to my coaches about leading a PBL initiative. This took extreme vulnerability on my part and letting go of control. As a principal, I am supposed to have the right answers, a master plan, and rule with an iron fist: Power Hoarding 101. But that doesn't work with school transformation. Instead, the process needs to be inclusive, democratic, and collaborative. I wasn't prescribing how to do PBL; I was saying, "We are going to figure it out together."

Three years later, after some extensive instructional leadership team development, we are still figuring it out, together—now with the effort led by teachers.

Equity Transformation Cycles: Loitering on the Street

> *To know exactly where you're headed may be the best way to go astray. Not all who loiter are lost.*
>
> —Sue Monk Kidd, *The Book of Longings*

Think about the equity transformation cycle as a positive form of loitering on the street. Instead of speed-walking through school buildings and classrooms checking off tasks, lean into the luxury of slowing down and absorbing the little stories you encounter in the corridors and stairwells. Become an ethnographer rather than a building or classroom manager. Listen with a mindset of radical inclusion to cultivate awareness of students' micro-experiences at the margins of your community. **Uncover** with a mindset of curiosity to understand root causes and build capacity to analyze street data. Reimagine with a mindset of creativity to design *with* those at the margins as you dream together beyond the boundaries of current imagination. And move with a mindset of courage to take antiracist, equity-driven action, however imperfectly, always pausing to reflect.

If you are struggling with where to start, consider designing a local survey (map data) to assess patterns of inclusion/exclusion and equity/inequity. Panorama Education has developed a powerful equity and inclusion student survey with questions like, *How often do you have classes with students from different racial, ethnic, or cultural backgrounds? How fairly do adults at your school treat people from different races, ethnicities, or cultures? How confident are you that students at your school can have honest conversations with each other about race? How well does your school help students speak out against racism? How connected do you feel to the adults at your school? Overall, how much do you feel like you belong at your school?* (Panorama Education, n.d.)

As pain points arise from the data, you may choose to focus your first cycle on students with learning differences, LGBTQ+ students, African American students, Latinx students, long-term English Learners, ELs, or any group of children for whom your equity compass and existing data signal, STOP and listen deeply. No matter where you begin, keep these questions in mind:

- What is the student (or adult) *experience* being revealed to you?

- What are the student's (or adult's) strengths, assets, and sources of cultural wealth?

- What is getting in the way of the learner's well-being, cognitive growth, and agency?

- How might racism and white supremacy culture be at play here?

When gathering street data, it is important to manage your reactions, namely the emotional distress and urge to defend that can accompany hearing uncomfortable truths. A defensive response to candid street data takes us right into the belly of white supremacy culture and may catapult a return to "doing equity" rather than breathing through the emotional complexity of how to shift our mindsets and practices.

Listen With a Mindset of Radical Inclusion

Conversations with leaders and teachers sparked the question, Why do we have to wait to get student perspective? How do we use something like empathy interviews to get a better understanding of where students are at?

—Chris Maldonado, deeper
learning coach, San Francisco

Empathy Interviews

Empathy interviews, a cornerstone of design thinking, help us listen for how a person *feels* and *perceives* the equity challenge we are trying to address, as well as access their creative thinking around how to approach it. These interviews are typically one-on-one for thirty minutes up to an hour—ideally in-person, but over the phone or video can work as well. Whatever format you use, study the speaker's body language, tone, and emotional reactions as well as capture their words. Remember: where vulnerability is at play, nonverbal cues (55 percent) and tone (38 percent) account for a vast majority (93 percent) of the meaning conveyed, not the spoken word (only 7 percent!) (Mehrabian, 1981). We are hardwired to read each other's subtle, implicit messages, which is why so-called microaggressions can be so damaging. You might even decide to pair up and have a partner take notes so that you can fully listen with all your senses.

In preparation for empathy interviews, identify at least five focal students or adults whose voices will bring insight to the equity challenge at hand. Next, craft a set of five to eight open-ended questions that prepare you to *listen* far more than talk.[1] During the interviews, encourage storytelling ("tell me more about . . .") to prevent generic responses and continually observe body language. If the speaker falls silent, allow them time to reflect and compose their next thought. Be

---

[1] In *The Listening Leader* (Safir, 2017), I shared the 90/10 rule from my community organizing days with the San Francisco Organizing Project: Listen for at least 90 percent of the meeting and talk for no more than 10.

sure to buffer your interviews with at least ten minutes to breathe, stretch, drink water, snack, and re-center yourself. This is an opportunity to practice humble, culturally affirming listening, which requires that we are rooted in our intentions and open in our demeanor. After the interviews, reserve at least ten to fifteen minutes to reflect on the data, either journaling or in dialogue with a colleague.

See Appendix 8.1 for an example of an empathy interview transcript that includes my think-aloud in the right-hand column.

Co-generative dialogues

The structures in place in traditional urban classrooms do not lend themselves to giving students a voice or a space in which to be valued and respected for their experiences. Students who populate urban schools are generally beholden to a "pedagogy of poverty" that rewards them for being docile and punishes them for being overly vocal or expressive. In response . . . many learn to repress their voices in order to not make any trouble.

—Christopher Emdin

Co-generative dialogues, or cogens, are another powerful way to listen with a mindset of radical inclusion. Developed by educator-scholar Christopher Emdin, cogens serve as an emancipatory practice inspired by two rituals: the hip-hop cypher and the culture circle. Emdin defines a rap **cypher** as a codified style of communication that many urban students of color (who Emdin calls the neoindigenous) use on street corners to engage in playful, dynamic dialogue. A **culture circle**, first described by Brazilian educator and philosopher Paulo Freire, is an informal space where adults who were learning to read and write came together to share their understandings of the world and their place within it (Emdin, 2017). From these models, Emdin coined the pedagogical practice of **cogens**: simple, informal conversations between a teacher and a small group of students with the goal of providing feedback and co-generating a plan of action.

If you want to work with this strategy, prepare yourself for critical feedback. Cogens require us to be ego-distant, resisting the pull to defend our current practices and choosing vulnerability and openness to student perspectives. Revisiting the stance of deep listening from Chapter 4 will help! Note that the cogen structure can be equally transformative for school and district leaders to use with teachers and principals.

Here are a few steps to experiment with cogens as a listening strategy:

- Identify a group of four to five students (or adults) who represent a cross-section of perspectives, demographics, and ability levels. Be sure to include some of the least heard voices.

- Arrange an initial meeting, outside of class time, and make a personal invitation to each student: "I am working on improving my teaching (or leadership) and really value your perspective."

- Set ground rules for the discussion, such as "Only one person speaks at a time," "Everyone has an equal voice," and "If you have a critique, offer a suggestion."[2]

- Brainstorm issues the group could work on together. Take deep breaths and listen deeply for what is said and not said. Invite candor from participants.

- Invite the group to choose a small classroom (or leadership) issue to work on together. Ask for their ideas around how to improve the issue.

- Meet with the group at least four times, roughly once a week, or until you all feel successful at improving the identified issue. In the final session, celebrate impact and reflect on learning: "What was this experience like for you? What did we learn together?"

- Invite a new, representative group into a new cogen with you. Rinse and repeat!

Uncover With a Mindset of Curiosity

 As we gather street data through listening, we enter the "uncover" phase of the cycle. This is the moment when we step back from the data and peel the layers to reveal hidden narratives and patterns, including root causes of inequity. Diagnosing root causes will help us evade the boomerang trap in Chapter 2, where we revert to past practices to protect ourselves from the pain and vulnerability of change. It's easy to get pulled back into default ways of teaching, leading, and being; fear drives us there. Shouldering up

---

[2]Emdin notes that urban youth who have participated in a rap cypher know the rules of engagement, which easily extend to the cogen. For example, the idea that only one rapper has the mic at a time lines up beautifully with the cogen norm of one speaker at a time.

with colleagues to use the tools described in the following section will keep your feet planted firmly on the street, unpacking the stories that emerge on each block.

Street Data Analysis: A Simple Protocol

Analyzing your fresh collection of street data will help you distill themes and patterns. Like any qualitative researcher, you'll need a highlighter (or several in different colors!) and maybe a pair of scissors to cut and sort the data. There are plenty of tech platforms to support more sophisticated approaches to data combing, but I prefer good, old-fashioned highlight, cut, and sort. The most important thing at this phase is to slow down, feel all your feelings, and check your assumptions, staying grounded in what the data actually says. Table 8.2 offers a basic protocol for analyzing street data.

TABLE 8.2	Street Data Analysis Protocol	

Time: Minimum 45 minutes to an hour

Roles:

- Facilitator (who sometimes participates, depending on the size of the group)
- Data gatherers (whose street data is being analyzed by the group)
- Thought partners

Preparation: If needed, have copies of the data available, plus highlighters and scissors. Consider having participants review the data in advance to expedite the observe step.

TIME	PROTOCOL STEPS	FACILITATOR TIP
10 minutes	**Connect (check-in, community circle, or dyad[3]):** What was the process of gathering this street data like for you? What do you predict the data may reveal?	*Frame as an opportunity to practice vulnerability. Go first to model vulnerability.*
15 minutes	**Observe:** What are we hearing from our students (or colleagues)? • Read through the data with a highlighter. Look for patterns (e.g., repeating words, narratives). • Consider having folks work with scissors in pairs first to cut and cluster the data into themes. • Reflect as a group: *What stands out from the data?*	*Frame the importance of staying low inference. Provide an example of a low-inference versus a high-inference statement.[4]*

[3]For a reminder on this structure, revisit the Chapter 4 description of listening dyads.

[4]A low-inference statement might sound like, "Four of the 5 students we spoke with said they feel afraid to raise their hands and speak in class." A high-inference version might sound like, "Most of the students feel uncomfortable in their classes."

TIME	PROTOCOL STEPS	FACILITATOR TIP
20 minutes	**Interpret:** What does this data reveal about the experiences of our most vulnerable learners (or community members)? • Ask them to try to name the patterns/themes in three words or less, using sticky notes. • If more than three or four themes emerge, ask the group: *Which theme/pattern feels most important and why?*	*Use a poster, whiteboard, or shared digital document to track the group's discussion.*
5 minutes	**Feel:** What feelings does this data evoke for you? • Encourage folks to sit with their feelings, taking a few deep breaths and noticing sensations in the body. • Use a listening dyad again or a community circle to allow people to share uninterrupted.	*Ask people to resist the tendency to self-anesthetize in the face of discomfort or pain.*
10 minutes	**Reflect/consider (possible questions):** What matters about this data? How does it (or doesn't it) stand up to our vision? Where is our greatest opportunity? What will help us learn more? What will help us move toward the pedagogy of voice? What steps or actions might come next?	*To bridge to the reimagine phase, offer possibilities for next steps—for example, another round of data-gathering; a team focus group with some of the students; an invitation to the students to meet and brainstorm approaches to the issues at play.*

CASE STUDY: UNCOVERING BLACK STUDENTS' LITERACY EXPERIENCES

Emma Dunbar, a principal in San Francisco, leads a large, comprehensive middle school with a persistent achievement gap—"Historically," she shares, "a fifty-percentage point gap in English and Math performance between the highest-achieving students and our African American students." As an equity-designated school, Emma enjoys district support and resources to address systemic inequities. In August 2019, she engaged me and Jamila to introduce her entire staff to the street data model and from there, Jamila began to coach her in facilitating schoolwide equity transformation cycles.

Aligned with the district's graduate profile, Emma's school had set a priority around increasing student connectedness to school. Listening to street data from teachers, she noticed a tendency to focus on student

(Continued)

(Continued)

connections <u>outside</u> the classroom—clubs, teams, extracurriculars. As an instructional leader, she had to reset her sights on the equity challenge she wanted to solve: creating success and opportunity for African American and Latinx students. She knew this challenge required drilling down to the classroom:

We can offer clubs and places to find affinity and to explore identity . . . those are really important and need to exist, but the majority of a student's day is inside the classroom. What are the moves? What are the adjustments in curriculum? What are the adjustments in structure? Where are our kids of color feeling included and valued and a part of the classroom community?

*In September, Emma helped her instructional leadership team (ILT) conduct empathy interviews with Black focal students[5] around their classroom literacy experiences. The ILT analyzed the empathy interview data, highlighted excerpts of student voice, and zeroed in on a key theme: the connection between oral tradition and academic conversation for many African American learners. Focal students articulated that they felt most comfortable and most enjoyed classes where they could share their ideas, but they overwhelmingly lacked the opportunity to do so. Through this process, academic conversation had risen to the top as a missing, yet crucial area of culturally responsive pedagogy. These conversations helped the ILT shape a sharper set of interview questions and a core stance to guide their work: "**Literacy** means that everyone is a literacy teacher, and **equity** means that we ask, How is everyone becoming an equity-focused literacy teacher?"*

Next, ILT members met with their respective grade-level teams and asked teachers to identify two focal students, including at least one African American learner, with whom to do empathy interviews. They asked colleagues to use the newly revised questions and to record their notes. Before jumping into the work, however, ILT members took their colleagues through a reflective process to open space for vulnerability:

- **ILT framing:** *Remember that our focal students as a school are African American as well as Latinx, English Learners, and students with special needs.*

---

[5]Focal students is a strategic approach to engaging in cycles of inquiry that help educators "go small to go big." By closely studying the experiences of a handful of learners, we discern patterns and root causes that catalyze larger shifts in practice, systems, and learning conditions.

- *Journal reflection*
  - ○ *Think of a student who you are trying to reach.*
  - ○ *What are some of the literacy skills that they need to develop?*

- *Share out to get a sense of patterns of struggle and to promote vulnerability.*

- *Set a goal*
  - ○ *Remember that our goal is to help focal students become strong readers, writers, speakers, and listeners. Review the schoolwide instructional rubric for structured talk and academic conversation:*
    - ❖ *What's one area or practice you could work on this year?*
    - ❖ *In which strategies here have you had success?*
    - ❖ *Which strategies would you like to learn more about?*

With this framing in place, teachers across the school set out to do empathy interviews.

ILT'S EMPATHY INTERVIEW QUESTIONS (MID-SEPTEMBER)	REVISED EMPATHY INTERVIEW QUESTIONS FOR GRADE-LEVEL TEAMS (MID-OCTOBER)
• *What do you like to read and why?* • *How does Presidio Middle School/your teachers help you with your reading?* • *If you could write a letter to someone, who would it be?* • *What kind of things do you like to write, and why?* • *How often and in how many classes do you write?* • *When you catch yourself daydreaming, what helps you pay attention?* • *How do you feel about speaking out in class?*	• *What do you think academic conversation is?* • *How much do you participate in academic conversation in class?* • *Who is first to talk in class, you or your teacher?* • *What helps you feel confident to speak in class?* • *When do you have the opportunity to have academic conversation in class?* • *How is class structured so that you can talk about what you're learning?*

(Continued)

(Continued)

Data from schoolwide empathy interviews continued to reinforce the importance of academic conversation for all focal students but particularly for African American scholars. This bridged into the reimagine phase, as departments began to send representatives to an academic conversation training with author Jeff Zwiers and pilot different approaches. At the same time, Emma engaged focal students in what are typically adult-only processes: learning walks and instructional rounds. As Emma has continued this work, she finds it necessary to keep staff vulnerability in the front of her mind. The work requires strategy and a focus on helping staff resist shame in the process.

Equity Learning Walks and Instructional Rounds: Students as Colleagues

If we want to understand the student experience, we need student observers by our side. When it comes to perceiving subtle micro-interactions in the classroom, students have the keenest eyes. Learning walks and instructional rounds exist in various forms in most schools. The pivot here is to engage *students* in these processes from the get-go, investing in their development as instructional leaders. I can't offer you an exact number, but your ratio of students to adults should trend toward more students over time. Invite students to articulate *their* lenses and questions by asking, "What should we be paying attention to when we walk into classrooms?" As young people build capacity to engage in these processes, consider bringing parents into the mix as well.

An *equity* learning walk is an informal series of classroom observations with an explicit equity lens. The learning walk team might look for

- Patterns of participation, broken down by race, gender, ELL status, and so forth

- Patterns of teacher feedback (i.e., affirmative versus negative interactions with students), broken down by race, gender, ELL status, and so forth

- Small-group peer interactions that manifest implicit biases and microaggressions, or microaffirmations—small acts of inclusion that add up to an overall feeling of inclusion for everyone

- Actual use of academic language by English language learners (given that oral production is critical to developing fluency)

To maximize the impact of this strategy, build a simple learning walk tool that is grounded in your equity imperative and instructional values. Use the six simple rules of a pedagogy of voice if they serve you! The San Francisco middle school network we met in Chapter 6 has three strategic priorities: literacy, deeper learning, and African American student achievement and belonging. The learning walk tool they built directly reflects these priorities with space for observers to capture a Likert scale rating (0–4, with only an exemplary "4" described) and narrative notes for each. You'll also see a specific section to capture data on Black student engagement. While the network uses a Google Form for leaders to capture this data, it's fine to print hard copies as well.

Instructional rounds, a practice developed by Elizabeth City, Richard Elmore, and their colleagues at Harvard University, takes participants through a robust process of observing, analyzing, and making meaning of classroom street data (City et al., 2009). Elmore envisioned rounds as a professional-learning design for school leaders (mainly superintendents), but we propose to use it at a district or school level with students as colleagues and co-observers. Though the full extended process may be more appropriate for secondary students, I would consider inviting third through fifth graders on modified instructional rounds. You can learn about rounds by reading Elmore's work, and Table 8.3 offers an example of an observation tool you might use with students during rounds. See Appendix 8.2 for a process guide to instructional rounds.

As you invite students into these processes, keep a few things in mind:

- As with cogens, engage students who represent a diversity of experiences and backgrounds—not just high performers.

- To center voices from the margins, engage students who are often referred out of class or *choose* to leave class because they find the hallways more rewarding.

- Aim to visit around three classes each time to get a triangulated data set. Let students know we are "going small to go big": we will study a few examples to uncover patterns.

- Before the learning walk or instructional round, bring student and adult participants together to share the purpose, goals, and tools. But don't stop there!

FIGURE 8.2 Middle School Leadership Team Look-Fors

Literacy: Academic conversations (circle only one)

Not Observed	0	1	2	3	4	Exemplary

Exemplary: Students are exchanging ideas with a peer(s) by engaging in fluid conversations and using academic language.

Notes:

Deep learning: Sustained inquiry around an essential, deep-learning question (circle only one)

Not Observed	0	1	2	3	4	Exemplary

Exemplary: Students are exploring a complex essential question in multiple ways throughout the lesson.

Notes:

African American Student engagement: Participation tracker (spoke around content w/partner or to whole class) (mark only one)

◯ AA Students spoke 0 times

◯ AA Students spoke 1–2 times

◯ AA Students spoke 3+ times

Notes:

Adapted from the San Francisco Unified School District MSLT Look-Fors document.

TABLE 8.3	Instructional Rounds: Observation/Scripting Form

Room: _____ Subject: _____ Grade: _____

School's Problem of Practice

Example: How are students equitably engaged in reading, writing, and academic conversation?

- How do students respond to and build on their peers' ideas?
- To what extent do students talk about academic content with each other versus with their teacher?
- To what extent do students provide meaningful written evidence to support their thinking?

STUDENT ACTIONS	TEACHER ACTIONS	NOTES AND QUESTIONS

Source: Tool developed by Davina Goldwasser, San Francisco Unified School District.

- Ask students: What else should we be looking for as we observe? What data points should we track that will help us understand how equity and racism play out in the classroom? Invite them to name less obvious data like nonverbal signals and tone.

- Afterwards, facilitate an inclusive debrief with students. Set a clear ground rule that each time an adult speaks, a student gets the mic next. Teach students how to analyze the data!

Reimagine With a Mindset of Creativity

As we uncover hidden narratives, the question becomes, what are we going to DO about it? At this point, it is seductively easy to tap or appoint an equity "expert" (remember Jamila's Lone Ranger of Color and Great White Hope tropes?) to come up with solutions in isolation. This is where **power-sharing**, the antidote to white supremacy culture's power *hoarding*, comes into play. We have to expand our planning and decision-making tables to include students, parents, paraprofessional staff, community elders, and other marginalized voices. To avoid the traps of the equity warrior (nesting equity with a single champion) or siloing equity (locating the work in a separate policy or team), we need to come together to reimagine current reality.

These next few strategies will help you enter the imaginative space *with* students. Young people have answers for us if we choose to listen. In a phenomenal piece for *Next Generation Learning*, educator Young Whan Choi (2020) talks about engaging students to help him lead a week-long project-based learning (PBL) institute for one hundred educators. He frames three ways to center student voice in teacher professional learning: setting the vision, reflecting on classroom learning experiences, and giving input on planning effective PBL units.

Student-Informed Curriculum

Young Whan had long considered himself an advocate for student voice but realized that he had failed to engage this resource at a critical point of impact: curriculum design. He writes, "Later in the week-long institute, we invited planning teams to invite a student to join them for a critique and revision session. Students were paid for their time and valued as consultants. They were given time during the professional development to sit down with teachers and listen to curriculum pitches. Teachers produced a small slide deck with information such as the essential question, the authentic product students would produce, and some of the key learning activities. Students provided feedback on what they thought would engage them and their peers." Feedback from participating teachers was overwhelmingly positive.

In addition to giving feedback on unit plans, students of all ages are perfectly capable of designing and leading lessons. Imagine inviting your second graders to pair up and rotate leading a community circle once a week. As an English teacher, I designed an instructional routine called Read and Lead to foster student agency and literacy. Students paired up to study a segment of the class text (we were reading *Beloved* and then *Othello* at the time) and design an interactive lesson for a small group of peers. Each pair had the opportunity to teach a lesson in which their peers would not only participate but would also provide feedback. It was so much fun, and I watched many a shy learner build moxie and confidence. The process also created a common language around teaching and learning in the classroom.

Student-Driven PD

Students are the best gauge as to whether instruction is interesting and relevant and pushes them appropriately, and student voice can reshape teacher professional development in radical ways. What if you invited a diverse group of third, fourth, and fifth graders to join PD for an afternoon? Small groups of students would meet with small groups of teachers to share what helps them learn, what makes them feel frustrated in class, and what contributes to feelings of inclusion or exclusion. One high school in Des Moines, Iowa, decided to try joint student-teacher professional learning. In their first attempt, administrators brought forty-five students into conversation with seventy-two teachers around how to make learning more culturally inclusive and engaging (Superville, 2019). The school's equity coach worked with the students behind the scenes to prepare them for this opportunity, including dress rehearsals with feedback. The dry run was so successful that soon, nearly one hundred students attended a staff PD to help teachers sharpen their lesson plans and make instruction more relevant.

It's worth noting that this initiative grew out of a local equity imperative around chronic absenteeism for Black boys. While the school's average absentee rate was 35 percent, for Black boys, it was 56 percent. This equity gap in attendance was linked to discipline referrals, and an initial set of empathy interviews revealed that students were skipping class for distinct reasons: "They didn't think teachers cared if they showed up, and many classes had no connection to their lives, experiences, and communities." There is no way to solve this complex challenge without centering the voices, stories, and experiences of students.

Student Design Challenges

Another way to reimagine instruction, school culture, and systems is to ask students to take on a design challenge in small groups. Put out a broad call to action for small groups of students to take up one of the following charges:

- Design the first week of school around the principle of radical inclusion

- Design an ideal school day that would promote well-being

- Design an equity-centered homework, tech, or attendance policy

- Design a project to highlight your community's cultural wealth

- Design an antiracist discipline policy

Be sure they have time, ideally a budget, and an authentic audience to present their ideas to.

Student-Led Conferences

Student-led conferences (SLCs) are a final, incredibly potent way to center student voice and share power. While the format may vary, SLCs always put students in the driver's seat of family-teacher conversations about learning. They create opportunities for students to share, reflect on, and explore evidence of their growth and learning. As such, SLCs are most powerful when tethered to a graduate profile or a performance assessment system, like portfolio defenses, as described in Chapter 6. Figure 8.3 includes a sample student self-assessment rubric and reflection from the middle school network we've been following.

FIGURE 8.3   Student Reflection Questions for Student-Led Conferences

Name: _____   Class: _____

After your SLC, think and write about how your conference went.

1. What went well? What I am proud of?

_____

_____

_____

_____

_____

_____

2. What do I want to improve on for next time?

_____

_____

_____

_____

_____

_____

_____

3. Look at your goal sheet. How do you think you will monitor these prior to your next conference?

_____

_____

_____

_____

_____

_____

_____

_____

HOW DID YOUR SLC GO? IN THE SELF-ASSESSMENT BELOW, CHECK THE BOXES WHERE YOU MET . . .	WOW	GOT IT	NEARLY THERE	OOPS	EXPLAIN WHY YOU GAVE YOURSELF THE RATING.
Career and Life Skills					
Managed my time to complete work ❑ I included all parts of my SLC project. ❑ I asked for help when I needed it.					
Communicated Clearly ❑ I spoke proudly. ❑ I did not read from cards. ❑ I practiced beforehand.					

(Continued)

(Continued)

HOW DID YOUR SLC GO? IN THE SELF-ASSESSMENT BELOW, CHECK THE BOXES WHERE YOU MET . . .	WOW	GOT IT	NEARLY THERE	OOPS	EXPLAIN WHY YOU GAVE YOURSELF THE RATING.
Sense of Purpose, Sense of Self					
Designed my future					
❏ I identified all my goals (personal and class).					
Used self-reflection					
❏ I identified what challenges I faced.					
❏ I identified successes in my goals.					
Creativity					
Risk taking					
❏ I made choices about what work to share.					
❏ I took risks to be my best.					
Leadership Empathy and Collaboration					
Working collaboratively with others					
❏ I gave and received feedback by practicing with a classmate before my conference.					
Global, Local, and Digital Identity					
Inclusivity					
❏ I thought about how I can connect with people who are different from me.					
Multilingualism					
❏ I said why I did my presentation in the language that I chose.					
Digital					
❏ I talked about how I use technology as part of my learning.					
Content Knowledge					
Think critically					
❏ I thought critically about my work this year.					

Move With a Mindset of Courage: Where the Rubber Meets the Road

The equity transformation cycle is where the rubber meets the road in our efforts to enact equity and deep learning for every child. We may talk the talk, but will we walk the walk? As we shift toward *moving* the work, we have an opportunity to get courageous and orient ourselves in a whole new direction. We may get sucked toward navel-gazing equity, keeping the work at the level of self-reflection without fundamentally changing instruction or school systems, or we may find ourselves in the blanket equity trope—investing in a program or curriculum rather than in the capacity of our staff. Now is the moment to resist the traps and tropes! It's time to take action, tolerate the possibility of failure, and embrace vulnerability.

Safe-to-fail experiments are your friend here: small, four- to six-week "hacks" that disrupt business-as-usual and give you fresh street data to study. You've listened at the margins, uncovered underlying patterns and roots causes, and reimagined (or flipped!) the proverbial table to center and collaboratively design *with* voices from the margins. Now give yourself permission to try something new. You can draw on any of the ideas in the reimagine section of this chapter as well as those in the table that follows. According to the National Equity Project (NEP) and the d.K12 Lab Network, "Oppression thrives on risk-averse behavior. It's important to fail fast. Small changes can have large effects, AND hacking oppression requires longshots" (Anaissie et al., 2016). Here are a few examples:

SCHOOL CULTURE	CLASSROOM/ PEDAGOGY	FAMILY ENGAGEMENT
Start every day for a week with a mindfulness meditation. See if discipline issues and behavior shift. Form listening circles with groups of six staff people, focused on healing. Every staff meeting, allow circles to meet and reflect, using the deep listening guidelines in Chapter 4. Organize a student-led antiracism campaign. Fund it!	Instead of Author's Chair, try a Story Chair: Every day or every meeting, a new child or adult gets to share and reflect on their story, including their identities, hopes, dreams, and struggles. Get rid of your desk! Seriously, though, try having a classroom or office for a few weeks with no desk to sit behind, only round tables. Transform power through physical space.	Do a positive phone call campaign. Each day, call one parent of a child at the margins and celebrate something specific about the learner. Be sure to also ask the caregiver, "What do you want me to know or understand about your child?" Do a cultural wealth teach-in. Ask parents to come to class to teach a twenty-minute lesson on *anything* they are passionate about. Be sure it's clear they don't need to have a college degree or be "professionals" to participate.

In closing, here are my three words of advice to you: Just start walking. The street is vibrant and full of color and texture and story. The path is jagged and perfectly imperfect. Your power to transform teaching and learning lies in your willingness to walk the path, arm and arm with colleagues, and increasingly with students and parents—acutely attuned to the songs of your students: each one different, each one beautiful, each one its own story waiting to be born . . .

GETTING UP CLOSE AND PERSONAL: REFLECTION QUESTIONS

1. How do you see white supremacy culture playing out in your context? What are you willing to do to disrupt it?

2. Reflect on a time where you were vulnerable around your practice. How did that feel? What will it take for you to continue to grow your vulnerability muscle?

3. Which step of the equity transformation cycle—listen, uncover, reimagine, move—most calls your attention right now and why?

4. Which strategies laid out in this chapter do you want to try next? Make a simple plan for doing so and hold yourself accountable to it.

STRATEGIES I PLAN TO TRY	POTENTIAL ROADBLOCKS	WAYS I'LL GET SUPPORT TO STAY THE COURSE

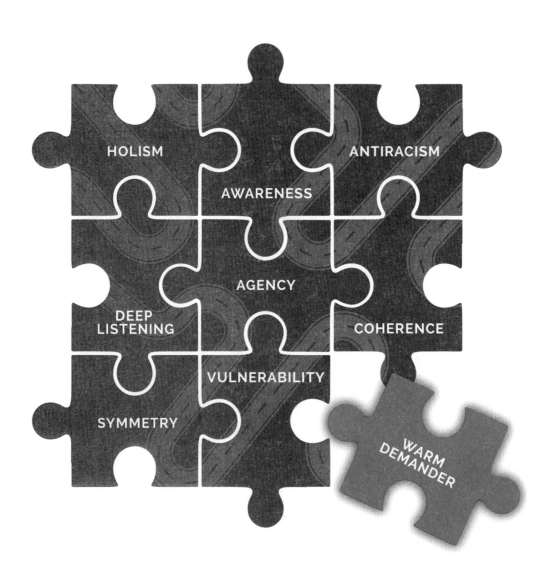

Calling Folks *In* and *Up* to Equity

9

Street-Level Conversations

Every moment is an equity moment.

Scene: A male student of African and Latino descent visits his white teacher after school to discuss his grade. Within minutes, the teacher asserts that the student is getting "angry" with her because he is "not getting the answer he wants." The student asks the teacher, "Are you scared of me?" The teacher responds, "No, why would you say that?" The student shares, "The other day, a woman walking past me on the street clutched her purse and crossed to avoid me." The teacher retorts, "I don't know why she would do that! You are not even that dark-skinned." The student walks out, hits a locker, and goes to the main office where Principal Jason R. finds him in tears.

> *Stop. Notice your body. Notice your heartbeat. Notice your breath. Are you clenching? If so, where? Are you angry? If so, where do you feel it in your body? If you're Black, Indigenous, Latinx, Asian, or Pacific Islander, does this story evoke a memory for you? What feelings wash over that memory? If you're white, do you feel embarrassed? Defensive? Ashamed? Notice your thoughts and imagine this teacher is your colleague. What will you do next?*

This scene is based on a real story from a Black male principal colleague of mine who works in an urban Midwestern district. In our closing chapter, we sit with this leader as he navigates a series of conversations—small moments really—that have a big impact on the teacher and student. We will think about how the student's intersecting identities as Black, biracial, and young contributed to his feeling of powerlessness and unsafety at first. We will study Jason's moves, witness a meeting he facilitates between the child's mother and the teacher, and unpack what it looks like to be a warm demander for equity.

In the last few chapters, we have talked about a pedagogy of student voice, a roadmap to instructional coherence, a public-learning model for educators, and concrete ways to operationalize the street data model. The connective tissue for all of this work is an **antiracist, antibias adult culture** in which educators develop the will, skill, vulnerability, and *courage* to uproot systemic racism and deep-rooted biases. In the absence of this cultural shift, street data runs the risk of becoming another reproductive tool—a framework to be "implemented" and then shelved. We can't afford to default to old ways of being or stay locked in the Western epistemology of classification, implementation, and compliance. We have a chance to do and *be* different this time, to radically reimagine school transformation. In that spirit, we end our reading journey by digging into the daily cultural work of calling ourselves and our colleagues in and up to justice.

As I finish this manuscript, the global and American landscapes have changed indelibly. We have experienced a collective trauma: COVID-19, ongoing police murders of Black people, a national uprising, and the shattering effects of climate change. We have been shaken to the core; yet as we look ahead, many of us are so mired in planning and damage control that we have forgotten the fabric of school transformation: small conversations that take our breath away. By the time this book is in your hands, I hope that a new educational reality is beginning to emerge—a focus on relationships before rigor, connection before content, human data before metrics, and healing the ripped-open wounds of oppression that Black, Indigenous, Latinx, Asian, Pacific Islander, and other people of color have been tending to for so long. I dream of collegial conversations that

- Center antiracism and antibias (ABAR) work

- Name and unpack whiteness and white supremacy as forces suffocating our communities

- Enable students and adults to grieve, cry, awaken, conspire across difference, find affinity within community, heal, humanize, and transform our schools

- Move the entire system toward a pedagogy of student voice and agency

We can do this together. It's going to take an unflinching commitment to stay on the ground, listening to and centering voices from the margins. It's going to take what Margaret Wheatley calls simple, human conversation (Wheatley, 2000)—that which we underestimate in its power to change the world.

The Core Stance of Warm Demander

The core stance of our final chapter is warm demander. From the moment he found a child in tears to the moment he facilitated a courageous conversation between mother and teacher, principal Jason R. exemplified what it means to be a warm demander. Author Lisa Delpit defines **warm demander teachers** as those who "expect a great deal of their students, convince them of their own brilliance, and help them to reach their potential in a disciplined and structured environment" (Delpit, 2013). **I build upon Delpit's frame by defining** warm demander *leaders* **(superintendents, directors, coaches, principals, assistant principals, teacher leaders) as those who expect a great deal of their colleagues, convince them of their capacity to grow as antiracist educators, and use street-level data and adaptive coaching moves to shift mindsets and practices**. Rather than call people *out*, warm demanders call folks *in* and *up* to the work of equity.

Becoming a warm demander is a critical approach for increasing equity in our schools. With roots in Native Alaskan and Inuit communities (Kleinfeld, 1975), this concept can be applied to teacher-to-student, leader-to-teacher, and as we'll see in Jason's story, even parent-educator interactions. Taking up the warm demander mantle will help you tune in to racial and other microaggressions that pack a macro impact, spirit-murdering (Love, 2019) so many students (and educators) by depleting their sense of hope and agency. As Jason reflected back on the teacher's "you're not even that dark-skinned" comment to her biracial student, he wondered, "How could we still be here? How do the same things keep happening? How much does the media influence what you feel or think about certain populations?" (personal interview, June 15, 2020). As a light-skinned Black man himself, Jason reflected on the painful ways that **colorism**—a practice of bias and discrimination by which those with lighter skin are treated more favorably than those with darker skin[1]—had impacted his life.

The warm demander framework will help us develop an antiracist culture in which people actively address racism and other forms of oppression at the individual and institutional levels, through courageous conversations as well as concrete policy shifts. Mind you, warm demander interactions won't dismantle white supremacy culture in and of themselves. They must rest on the twin pillars of structural/policy change (i.e., shifting from a punitive discipline approach to a restorative one or from a standardized testing system to a performance-based

---

[1]Note: Colorism is a product of systemic racism in the United States, in that it upholds white supremacy and white standards of beauty and benefits white people in institutions of oppression.

assessment one) and a commitment to building racial literacy and historical fluency through ongoing study. Still, our daily conversations are where the rubber meets the road. Will we have the courage to interrupt inequitable behaviors—even those of our close colleagues? Will we fight for the dignity and humanity of every child and adult? Will we make mantras like "Black Lives Matters" more than a hashtag?

FIGURE 9.1   Twenty Must-Read Books for Racial Literacy

1. Bettina Love (2019).*We Want to Do More Than Survive: Abolitionist Teaching and the Pursuit of Educational Freedom*, Beacon Press.

2. Michelle Alexander (2012). *The New Jim Crow*, The New Press.

3. Ibram X. Kendi (2016). *Stamped from the Beginning: The Definitive History of Racist Ideas in America*, Bold Type Books.

4. Ibram X. Kendi (2019). *How to Be an Antiracist*, One World.

5. Elaine Alec (2019). *Calling My Spirit Back.*

6. Ta-Nehisi Coates (2015). *Between the World and Me*, One World.

7. bell hooks (2000). *All About Love: New Visions*, William Morrow & Company.

8. Richard Rothstein (2017). *The Color of Law: A Forgotten History of How Our Government Segregated America*, Liveright.

9. Gholdy Muhammad (2020). *Cultivating Genius: An Equity Framework for Culturally and Historically Responsive Literacy*, Scholastic Teaching Resources.

10. adrienne maree brown (2017). *Emergent Strategy: Shaping Change, Changing Worlds*, AK Press.

11. Isabel Wilkerson (2020). *Caste: The Origins of Our Discontents*, Random House.

12. Eddie Moore, Ali Michael, and Marguerite W. Penick-Parks (Editors) (2018). *The Guide for White Women Who Teach Black Boys*, Corwin.

13. Ocean Vuong (2019). *On Earth We're Briefly Gorgeous: A Novel*, Penguin Press.

14. Patricia Baquedano-Lopez and Paul Garrett (2021). *On Becoming Bilingual: Learning from Children's Experiences Across Schools, Homes, and Communities*, Taylor & Francis.

15. Roxanne Dubar-Ortiz (2019). *An Indigenous Peoples' History of the United States For Young People*, Beacon Press.

16. Derald Wing Sue, *Microaggressions in Everyday Life: Race, Gender, and Sexual Orientation*, Wiley, 2010.

17. Jeff Chang (2016). *We Gon' Be Alright: Notes on Race and Resegregation*, Picador.

18. Cherríe Moraga and Gloria Anzaldúa (Editors) (2015). *This Bridge Called My Back, Fourth Edition: Writings by Radical Women of Color*, SUNY Press.

19. Grace Lee Boggs (2012). *The Next American Revolution: Sustainable Activism for the Twenty-First Century*, University of California Press.

20. Monique W. Morris (2016). *Pushout: The Criminalization of Black Girls in Schools*, The New Press.

My colleagues Matt Alexander and Jessica Huang, former co-directors of the June Jordan School for Equity (where I was a founding principal), offer four principles for becoming a warm demander:

1. **Believe in the impossible.** Do you believe every educator in your building can improve? If not, are you ready to coach or evaluate *out* those you don't believe in? Brain science and the concept of neuroplasticity[2] teach us that every human being has the ability

---

[2]Neuroplasticity (neuro: relating to the nervous system; plasticity: the quality of being easily shaped or molded) essentially means the brain's ability to form and reorganize connections, especially as a result of a learning experience.

to grow and change. When you believe this, you convey it. When you don't, it shows.

2. **Build trust.** Warm demanders understand that all growth and learning is rooted in **relational capital**, the "resource that leaders accrue when they take time to listen to and convey authentic care and curiosity toward others . . . If relationships function as currency in schools, relational capital is like a big savings account of trust and goodwill" (Safir, 2017b, p. 107). Trust is the foundation of all warm demander interactions.

3. **Teach self-discipline.** With trust, you can communicate high expectations to your colleagues: "I respect you, and therefore I am not going to lower my bar for you." The combination of belief and trust creates a platform on which to help ourselves and our colleagues develop self-discipline in our practice.

4. **Embrace failure.** Warm demanders model a growth mindset toward colleagues, encouraging a bias toward action and a willingness to move toward a pedagogy of voice. They end coaching conversations with questions like, "What's next in your development as an antiracist educator?" "What will you do to repair harm with the student (and/or parent)?" "How will you continue to build racial literacy and historical fluency?" In the realm of pedagogy, the warm demander might ask, "What street data strategy will you try this week to deepen your understanding of the student's experience?" "What pedagogical moves can you try out tomorrow to center student voice?" or "What's a stretch goal you can set for yourself as an aspiring antiracist educator?" Warm demanders don't expect their colleagues to change overnight, but they *do* expect them to take risks, look in the mirror, and build antiracist, anti-bias muscle. When it comes to microaggressions and other oppressive behaviors, they hold colleagues accountable to *do no harm* and to take full, unequivocal responsibility for the harm they may inadvertently cause.

These principles are powerful, but what do they look like in action? What are the listening and coaching moves of a warm demander? Let's get into it, using Jason's story as a case study. By the time Jason sat down with the teacher, he had lots of street data about the impact of her comment ("you're not even that dark-skinned") on the student. The student's mother, a Black woman and one of the more active parents on campus, had suddenly stopped coming to school. Whereas she normally came inside and talked to the staff, she had become visibly withdrawn and would opt to pick her son up at the curb. In addition, the student appeared deflated and disconnected whenever Jason would pass by him in the hallway. Jason knew he had to act, but how?

**CHALLENGE +
OFFER A CHOICE**

Help the person see the big picture; name systemic racism at play.

Flip the script, sharing power and cultivating a sense of agency.

Challenge and empower the person to make a choice/take a step.

Ask, "What kind of educator do you want to be?"

**LISTEN +
AFFIRM**

Listen to yourself and your body.

Listen with ears, eyes, undivided attention, and heart, paying attention to nonverbal cues.

Center voices at the margins.

Affirm the person's humanity and capacity to grow.

Inspired by the work of Matt Alexander and Jessica Huang at June Jordan School for Equity

**SHOW
STRENGTH**

Get grounded in your vision (graduate profile, instructional framework, equity values).

Don't capitulate to deficit language or white fragility.

Stay calm and clear-headed.

Use humor, intensity, and/or personal story to set the stage.

TRAVEL PLAN

WARM DEMANDER
FRAMEWORK

It's not enough to believe in your colleagues' ability to do better by kids. You have to proactively set the instructional tone and direction and then be willing to interrupt inequitable mindsets and practices when they surface. This requires us to cultivate what I call in *The Listening Leader* (Safir, 2017b) an **orientation to vision**—a leadership stance in which we define, coach toward, and message a vivid picture of success. Remember the graduate profile and performance assessment system you began to shape in Chapter 6. Get grounded in these visions as well as your image of an antiracist classroom that embodies the pedagogy of voice. Know it, live it, breathe it, and communicate it in every way you can: in meetings, on agendas, on the school walls, on classroom observation tools. Overcommunicate your vision so that when a breach happens, you are ready to show strength.

Showing strength means holding the line on equity and your vision of deep learning for every child and refusing to capitulate to deficit language or distorted views of student behavior. In Jason's story, the teacher first fell into what social psychologists call the **fundamental attribution error** (also known as correspondence bias): the tendency to explain someone's behavior based on *internal* factors, such as personality or disposition, and to underestimate situational explanations. She interpreted the student's advocacy around his grade as his being "angry for not getting what he wanted" instead of showing up as scholarly and self-possessed. She could have been impressed with this young man, but instead, implicit racial bias took over as she mapped his behavior right into a racist trope about "angry Black men." The warm demander has to *see* all of this, drawing on racial literacy and historical fluency around such tropes from our national legacy of dehumanizing portrayals of people of color in popular culture, the pseudoscience of eugenics, and centuries of violence against Black bodies. However, beyond drawing on one's racial literacy, warm demanders must be ready to interrupt such tropes head-on.

Strength can look extremely calm and grounded; you may choose to use humor, personal story, or emotional intensity to convey strength. On the other hand, anger, condescension, anxiety, or manipulation will distort our efforts to call the person *in* to equity. Before a warm demander conversation, be sure to take time to center yourself through breathing, meditation, visualization, journaling, or other forms of intention-setting. Jason "showed strength" in a number of nuanced and powerful ways. First, as soon as he saw the teacher's email communications with the mother, he took control of the situation. The teacher had sent the following email to the mom recounting the incident, including (shockingly to Jason) her own racist comment. It essentially said,

> *Hey, your son was very agitated. He was angry about his grade. He wouldn't let it go, and it wasn't the time or place. Then he asked me if I was scared of him, and I asked him, "Oh, why would I be scared of you?" He said, "Well, because the other day this white woman clutched her purse and moved to the other side of the street when I was walking by." So I asked him, "Well, why would she do that? You're not even that dark."*

Jason took one look at this piece of street data and knew he had to intervene quickly. Before he had a chance to engage, the teacher sent *another* email to the mom offering a sort of backhanded apology. When Jason saw this whole thread, he directed the teacher to please stop emailing the mother until they could sit down and have a meeting to discuss the situation.

Jason also showed strength by sitting down one-on-one with the teacher and interrupting her first response, which was to focus on her own feelings over the child's. When they first met, he found himself smack dab in the middle of **white fragility**—feelings of discomfort and defensiveness on the part of a white person when confronted around racial inequality and injustice: "I could tell she was visibly upset. She knew she had made a mistake, but she started crying right off the bat. I just remember stopping her. I said, 'This can't be about you right now. Yes, you made a mistake but let me tell you a story of what happened to *me* when I was this student's age.'" Jason leaned into vulnerability to center his own experience rather than the teacher's feelings. He shared how seeing her comment to the student took him right back to the second day of his own high school experience as he walked the halls with four white friends. A white male teacher stopped him but not his friends and said, "Hey, you don't go to this school," before asking Jason for identification. He shared the aftermath of this incident, including how it shaped his sense of belonging for years to come.

Jason taught his colleague self-discipline by refusing to enable her initial emotional response to take over and insisting that she listen and learn from his story. This required a lot of trust and vulnerability on Jason's part and in taking this risk, he humanized himself, the child, and even the teacher—deeming her worthy of his confidence and setting the stage for her to learn and grow. In his words,

"I think she realized this wasn't about *her* as much as about what she had communicated to this young man and how damaging that was."

Listen and Affirm: Centering Voices From the Margins

By shifting the teacher's response from defensiveness and fragility to listening, Jason opened up space for an authentic coaching conversation. First, however, he made a choice to engage the student's mother around her experience of her child's mistreatment. My June Jordan School for Equity colleagues call this part of the warm demander framework "listen and affirm," and I refer to it as deep listening in *The Listening Leader*: a type of listening that aims to relieve the suffering of the other person, supporting personal healing and the development of relational trust (Safir, 2017b). In my coaching, I see many leaders leapfrog this step, perhaps because they fear the emotionality that may emerge. Racism and other forms of oppression are lived, visceral, somatic experiences, a point to which author Ta-Nehisi Coates speaks eloquently in his writing (2015). **If leading for equity is inherently emotional work, we must cultivate our capacity to sit with and honor people's feelings. Otherwise, we risk erasing their experience.**

When we practice deep listening, we tune into the message *beneath* the words, paying close attention to the speaker's nonverbal signals and affirming his or her capacity to grow and find a sense of agency. What does the person's facial expression and body language reveal? What about their tone? As you assess these street data indicators, try to understand the other person's experience and model empathy in any of the following ways:

- Demonstrating care and compassion

- Being vulnerable and sharing a piece of your own story and struggle

- Reflecting back nonverbal cues to activate mirror neurons, a unique type of brain cell that fires when we observe an action or emotion

- Practicing active listening by paraphrasing and summarizing what the speaker has said ("What I hear you saying is . . .")

- Using affirmative language to reinforce that you value and believe in the person ("I really appreciate how you . . ." "I know this is difficult, and I thank you for . . .")

Jason chose the margins when he decided to listen to the student's mother before bringing her face-to-face with the teacher. After meeting with the teacher, he scheduled a follow-up with the teacher *and* the mom. He intentionally asked the mom to come in twenty minutes early to gauge where she was at emotionally. When she first arrived, Jason noticed that her leg kept twitching, a street-level indicator that she felt anxious and unsettled. In their brief time together, Jason shared his personal story of racism in high school and discovered that the mom had a similar story in her background. He created space for her to be vulnerable, to metabolize the stress she was carrying in her body, and to get ready to speak to the teacher. She told Jason she was upset but mostly that she didn't want this type of incident happening to other children. She wanted to address it with the teacher and then move on. By the end, Jason shares, her leg had stopped twitching and she was focused and rooted in what she wanted to say to the teacher.

In addition to listening to the mother, Jason listened deeply to *himself* and affirmed his own story as source of cultural wealth that would help him shape his leadership moves. Before sitting down with the teacher the first time, he was wracked with anxiety:

> I remember thinking the whole week, *How am I going to address this so that she understands what she did, why it was wrong, and the impact it could have on this young man?* The week went by, and then Monday came and I was still nervous. I said to myself, *Why am I nervous about this? I didn't do anything wrong.*

In this moment of self-awareness, Jason realized he, a Black man, was carrying the emotional labor for the teacher, a white woman. He needed to take a deep breath and trust himself and his leadership while still acknowledging that addressing racism is difficult work.

All of Jason's moves helped him build enough trust with the student's mother that she was able to find her own agency to address the teacher. This was key in that it allowed Jason to share power rather than hoard it, and to disrupt white supremacy culture at work. His facilitation, in turn, created a trust-building opportunity between teacher and parent. In focusing *first* on building trust with the student's mother, Jason exhibited the mindset of radical inclusion. He also activated **mature empathy** (Safir, 2017b)—the ability to form a mental picture of another person's experience by drawing on one's own schemas—by reaching out to his own mom to hear what *she* would have wanted when her own son experienced a similar microaggression by a white teacher. She said clearly: "To be able to advocate for you." That street data shaped his next move.

Challenge and Offer a Choice: Building Student and Teacher Agency

When a person feels seen and heard, something magical happens. Often, they can breathe deeply once again. They might cry, sigh, shift their posture, or release physical tension in a way that signals increased openness. Look for that signal; it is your opportunity to engage in **strategic listening**, a style of equity-centered coaching that employs reflective questions and a bias toward experimental action to help the person build capacity and agency (Safir, 2017b). This is your entry point for the third part of the warm demander framework, "challenge and offer a choice." The nuance here is we are attempting to call somebody *in* and *up* to their fullest potential, not to call them *out*.[3] This is the moment to re-anchor the conversation in your vision and values—the graduate profile, the pedagogy of voice, and/or an emerging set of values around equity and antiracism.

One way to challenge people is to focus the conversation on their *impact* rather than their *intent*. Microaggression theory has long uplifted the idea of impact versus intent, and it can be an incredibly helpful frame. If you are engaging in a warm demander conversation and the person says, "But I didn't *mean* to upset him" or "I don't have a biased bone in my body," here's a way to challenge and pivot. "I understand that you may not have intended to cause harm, but what matters most here is the impact you've had. How can you take responsibility for your impact? What would that look and sound like? How can you prepare yourself for the vulnerability this requires?" Research on implicit bias can be another useful frame: "Research has shown that we all have biases, and it's our responsibility to look in the mirror and reflect on them regularly rather than deny they exist." To model

---

[3]Note: There is definitely a place for calling people *out* and holding them accountable. We may have to call out board members for upholding biased policies or not responding swiftly in the wake of racist events. We may have to call out positional leaders for being complicit in ongoing racist or exclusionary behaviors. Inside our school buildings, relying on "calling out" strategies runs the risk of leaving behind a trail of distrust and fear that doesn't serve our greater mission. Think of it like constantly living in "fight" mode among "fight, fight, or freeze" responses. Warm demander offers a fourth path, rooted in our moral imperative to address oppression while building the capacity of the people around us.

vulnerability, I might name a time when my own intentions didn't align with my impact: "We are all capable of causing harm without intending to. As a teacher/leader, I too have misstepped and had to push myself to stop, reflect, and grow from it." Then, I would push the discourse toward street data: "How do you understand the impact this experience had on the student (or colleague)? If you don't know, how could you find out?"

We can also challenge people by posing probing questions that invite them to reframe their thinking about the situation, such as the following:

- If you step back for a moment, what's a different way of seeing this student's behavior?

- What might be getting in the way of . . . (e.g., you building a strong relationship with the student or parent)?

- When have you been successful in addressing a similar situation, and what can you learn by studying that?

In this "challenge and offer a choice" moment, the warm demander always moves the conversation toward responsive action. Remember the principle of embracing failure? This is where you plant that seed! Offer the teacher small action steps to consider, or better yet, ask, "What is a next step you could try?" or "What is another form of street data we could gather to help us understand this situation?" or again, "How will you continue to develop your practice as an antiracist educator?" Affirm that you believe in the person's capacity to grow and that it is indeed safe to try and even sputter along the way—but never at the expense of a student's dignity. Schedule another time to meet and continue reflecting.

In his one-on-one with the teacher, Jason seized the moment to challenge the teacher and offer her a choice: How was she going to move forward? He shared with me that he wanted to create a learning experience for her without letting her off the hook: "I think I gave her the information to understand the reaction she got. I don't think I gave her a break . . . Like I said, she's a human being too. She can make mistakes, but it's like, how do we come back from that? Does our thinking continue to be the same, or do we change by seeing the hurt that we put on a young man's face?" Even as his own schooling memories as a young Black man surfaced, Jason continued to believe the teacher could grow and held her accountable to do so.

He had paved the way to this moment by showing strength and listening to and affirming his own experience, the mom's experience, and his own mother's experience. Now he needed to cultivate the teacher's agency and coach her toward her next move. Jason asked her to think deeply about her identity (the first component of our agency framework): "What kind of teacher do you want to be right now?" In his words, "At that point, we started having a real discussion. 'Do you want to be that teacher who made a mistake and didn't know what you were saying was wrong, or do you want to be that teacher I had in high school who basically told me he couldn't care less about my feelings . . . What will tomorrow look like for you?'" This conversation became a pivot point for the teacher and primed her to later sit down with the mother from a place of humility and deep listening. When Jason asked the teacher if she'd be willing to meet with him and the mom to mend the relationship, the teacher said an unequivocal yes.

The stage was set for another warm demander conversation, this time led by the mom. By meeting with the mom in advance as described earlier, Jason had empowered her to speak to the teacher from a place of conviction and strength. When the teacher first entered the meeting, she tried to put the student's academic work on the table, perhaps in an effort to avoid the more painful conversation about her own behavior. Jason again showed strength by saying, "No, you can put that away. We need to talk about what happened." Sitting together around a table, the mom spoke frankly to the teacher, letting her know that what she said was very inappropriate and that she didn't want it to interfere with her son's education nor anyone else's. She held a high bar for the teacher, stating directly, "I have my son here for a reason, and I need you to be at your best." The teacher, having been coached and prepared by Jason, just listened and took it in—no tears or defensiveness.

By the end of the meeting, something had shifted. The mom was breathing more deeply and appeared relaxed. She even asked the teacher what she could help her with: field trips or other class activities. As the school year progressed (until the pandemic hit and school buildings closed), Jason began to see the mom on campus more and more—back to her regular, engaged self. The teacher, instead of shutting down and becoming defensive, began to check in regularly with Jason, showing a desire to continue learning and growing. Most importantly, the student showed street-level signs of restored confidence, what Jason calls "the return of his youthfulness and teenage innocence." Jason saw him laughing, making jokes, and playing sports with friends again, returning to his normal, confident, academically successful self.

All the street data pointed toward a healing breakthrough. Jason's adept moves as a warm demander restored dignity and healing to all parties involved.

From the Micro to the Macro

I am no longer accepting the things I cannot change. I am changing the things I cannot accept.

—Angela Y. Davis

I recently caught up with Jason, in the wake of another spate of police killings of Black lives. He shared with me his thoughts and feelings about raising a Black son: "I'm raising a young, Black male and teaching him. I don't know what a white man teaches his son, but I'm teaching my son not how to just live and be a productive citizen. I'm teaching him how to *survive* at age nine, and that's ridiculous." For anyone who resists the call to engage in the types of conversations outlined in this chapter, I ask you to dig deep. Find the courage and build your will and skill to address racism, homophobia, and other forms of oppression—people's lives depend on it. Students' right to live with dignity and find agency in the world depend on it.

As I reflected with Jason in that conversation, it's a reification of white privilege that white people can choose *not* to have "The Conversation" about survival and police brutality with their kids. But when we as white people are silent about these issues, we reinforce the whole paradigm by raising children who lack consciousness and are able to dismiss BIPOC stories with a "That's not real. You're making that up," or "You're just being sensitive." Let's all shoulder up to have the street-level conversations that matter.

The street data framework reminds us that equity isn't something "out there"—in a policy, strategic plan, memo, or agenda. It isn't something we "do" as Jamila argued so passionately in Chapter 2. It's in here, inside each of us, and it's right now, inside every classroom and leadership moment. Every moment is a chance to be an antiracist educator, to center the voices of the most marginalized (for readers of color, sometimes that may be your own voice), to bend the arc of education toward justice.

We can become warm demanders for equity by leading toward a clear vision and values, believing in the impossible, taking time to build trust, and cultivating a culture of risk-taking. This approach requires courage, deep listening, and an expanding set of coaching moves. Much of our equity work in schools focuses on the problems we need to solve: racism, sexism, homophobia, transphobia, ableism, exclusion, bias. Street data will help us develop a robust analysis of these equity challenges while the warm demander framework offers us a daily footpath rooted in hope and possibility. Imagine a school full of warm demanders, where teachers, leaders, and even students take the time to confront and transform deficit thinking and mindsets in themselves and their peers.

In her spectacular book *Emergent Strategy*, adrienne maree brown quotes podcast producer Kat Aaron:

> The micro reflects the macro and vice versa—Fibonacci patterns show up from space to cauliflower. The tiniest most mundane act reflects the biggest creations we can image. (a. m. brown, 2017)

As we take the time to invest in warm demander interactions, we grow a new way of being and learning together. We envision the seemingly impossible—a place where every student and every teacher is held to high expectations in a loving and supportive manner—and begin to enact it. Suddenly, the tiniest conversation will be reflected in the image of the schools we long to create.

WARM DEMANDER SCENARIOS

Review the scenarios below and choose ONE that feels familiar. Take time to reflect in writing: How would you approach the warm demander conversation? How might you show strength? Listen and affirm? Challenge and offer a choice?

Scenario A: You are the principal of a racially and economically diverse middle school that has a good reputation but a poor track record of serving students with learning differences. The father of a child with ADHD and generalized anxiety asks to meet with you to

(Continued)

(Continued)

share a recent experience his child had with a teacher around the time she began taking a new ADHD medication. When the student had to up her dosage, she had an adverse reaction and began shaking and twitching in class. She approached the teacher, visibly shaking, to ask for a pass to go to the office, and the teacher's response was to look away and say dismissively, "Whatever . . . You do you." By the time the father arrived at the school, the child was sobbing and entirely disregulated. The father is very upset and says his child doesn't feel safe in the class anymore. You are preparing to have a warm demander conversation with the teacher.

Scenario B: You recently attended your site's Coordination of Services Team (COST) meeting where you learned that a significantly large number of students have been identified as children of migrant families or newcomers to the country. The next day, you are walking by a colleague's classroom when you witness her yelling at a student for wetting her pants. From the COST meeting, you know this student is a child from a migrant family. Having been an immigrant yourself, you are filled with rage at seeing another adult in your school be so insensitive to a child. You wait a couple of days to try to center yourself before addressing the issue with your colleague. Now, you are preparing to have a warm demander conversation.

Scenario C: You are the teacher-leader of the fourth-grade team at an elementary school that has had a recent influx of newcomer students. One of your colleagues is a veteran teacher whom you respect and think of as skillful and caring. However, in recent team meetings, she has made comments about her newcomer students that trouble you and indicate she views them with pity. For example, "Luis has dealt with so much trauma, I don't want to challenge him too much with this writing assignment. I think I'll let him do an art project instead." Another time, she said, "I've decided to stop expecting my newcomer students to complete their homework because I know most of them don't have a good space to work at home." You are concerned that she is projecting implicit biases onto the students and failing to challenge them appropriately, and you're preparing to have a warm demander conversation.

Scenario D: You are a member of a grade-level team that has been using a PLC model to share and give feedback on each other's lessons. Your colleague comes to the meeting with a "Pilgrim lesson" that she has done for many years and wants to expand on. In the lesson, students are asked to draw a picture of where their ancestors came from and tell the story. You are disturbed by the lack of cultural and historical awareness about how this lesson might land, especially for African American students. At the next meeting, your colleague comes in upset, almost in tears, because an African American father has written to the principal to tell him he felt "heartbroken" when he saw the lesson and viewed it as "culturally insensitive at best." Your colleague feels hurt and wants you to empathize with her. How do you approach this conversation?

GETTING UP CLOSE AND PERSONAL: REFLECTION QUESTIONS

1. What ideas or pieces of Jason's story most stood out to you and why?

2. Share a passage that resonated with you with a colleague or small group. Allow others to comment on the passage before getting the final word to reflect on what it meant to you.

3. Which of the three components of the warm demander framework—show strength, listen and affirm, challenge and offer a choice—do you find most challenging to enact?

4. How will you build your capacity as a warm demander teacher or leader? Set a stretch goal.

5. Envision: what would it look like to have an entire school culture built around these ideas? Draw, journal, or meditate on a vision of what that would look and feel like.

Epilogue
The Journey Toward Liberation

In April 2019, I flew to Vancouver Island to join forty educators from the United States and Canada participating in the Deeper Learning Dozen (DLD) project out of Harvard University. We began Chapter 1 at the DLD gathering where First Nations elders and local leaders led us through a paradigm-shifting experience that made me interrogate all of my assumptions about education, knowledge, and data. In that vibrant community of practice, I met some of the most compelling and passionate educators I have ever encountered. One is Gail Higginbottom, district principal for Aboriginal Education in Kootenay Lake District, BC. At the end-of-year DLD virtual convening, amidst the heartache and uncertainty of a global pandemic, Gail shared a story with the group:

> Let me begin with a story.
>
> I was eight years old, driving with my gramma out on an old bush road. We arrived at my great uncle's house and there was a freshly hunted moose on the kitchen floor, skinning and butchering in place. While driving on that bumpy road, my gramma shared this with me: **Drink from a straw or you will chip a tooth**. I share this story as a reflective tool as I think about equity leadership and Aboriginal education in my district.

Gail went on to draw out three powerful metaphors. First, *harvesting the moose*: she reminded us that leading for equity is about translating our understanding of complex issues into digestible steps—common language, shared tools, individualized street-level data, and awareness.

Second, *drinking from a straw*: Gail honored that fact that equity work is vulnerable work, and creating emotional safety is essential in working with families, communities, and students as we navigate their needs, hopes, and dreams. Finally, *on that bumpy road*: Gail acknowledged that her team has worked with the best intentions, *and* they have more work ahead to see and hear results in closing the opportunity gap between Indigenous and non-Indigenous learners. She publicly committed to continue to build trust and equity awareness districtwide (DLD virtual convening, June 16, 2020).

Close your eyes for a moment and take in the images Gail offers: harvesting the moose, drinking from a straw so that we don't chip our teeth, navigating that bumpy road toward equity and transformation. These metaphors speak volumes about our collective need to slow down so that we can *see* the whole learner (adult and child), *tend* to every part of the system, *grow* our fluency around equity, and not *harm* ourselves and each other by moving with the "urgency," "efficiency," and "perfectionism" privileged by white supremacy. This is the work of **seventh generation principle**, based on an ancient Haudenosaunee (Iroquois) philosophy that the decisions we make today should result in a sustainable world seven generations into the future.

Our ancestors and predecessors fought to create space for the dignity and humanity of Black, Indigenous, brown, immigrant, working-class, LGBTQ+, students with learning differences, and others at the margins. We stand on the shoulders of *generations* of courageous, anti-racist educators who refused to uphold a system rooted in oppression and the devaluation of Black and brown lives. Street data is just one more tool in this legacy of resistance—a way to unify our vision of a different world with our daily actions. We hope this book will offer you a gentle path forward to witness and uplift the brilliance and cultural wealth of your students, colleagues, and families.

We *can* embrace a new way of being together. We must. If not now, when?

I close with the words of my brilliant friend Denise Augustine, a secondee for Indigenous Education with the Ministry of Education in British Columbia:

> Deeper learning requires first that we *listen* deeply. That we open our hearts and minds. That we enter into relationship.

We also need to *trust* the person whom we are listening to—that they know best where their learning needs to go, where their attention and energy is best spent.

All of that means little if we don't *act* on what we have learned. This makes me ask myself the questions, "As a member of the leadership team, what am I *doing* to demonstrate that I am listening and trusting the educators in our organization? How am I showing/modeling that I *value* deeper learning? What decisions are we making about how resources are allocated, who we hire, whose voices we include (or do not include) in decision-making?"

Listen deeply. Trust the people. Act on what you learn. With that invocation, I invite you to walk forward on your street data journey with clear eyes and a full heart, knowing that the biggest mistake we can make is to cling to the status quo. Be brave, be bold, be visionary. We've got this.

Appendices

Appendix 6.1

Elementary Example of a Graduate Profile

The Katherine R. Smith School is a public elementary school in San José, California, serving predominantly Latinx students, that has been recognized as both a California Distinguished School and a National Blue Ribbon School of Excellence. An innovator and early adopter of project-based learning methods, Katherine Smith's leaders developed a graduate profile that conveys to families and students the importance of thinking, learning, working, communicating, collaborating, and contributing to their community. All of their professional learning, curriculum planning, and student engagement is oriented toward this framework.

Kevin Armstrong and Rachel Trowbridge, co-principals of Katherine R. Smith, reflected with me on the impact of the graduate profile:

> When our school went through a significant reinvention eight years ago, our staff became anchored in a shared belief about the learning and overall school experience we wanted for our students. What we *didn't* have was specific language describing measurable outcomes that could not only bring our initial vision to life but provide guidance for the direction of adult learning, cohesion across all classrooms, and a fully embraced sense of purpose for everyone on campus.

> The beauty of the K Smith Habits is that they are easily built into our projects as learning targets—academic, social-emotional, and personalized—and they translate across grades and school systems, such as PBIS (positive behavior interventions and supports), so they never become "just another thing." Some might call it brainwashing, but we spend significant time in every classroom and collectively helping our staff to internalize these attributes, beliefs, and skills. In essence, if a piece of work is *not* focused on the profile outcomes, we know we can take it off our plate.

Katherine Smith School
DESIGNED FOR THE 21ST CENTURY LEARNER

THINK critically. Ask questions and use evidence to describe and support claims. Be flexible and innovative to design solutions to complex problems. Reflect and critique ideas.

LEARN continuously. Develop strong foundational skills to master significant content. Make mistakes. Build on knowledge and apply to new situations.

WORK intentionally. Be persistent and self-directed. Manage impulsivity and set goals. Strive for accuracy and apply effort to continuously improve. Take risks and create beautiful work.

COMMUNICATE effectively. Speak and write with clarity. Listen actively. Know your audience, understand the purpose, and choose precise language. If appropriate, incorporate media to enhance ideas.

COLLABORATE constructively. Take responsibility for yourself and your team. Listen with empathy and understanding with a commitment to shared success. Give and receive feedback.

CONTRIBUTE globally. Apply your work to real-world situations to serve an authentic purpose. Be kind to others and empowered to make a difference. Recognize your place in the community.

Appendix 6.2

Student-Authored Descriptors of the Art of Social Justice Teaching

WARM DEMANDER & SAFE CLASSROOM COMMUNITY	STUDENTS AS INTELLECTUALS & TEACHER AS COACH	KNOWLEDGE OF STUDENTS & SOCIAL JUSTICE CURRICULUM
TEACHER • Is in control • Treats students like family • Takes consideration of students' feelings • Is understanding • Shows respect • Brings positive energy	**TEACHER** • Supports students • Gives clear instructions • Hopes the best for their students • Sees the different skills students have • Phrases things in a way that makes students think critically	**TEACHER** • Leads class discussions & encourages students to speak up about their opinions (Talking Circles) • Pre- and post-discussion briefing • Real-world curriculum • Relevance to our modern society
STUDENTS • Equality for all students • Safe environment • Happiness and quiet • Feels like a family • Closeness with each other • Stronger mindsets	**STUDENTS** • Critical thinking • Their voices are heard • Their opinions matter • Constant questioning • Discussion • Students expanding their minds to think bigger	**STUDENTS** • Having class discussions • Lots of students talking • Teachers listening • Students teaching each other • Students being engaged

These descriptions were created by the JJSE eleventh-grade Peer Resources class in May 2015.

Appendix 8.1

Empathy Interview Transcript
With Teacher Think-Aloud

Note: This interview is adapted from a real transcript from a middle school teacher's empathy interview with his student. The student's name has been changed to protect anonymity. I added the third column to show how the teacher might analyze the rich street data presented.

QUESTION	QUOTE	THINK-ALOUD ANALYSIS
Can you introduce yourself?	Hi. My name is Alejandro. Me and my class are currently working on this project about doing a podcast. We are also including interviews. I would like to include my mom in this interview because she is the one who I will be interviewing. I want to ask her about her culture or any tradition she's had, basically, her past life. I would like to learn about this because I would like to know her strengths, her hopes, of what she has done back in the past, and what made her achieve herself to where she is today.	*I love that Alejandro is intuitively tapping into his mom's community cultural wealth. He is using such a strong asset frame on his own.*
What are some important activities you have done in this project?	Some important activities that I've done in this project is writing an introduction, choosing some song intros. Also, practicing my work that I've done with fellow peers. Let's say I wrote an introduction and to make sure there are no mistakes to try and correct myself to better it, I practice reading it out loud to a fellow peer or teacher. I'm trying to gain feedback from others to see what I can improve or change.	*This street data tells me that Alejandro values and actively uses practice and feedback as strategies for improvement. He does not approach learning as a one-and-done, which is a huge strength. Specifically, I can infer that reading a piece of writing out loud to a peer or teacher helps him hear his own writing voice and get feedback.*
What's something in this project that you feel you have been successful in?	I feel I've been successful in two things. One, finishing a sheet filled with questions that I may include during the interview, and also preparing myself an introduction for the beginning, and what I have planned for a start.	*This helps me see Alejandro's growing sense of efficacy as a key element of agency. He uses two verbs to signal efficacy: "finishing" and "preparing." I want to help him continue to build on these things.*

(Continued)

(Continued)

QUESTION	QUOTE	THINK-ALOUD ANALYSIS
What has helped you be successful? Why do you think you've been successful with those things?	Well, one thing that I don't occasionally get; I just need to complete any assignment that I may struggle with, perhaps. What I need is time and patience. That could benefit myself to see how I can be better in these activities.	*Here, Alejandro is giving me insight into two growth areas: time and patience with himself. He understands that to improve on assignments that he is struggling with, he needs to slow down his pace and be patient with himself.*
What have you found challenging in the project?	I found it challenging in trying to start a song intro . . . podcast intro. When we created it in our computers, I didn't really have any time to try finishing one of those. I struggled to find the right way of trying to see what could be useful and what could be negative. I haven't finished my podcast intro on the computer because I can't seem to find . . . I can't find the right theme that could fit properly into my intro.	*Here again, the theme of time and pacing comes up in Angel's narration. I can see how important it will be to reassure him that I value quality and process over quantity and product. I also may need to do a mini lesson with him and other students around theme.*
What's something you learned in this project that you're proud of?	Well, to be honest, there isn't really anything I'm proud of this. I just feel great about it but not proud.	*This makes me wonder if "pride" is an individualistic trait and not culturally congruent for Alejandro. Maybe pride is part of Western epistemology, and I should think about how to reframe that question!*
Okay what's something you learned?	Something that I knew already was trying to find an intro. Just to start the beginning of my topic to try and drag people's attention to it. Yes, that's something that I've already learned and pretty much accomplished well.	*Alejandro is really tuned in to the "hook" for this podcast project, and I love his description of "dragging people's attention to it." I can sense his growing confidence and agency in his final sentence. Going forward, I want to help him build on his many strengths and feel comfortable slowing down and being patient with himself as a learner.*

Appendix 8.2 Process Guide to Instructional Rounds

School's Problem of Practice
Example: How are students reading, writing, and engaging in academic conversations?
• How do students respond to and build on their peers' ideas?
• To what extent do students talk about academic content with each other versus with their teacher?
• To what extent do students provide meaningful written evidence to support their thinking?

TIME	TOPIC

Facilitator Welcome & Overview
 	
(8 min.)
 	
Time: _____
	Welcome
	
	1. **Introductions**
	
	2. **Objective**
	
	Provide a learning space that is evidence based and structured by using a common protocol to investigate a school's problem of practice using the insights of a diverse team comprised of school administrators, which can support the hosting school with new insights into how to continuously improve.
	
	3. **Norms**
	   • Respect the start and end time of every visit.
	   • Actively cultivate a safe space for learning.
	   • Push yourself to take risks and grow.
	   • Maintain confidentiality. Limit all discussion to the debrief and avoid hallway talk.
	   • Stay true to the role of data collector and "fly on the wall" in classrooms (do not help students with their work, intervene in the lesson, or engage with the teacher).
	
	4. **Agenda Overview**
	
	Introduction (30 min.)
	   • Facilitator overview
	   • Presentation of problem of practice
	   • Preparing for observations .
	   • Logistics
	
	Classroom observations (60 min.)
	
	Debrief (120 min.)
	   • Patterns
	   • Analysis
	   • Summary of patterns
	   • Debrief fishbowl conversations
	   • Closing, online feedback

(Continued)

(Continued)

TIME	TOPIC
Presentation of Problem of Practice & Preparing for Observations (15 min.) Time: _____	**Problem of Practice (POP):** Host reviews the POP and identifies the focal questions for the team. What is the current context? When we think of this POP, our school is working to hone in on _____. **Building Shared Understanding:** Facilitator guides the team and charts responses to these questions. Participants take notes in their agenda packet. • What would it look like in every classroom if this problem of practice were resolved? • What teaching practices and student practices do we hope to see related to this POP? What is possible in the constraints of a ten-minute observation? • Facilitator guides T-chart of observable student and teaching practices.
Preparing for Observations (5 min.) Time: _____	**Classroom Observation Logistics** • Review observation schedule and observation/scripting form. • Review of process: We collect evidence on what we *do see* that is related to the POP. Focus most on what students are doing. Notes are confidential and will be shredded after rounds. Remember classroom and hallway norms. • Report back time. _____

Observations

(60 min.)

Notes about the classrooms I will visit or campus logistics:

Time to report back: _____

Instructional Rounds Debrief

| **Prepare for Debrief**

(8 min.)

Time: _____ | **Partner Discussion:** What was it like to observe in classrooms using this problem of practice as a focus. How was it helpful? How was it challenging?

Facilitator outlines the steps of the debrief.

1. Individually sift through all of the evidence from each classroom observation that relates to the POP.

2. In small groups
  • Analyze data to organize into similar buckets
  • Summarize evidence into pattern statements on a poster
  • Present poster to the whole group

3. In small groups
  • Summarize one bucket of patterns from all the posters into one summary sentence

4. Facilitator uses group input to summarize all ideas from the buckets into one overall summary poster. |

TIME	TOPIC
Description of Evidence & Finding Patterns (40 min.) Time: _____	**Description** Individual review of evidence (8 min.) • Review the POP. • Mark/highlight evidence related to the POP that shows up in your notes. • Select one to two pieces of evidence from each classroom and write each one on its own post it. But you should have no more than ten sticky notes total. *Is my evidence specific, descriptive, and non judgmental? Is it useful?* **Analysis** *How can we organize our ideas to make sense of what we saw? Which could be a high level pattern that might help the school get unstuck?* Small groups construct pattern statements (30 min.). • Share sticky notes and organize into similar buckets using the sticky note categories. • Summarize evidence from each row into a pattern statements on the poster.
Summary of Patterns (15 min.) Time: _____	**Summary of Patterns** Each team shares their poster. In small groups • Summarize one bucket of patterns from all the posters into one summary sentence • Facilitator uses group input to summarize all ideas from the buckets into one Overall summary poster
Discussion on Next Steps (25 min.) Time: _____	**Discussion and Reflection** **Participant Discussion:** All principals discuss while facilitator takes notes. (20 min.) Participants, including host principal, use the guiding questions in this section to support their fishbowl conversation. What suggestions can we offer our host school that can support these hack mindsets in the following list? (Fail Forward and Learn) (Start Small) (Bias to Action) • What assets could the school build upon? • What might help get some changes going?

(Continued)

(Continued)

TIME	TOPIC
	• What strategies have we seen succeed in a similar context that could be helpful for addressing the patterns around this school's POP?
	• How does the context of this school inform our suggestions around next steps?
	• What assets could the school build upon?
	• What resources/support are we aware of within SFUSD that might be helpful?
	Hosts Reflection (5 min.)
	What resonated from the discussion? Use the prompts that follow to guide your reflection.
	• What is in your sphere of influence related to this POP? What leadership actions are you willing to test out?
	• What feels like one small doable step that will help build momentum toward engaging in this work?
	• How might you share the patterns collected today with your ILT/larger staff? What needs to happen to propel this work forward?
	• What would happen if we continued on without changing?
	• If students did everything that was asked of them, what would they know and be able to do?
Closing (10 min.) Time: _____	**Appreciations and Personal Learnings** (5 min.) What is something you appreciated about our time learning together today? What are you taking away from today that connects to your own work? **Feedback Online Form** (5 min.)

Glossary

adaptive expertise: A broad construct that encompasses a range of cognitive, motivational, and personality-related components, as well as habits of mind and dispositions. Generally, people demonstrate adaptive expertise when they are able to efficiently solve previously encountered tasks and generate new procedures for new tasks.

agency: The idea that people have the capacity to take action, craft and carry out plans, and make informed decisions based on a growing base of knowledge. Also, the street data metric offered as an alternative to satellite metrics and in relationship to a pedagogy of voice.

anti-Black racism: A feature of white supremacy, anti-Blackness is a two-part formation that both strips Blackness of value (dehumanizes) and systematically marginalizes Black people. This form of racism is overt, historical, and embedded in all of our institutions. Beneath anti-Black racism lies the covert structural and systemic racism that is held in place by anti-Black policies, institutions, and ideologies. Anti-Blackness is also the disregard for Black institutions and policies privileging outside practices over Black traditions.

antiracist, anti-bias adult culture: A culture in which educators develop the will, skill, vulnerability, and courage to uproot systemic racism and deep-rooted biases.

antiracist stance: The idea that racial groups are equals, none needs developing, and the commitment to support policy that reduces racial inequity (Kendi, 2019).

artifact: Anything created by human beings that yields information or insight into the culture and/or society of its creator and users.

audacious hope: An idea that educators must reconnect to collective experience by struggling alongside one another, sharing in the victories and the pain (Duncan-Andrade, 2009).

banking model of education: A pedagogical model that positions the teacher as subject and active participant and the students as passive objects. Education is viewed as a process of depositing knowledge into students' brains, with little to no attention to students' preexisting knowledge and cultural schema (Freire, 1970).

belonging: A component of agency in which students feel deeply connected to their school, classroom(s), peers, and teachers and can say, "I see myself, and I am seen and loved here."

BIPOC: Black, Indigenous, and People of Color (BIPOC) is used to highlight the unique relationship to whiteness that Indigenous and Black (African Americans) people have, which shapes the experiences of and relationship to white supremacy for all people of color within a U.S. context (https://www.thebipocproject.org/, 2020).

blanket equity: Investing in a program or curriculum rather than building the capacity of your people to address equity challenges as complex and ongoing places of inquiry.

boomerang equity: Investing time and resources to understand your equity challenges but reverting back to previous mental models in ways that lead to unintentionally harmful solutions (e.g., measuring progress toward equity solely through state testing exams).

co-generative dialogues (or cogens): A pedagogical practice of simple, informal conversations between a teacher and a small group of students with the goal of providing feedback and co-generating a plan of action. Can also be adapted for leaders to use with staff (Emdin, 2017).

coherence: The act or state of binding one thing with another; in schools, a shared depth of understanding about the purpose and nature of the work in the minds and behaviors of educational actors, individually and especially collectively (Fullan & Quinn, 2015).

colorism: Prejudice or discrimination against individuals with a darker skin tone, which can also result in exclusion of those with lighter skin tone.

community cultural wealth: An array of knowledges, skills, abilities, and contacts possessed and used by communities of color to survive and resist racism and other forms of oppression (Yosso, 2005).

complex challenges: The solution to the challenge is not known and can only be seen or known during or after the action unfolds. Equity challenges are complex in nature. There is no set of steps or algorithm that will tell you how to respond.

complicated challenges: The solution to the challenge is not immediately obvious but can be known prior to taking action. These challenges are hard to solve but can be addressed by assembling the right technical expertise.

courage: A mindset connected to the move phase of the equity transformation cycle, signifying the need to act without complete information, the perfect design, or a predetermined outcome.

creativity: A mindset connected to the reimagine phase of the equity transformation cycle, signifying use of the collective imagination and/or original ideas to transform student experience.

critical pedagogy: A teaching approach popularized by Paolo Freire that helps students question and challenge the status quo, develop habits of mind that go beneath surface meaning, uncover root causes of oppression, engage in deep thinking, and create counter-narratives about their lived experiences.

culturally responsive education (CRE): A pedagogy that recognizes the importance of including students' cultural references in all aspects of instruction and calls for deep cognitive engagement of learners whose culture and experiences have been relegated to the margins (Ladson-Billings, 1994).

culturally responsive pedagogy (CRP): Dr. Geneva Gay defines culturally responsive pedagogy as "using the cultural characteristics, experiences, and perspectives of ethnically diverse students as conduits for teaching them more effectively" (Gay, 2002). CRP points toward teaching practices that attend to specific cultural differences among students, including values, traditions, languages, communication and learning styles, and relational norms.

culture circle: First described by Brazilian educator and philosopher Paulo Freire, Emdin defines a culture circle as an informal space where adults who were learning to read and write came together to share their understandings of the world and their place within it (Emdin, 2017).

culture of compliance: A culture focused solely on satellite data, program implementation, and power-hoarding or top-down mandates.

culture of public learning: A culture that centers student voice, cultivates curiosity, and moves professional learning beyond the low bar of implementing "best practices" to a high bar of cultivating practitioner knowledge about how their students learn.

curiosity: A mindset connected to the uncover phase of the equity transformation cycle, signifying a strong desire to know or learn something and a willingness to dig beneath the surface to identify root causes.

cypher: A rap cypher is a codified style of communication that many urban students of color use on street corners to engage in playful, dynamic dialogue (Emdin, 2017).

deep listening: A type of listening that aims to relieve the suffering of the other person, supporting personal healing and the development of relational trust (Safir, 2017b).

default practices: Practices that we automatically do.

defense: A defense involves a student revising and preparing over weeks or even months to share polished pieces of academic work before a committee or "panel." Panels typically include peers, teachers, a significant adult, and a community member.

doing equity: Treating equity as a series of tools, strategies, and compliance tasks versus a whole-person, whole-system change process linked to culture, identity, and healing.

efficacy: A component of agency in which students feel able to identify what matters to them, take action, and say "I can make a difference"; the ability to produce a desired or intended result.

emergence: The theory that simple rules interact with one another in complex ways to shape a change process, the outcome of which cannot be predicted.

empiricism: A theory developed in the seventeenth and eighteenth century emphasizing the role of sensory evidence and patterns in the formation of ideas rather than innate ideas or traditions.

epistemology: The theory of knowledge, especially with regard to its methods, validity, and scope. Epistemology is the investigation of what distinguishes justified belief from opinion.

equity: An approach to ensuring equally high outcomes for all by removing the predictability of success or failure that currently correlates with any racial, social, economic, or cultural factor.

equity-centered transformation cycle (ETC): A fluid yet structured process that centers street data in a journey of listening deeply to voices at the margins, uncovering root causes of inequity, reimagining current approaches in partnership with stakeholders, and moving a change agenda.

equity learning walk: An informal series of classroom observations with an explicit equity lens. The learning walk team might look for patterns of participation broken down by race and gender; patterns of teacher feedback (i.e., affirmative versus negative interactions with students); small-group peer interactions that reflect implicit biases; or actual use of academic language in classes with English language learners.

equity transformation cycle: The equity transformation cycle (ETC) is the central process tool in this book. The cycle represents a fluid yet structured process that is grounded in core values—radical inclusion, curiosity, creativity, and courage—and centers street-level data. As you move through the cycle, you will learn to listen deeply to voices at the margins, uncover the root causes of inequities, reimagine your current approaches in partnership with key stakeholders, and move a change agenda with courage.

equity warrior: Nesting equity within a single champion and holder of the vision.

false generosity: Paolo Freire's concept defines false generosity as charity that targets the symptoms of an unjust society. Examples include donating to shelters for the homeless or creating a foundation to eradicate malaria. False generosity isn't false because it doesn't help people; it can and often does save lives. Rather, it's "false" because, by addressing symptoms rather than underlying causes, it functions to maintain oppression.

focus: The ability to know where we are going as a community and reinforce it consistently through our messages.

fractals: Never-ending patterns that replicate across different scales and every level of the system—for example, the tiniest broccoli flower mirrors the largest floret.

fundamental attribution error: Also known as correspondence bias, fundamental attribution error is the tendency to explain someone's behavior based on internal factors, such as personality or disposition, and to underestimate situational explanations.

graduate profile: An accessible, succinct description of what every graduate must know, understand, and be able to do. It can be developed at every level of the educational system.

holism: A tenet of Indigenous epistemology, holism helps us account for the whole of the system and the individual learner—the emotional, spiritual, physical, intellectual, and cultural dimensions—rather than fragment into parts. The theory that parts of a whole are in intimate interconnection, such that they cannot exist independently of the whole or cannot be understood without reference to the whole, which is thus regarded as greater than the sum of its parts. Holism is often applied to mental states, language, and ecology.

iceberg: Designed by systems theorist Peter Senge, the iceberg protocol helps us move from an event we might typically react to into the deeper waters of patterns, trends, systemic structures, and mental models that shape our thinking. When we encounter an iceberg, only a small portion (that which surfaces above sea level) is visible from a distance.

identity: A component of the agency framework signifying that a student feels their ways of being, learning, and knowing in the world are valued.

implicit bias: Implicit biases stem from implicit associations we harbor in our subconscious that cause us to have feelings and attitudes about other people based on characteristics such as race, ethnicity, age, and appearance. These associations are activated involuntarily and without individual awareness as they develop over the course of a lifetime, beginning at an early age through exposure to direct and indirect messages.

improvement science: A problem-solving approach in education that encourages practitioners to test new ideas in rapid cycles—often referred to as plan-do-study-act (PDSA)—in which they develop a change idea, test it, collect data on it, and reflect on whether it worked.

instructional rounds: A structured practice that takes participants through a robust process of observing, analyzing, and making meaning of classroom street data (City et al., 2009).

intentional practices: Practices that we choose to do in order to transform the way we show up in the world and that are an essential element of antiracist work. Intentional practices give us the opportunity to increase choice and alignment with values (Maina & Haines, 2008).

intersectionality: Intersectionality is a theory and way of framing the various interactions between race, gender, and other identities as well as explaining how systems of oppression interact with each other in complex ways to impact people's lived experiences.

learning spirit: An Indigenous concept that spirits travel with individuals and guide their learning, providing inspiration and the unrealized potential to be who we are.

literacy: The ability to read, write, and express oneself; competence or knowledge in a specified area.

map data: Data that hover closer to the ground, providing a GPS of social-emotional, cultural, and learning trends within a school community. Map data include literacy levels gathered through "running records" where teachers listen to and code students reading aloud, rubric scores on common assessments, and surveys that reveal student, parent, or staff perception and satisfaction levels.

margin: Māori scholar Linda Tuhiwai Smith writes that the metaphor of the margin has served as a powerful symbol for understanding social inequality, oppression, disadvantage, and power as well as hidden sources of wisdom. Xicana writer Gloria Anzaldua invoked the idea of the frontera, or borderland, for this same purpose, while African American author and activist bell hooks wrote of the "radical possibility of 'choosing the margin' as a site of belonging as much as a site of struggle and resistance" (Smith, 2012, pp. 204–205). Far from places of weakness or impoverishment, the margins are sites of deep cultural wealth and community wisdom.

mastery: A component of agency in which students are able to build knowledge, demonstrate their understanding as a learner, and show what they know in nontraditional ways.

mature empathy: The ability to form a mental picture of another person's experience by drawing on one's own schemas (Safir, 2017b).

mental models: Personal, internal representations of reality that people use to interact with the world around them, constructed by individuals based on their unique life experiences, perceptions, and understandings of the world (Jones, Ross, et al., 2011).

microaggressions: Subtle, everyday slights or insults that convey a hostile or derogatory message to targeted persons based on identity as part of a marginalized group.

mixed methods: A form of research that integrates quantitative and qualitative methods to enact a more holistic approach.

navel-gazing equity: Keeping the equity work at the level of self-reflection and failing to penetrate the instructional core and school systems and structures (e.g., master schedule, tracking).

neuroception: A scientific term describing how our neural circuits perceive and distinguish, often automatically, whether situations or people are safe, dangerous, or life-threatening.

observer: A person who watches or notices something.

oral tradition: A form of human communication wherein knowledge, art, ideas, and cultural material is received, preserved, and transmitted orally from one generation to another. The transmission is through speech or song and may include folktales, ballads, chants, prose, or verses.

orientation to vision: A leadership stance in which we define, coach toward, and message a vivid picture of success (Safir, 2017b).

outlier syndrome: A systemic pattern in which a few exceptional teachers work their magic in a handful of classrooms.

pedagogy of compliance: A pedagogy that continues to dominate the majority of American classrooms, particularly at a secondary level, characterized by lecture-style instruction, students in rows looking toward the teacher as epistemological expert, and teachers carrying the cognitive load.

pedagogy of voice: A pedagogy that emerges at the intersection of critical pedagogy and culturally responsive education, offering an instructional technology and a way of being that shifts the locus of learning and power to the student's voice. A pedagogy of voice transcends numbers and metrics to create street-level learning experiences that foster healing, cognitive growth, and agency.

peeling the onion: Peeling the onion protocol provides a structured way to look at a problem without immediately trying to solve it. It includes a series of timed steps that help you get to the heart of an issue.

performance assessment: The demonstration and evaluation of applied skills in authentic settings.

positivism: A philosophical system that holds that every rationally justifiable assertion can be scientifically verified or is capable of logical or mathematical proof and that therefore rejects metaphysics and theism.

power-sharing: An antidote to white supremacy culture's power hoarding; a stance of redistributing power, access, and voice to others, particularly those currently at the margins.

program-itis: A phenomenon whereby layer upon layer of underfunded mandates are piled on teachers as demands to personalize learning for an increasingly diverse student body mount (Berry, 2020).

public learning: A transformation model for professional learning that centers student voice and teacher agency. An opportunity to shine a light on a dilemma or challenge and think it through collaboratively with the benefit of street data.

qualitative research: An approach that investigates questions about why and how people behave in the ways that they do, mining for insight into the messy interplay of human relationships. Qualitative researchers collect and analyze non-numerical data in an effort to gain insight into social conditions and behaviors.

quantitative research: Attempt to explain patterns through the collection and statistical analysis of numerical data.

radical inclusion: A mindset connected to the listening phase of the equity transformation cycle, described as the intentional act of interrupting inequity where it lives by recognizing the multiplicity of stories, truths, their proximities, their intersections, and the people who own the stories (Ortiz Guzman, 2017).

reimagining: The act of reinterpreting (an event, work of art, etc.) imaginatively; rethinking.

relational capital: The resource that leaders accrue when they take time to listen to and convey authentic care and curiosity toward others. If relationships function as currency in schools, relational capital is like a big savings account of trust and goodwill (Safir, 2017b).

routine expertise: Knowing the best practices, staying on the pacing guide, and fixating on standardized test scores as the primary indicators of learning. A routine expert can master procedures in order to become highly efficient and accurate (but not flexible or adaptable in situations that are outside the routine). People who are routine experts can accelerate efficiency through well-practiced routines.

safe-to-fail experiments: Small, four- to six-week "hacks" that disrupt business-as-usual and give you fresh street data to study.

satellite data: Data that hover far above the classroom and tell an important but incomplete story of equity. Satellite data encompass broad-brush quantitative measures like test scores, attendance patterns, and graduation rates, as well as adult indicators like teacher retention, principal attrition, and parent participation rates.

scientific colonialism: An approach to scientific inquiry in which the center of gravity for the acquisition of knowledge about a people is located outside of that people's lived reality (McDougal III, 2014).

sense of purpose: The quality of having a definite reason for being.

sense of self: The way a person thinks about and views his or her traits, beliefs, and purpose within the world.

settler colonialism: The removal and erasure of Indigenous peoples in order to take the land for use by settlers in perpetuity. Settler-colonialism plays out in the erasure of Indigenous presence and the ongoing dispossession of land and other resources from Indigenous peoples.

seventh generation principle: A principle based on an ancient Haudenosaunee (Iroquois) philosophy that the decisions we make today should result in a sustainable world seven generations into the future.

showing strength: A component of the warm demander framework in which a person holds the line on the vision and does not capitulate to deficit language or distorted views of student behavior.

siloing equity: Locating the equity work in a separate and siloed policy, team, or body.

single-point rubric: A reflection that breaks down the components of an assignment into different criteria but only describes the criteria for proficiency; it does not attempt to list all the ways a student could fall short, nor does it specify how a student could exceed expectations (Gonzalez, 2014).

simplexity: A way to navigate complex realities with simple rules, by identifying a small number of core factors that constitute your focus (the simple part), recognizing that the challenge is how to make them coalesce in actual learning spaces (the complex part) (Fullan, 2009).

spray and pray equity: Engaging "equity experts" to drop in for a training with no ongoing plan for learning and capacity-building.

spirit murdering: The denial of inclusion, protection, safety, nurturance, and acceptance because of fixed yet fluid and moldable structures of racism in schools (Love, 2013).

stereotype threat: A theory developed by social psychologist Claude Steele to describe how the performance of women, people of color, and others often decreases in the face of the psychic threat of being viewed as inferior. The perceived risk of confirming negative stereotypes about one's racial, ethnic, gender, or cultural group that leads to diminished performance on tasks and increasing privatization of one's practice (Steele & Aronson, 1995).

storientation: A concept signifying close attention to the role of stories in equitable school transformation (Safir, 2017b).

strategic listening: A style of equity-centered coaching that employs reflective questions and a bias toward experimental action to help the person build capacity and agency (Safir, 2017b).

street data (or street-level data): The qualitative, systematic, and experiential data that emerges at eye level and on lower frequencies when we train our brains to discern it. Street data is asset-based, building on the tenets of culturally responsive education by helping educators look for what's right in our students, schools, and communities instead of seeking out what's wrong. Street data embodies both an ethos and a change methodology that will transform how we analyze, diagnose, and assess everything from student learning to district improvement to policy. It offers us a new way to think about, gather, and make meaning of data.

structural equity: Redesigning systems and structures (e.g. master schedule) without investing in the deeper personal, interpersonal, and cultural shifts.

superficial equity: Failing to take time to build equity knowledge and fluency, leading to behavioral shifts without understanding deeper meaning or historical context.

systemic oppression: When laws and policies lead to unequal treatment and disadvantaging of a specific group of people based on their identity (gender, race, class, sexual orientation, language, etc.).

systemic racism: A theory that addresses individual, institutional, and structural forms of racial inequality and was shaped over time by scholars like Frederick Douglass, W. E. B. Du Bois, Oliver Cox, Anna Julia Cooper, Kwame Ture, Frantz Fanon, and Patricia Hill Collins, among others. Sociologist Joe Feagin built on this legacy to offer this framing: Systemic racism includes the complex array of antiblack practices, the unjustly gained political-economic power of whites, the continuing economic and other resource inequalities along racial lines, and the white racist ideologies and attitudes created to maintain and rationalize white privilege and power.

tokenizing equity: Asking leaders of color to hold, drive, and symbolically represent equity without providing support and resources nor engaging the entire staff in the work.

trap: A mechanism or device designed to catch and retain.

trope: A recurring theme we've seen happen before.

uncover: A phase of the equity transformation cycle in which educators mine the street data to identify root causes and/or discover something previously unknown or misunderstood.

vulnerability: Defined by qualitative researcher and author Brené Brown as an unstable feeling of uncertainty, risk, and emotional exposure that we get when we step out of our comfort zone or do something that forces us to loosen control (B. Brown, 2015).

warm demander leaders: Leaders, such as superintendents, directors, coaches, principals, assistant principals, who expect a great deal of their colleagues, convince them of their capacity to grow, and use street-level data and adaptive coaching moves to transform mindsets and practices. Rather than call people out, warm demanders call folks in and up to the work of equity.

warm demander teachers: Teachers who expect a great deal of their students, convince them of their own brilliance, and help them to reach their potential in a disciplined and structured environment (Delpit, 2013).

well-being: A state in which educators and students experience healing, agency, joy, and connection as they dismantle oppressive practices and structures and make deep learning available for all. An experience of holism as integration of mind, body, spirit, and identity.

white fragility: Feelings of discomfort and defensiveness on the part of a white person when confronted around racial inequality and injustice (DiAngelo, 2018).

white supremacy: The global system that confers unearned power and privilege on those who become identified as white while conferring disprivilege and disempowerment on those who become identified as people of color.

white supremacy culture (WSC): Ideas, thoughts, beliefs, habits, and actions grounded in whiteness that are perceived to be superior to the ideas, thoughts, beliefs, and actions of people and communities of color. One does not have to be a white supremacist or even white to embody or enact white supremacist culture (Jones & Okun, 2001).

wise feedback: A way of providing students of color with structured, empowering explanations that mitigate stereotype threat and reduce the possibility that feedback is experienced as biased (Cohen, Steele, & Ross, 1999). This process includes three instructional elements: describe the nature of the feedback being offered; emphasize and explain the high standards used to evaluate the student work and organize the feedback; explicitly state a belief that the student has the skills needed to meet those standards.

working toward equity: A practice that requires us to (1) acknowledge that our systems, practices, and narratives are designed to perpetuate disparities in outcomes for non-dominant students; (2) deliberately identify barriers that predict success or failure and actively disrupt them; (3) consistently examine personal identity, bias, and both personal and collective contributions to the creation and/or reproduction of inequitable practices; (4) (re)allocate resources (tools, time, money, people, support) to ensure every child gets what they need to succeed to thrive socially, emotionally, and intellectually; and (5) cultivate the unique gifts, talents, and interests that every person possesses.

Bibliography

Albert, T., & Ramis, H. (Producer), & Ramis, H. (Director). Ramis, H., & Rubin, D. (Writers) (1993). *Groundhog Day* [Motion picture]. United States: Columbia Pictures.

Alexander, M. (2016, April 13). *The warm demander: An equity approach*. Retrieved from https://www.edutopia.org/blog/warm-demander-equity-approach-matt-alexander

Anaissie, T., Cary, V., Clifford, D., Malarkey, T., & Wise, S. (2016). Liberatory design: Your toolkit to design for equity. Version 1.0. (Card 34). National Equity Project and Stanford d.school's K12 Lab.

Annie E. Casey Foundation. (2012, December 3). Youth unemployment soars in past decade. *[Web log post]*. http://www.aecf.org/blog/youth-unemployment-soars-in-past-decade/

Antell, R. (2001). *"I am somebody": Closing the achievement gap* [Video featuring students from Balboa High School in the community organizing process that led to the opening of June Jordan School for Equity]. https://www.youtube.com/watch?v=hzn6KITE-A8

Antoine, A., Mason, R., Mason, R., Palahicky, S., & Rodriguez de France, C. (2018). *Pulling together: A guide for curriculum developers*. Victoria, BC: BCcampus. https://opentextbc.ca/indigenizationcurriculumdevelopers/

Applied Research Center. (ARC). (2011). *Historical timeline of public education in the US*. https://www.raceforward.org/research/reports/historical-timeline-public-education-us

Aronson, B. A., & Boveda, M. (2017). The intersection of white supremacy and the education industrial complex: An analysis of #BlackLivesMatter and the criminalization of people with disabilities. *Journal of Educational Controversy, 12*(1), 6.

Bakari, R. S. (1997). *Different perspectives on majority rules*. Epistemology from an Afrocentric perspective: Enhancing black students' consciousness through an Afrocentric way of knowing. 2nd Annual Conference on People of Color in Predominantly White Institutions.

Bandura, A. (1997). *Self-efficacy: The exercise of control*. New York: W.H. Freeman and Company.

Bay Window 112. (1999). *Making the grade*. Boston, MA; KQED, American Archive of Public Broadcasting (WGBH and the Library of Congress), Boston, MA, and Washington DC. Retrieved from http://americanarchive.org/catalog/cpb-aacip-55-76rxx8mg

Berner, A. (2017, September). *Would school inspections work in the United States?* Johns Hopkins School of Education, Institute for Education Policy. https://edpolicy.education.jhu.edu/wp-content/uploads/2017/05/Inspectorate2.pdf

Berry, B. (2020). *Whole child education, the future of schooling, and a reinvented teaching profession*. Background paper for the ALL4SC. Columbia: University of South Carolina.

BIPOC Project. (n.d.). Retrieved from https://www.thebipocproject.org/.

Birchall, T. (2018, May 15). *How to conduct empathy interviews*. Retrieved from https://www.zionandzion.com/how-to-conduct-empathy-interviews/

Blackstock, C. (2007). *The breath of life versus the embodiment of life: Indigenous knowledge and Western research*. ResearchGate. https://www.researchgate.net/publication/237555666_The_breath_of_life_versus_the_embodiment_of_life_indigenous_knowledge_and_western_research

Boyle, G. (2010). *Tattoos on the heart: The power of boundless compassion* (p. 17–19). New York, NY: Free Press.

Brazas, C., & McGeehan, C. (2020). What white colleagues need to understand. *Teaching Tolerance, 64*, 55–58. https://www.tolerance.org/magazine/spring-2020/what-white-colleagues-need-to-understand

Brown, A. M. (2017). *Emergent strategy: Shaping change, changing worlds* (p. 9–10). Chico, CA: AK Press.

Brown, B. (2015). *Daring greatly: How the courage to be vulnerable transforms the way we live, love, parent, and lead.* New York: Avery.

Brown, B. (Host). (2020, June 3). *Unlocking us: Brené with Ibram X. Kendi on how to be an antiracist* [Audio podcast]. Retrieved from https://brene brown.com/podcast/brene-with-ibram-x-kendi-on-how-to-be-an-antiracist/

Brown, J. (2019, November 14). Opening remarks in session called "Community-centered public education and inclusive decision making in Chicago and beyond." Partnership for the Future of Learning Convening.

Choi, Y. W. (2020, February 24). *Student voice in teacher professional learning.* Retrieved from https://www.nextgenlearning.org/articles/stu dent-voice-in-teacher-professional-learning

Christie, C. (2019, December 22). Lecture on program evaluation and mixed methodologies. UCLA Luskin Center.

Chun, M. (2010, March/April). Taking teaching to (performance) task: Linking pedagogical and assessment practices. *Change: The Magazine of Higher Education, 42*(2), 22–29. Retrieved from http://jcsites.juniata.edu/faculty/kruse/misc/Chun_Change_TakingTeachingToTask.pdf

City, E., Elmore, R., Fiarman, S., & Teitel, L. (2009). *Instructional rounds in education: A network approach to improving teaching and learning.* Cambridge, MA: Harvard Education Press.

Coates, T.-N. (2015). *Between the world and me.* New York: One World.

Coffey, K. (2015, January 15). *Perennial pioneers: The sisters of St. Ann.* Retrieved from https://www.globalsistersreport.org/news/trends/pere nnial-pioneers-sisters-st-ann-17836

Cohen, J. S. (2020, July 14). *A teenager didn't do her online schoolwork. So a judge sent her to juvenile detention.* ProPublica. Retrieved from https://www.propublica.org/article/a-teenager-didnt-do-her-online-schoolwork-so-a-judge-sent-her-to-juvenile-detention

Cohen, G. L., Steele, C. M., & Ross, L. D. (1999). The mentor's dilemma: Providing critical feedback across the racial divide. *Personality and Social Psychology Bulletin, 25*(10), 1302–1318.

Cole, N. L. (2020, July 21). *Definition of systemic racism in sociology: Beyond prejudice and micro-aggressions.* ThoughtCo. Retrieved from https://www.thoughtco.com/systemic-racism-3026565

Collective Teacher Efficacy (CTE) according to John Hattie. (2018, March). *Collective teacher efficacy (CTE) according to John Hattie.* Visible Learning. Retrieved from https://visible-learning.org/2018/03/collective-teacher-efficacy-hattie/

Cook, A., & Tashlik, P. (2004). *Talk, talk, talk: Discussion-based classrooms.* New York: Teachers College Press.

Crenshaw, K. (1989). Demarginalizing the intersection of race and sex: A black feminist critique of anti-discrimination doctrine, feminist theory and anti-racist politics. *University of Chicago Legal Forum, 1989*(1), 139–167.

Crenshaw, K. (1991). Mapping the margins: Intersectionality, identity politics, and violence against women of color. *Stanford Law Review, 43*(6), 1241–1299.

Cross, T. L. (1997, May/June). Relational worldview model. *Pathways Practice Digest, 12*(4). National Indian Child Welfare Association (NICWA). Retrieved from https://issuu.com/nicwa

Darling-Hammond, L. (2002). *10 features of good small schools: Redesigning high schools: What matters and what works.* School Redesign Network. Retrieved from https://edpolicy.stanford.edu/sites/default/files/10-features-good-small-schools-redesigning-high-schools-what-matters-and-what-works_0.pdf

Darling-Hammond, L., & Friedlaender, D. (2008, May). Creating excellent and equitable schools. *Educational Leadership, 65*(8), 14–21.

Delpit, L. (2013). *"Multiplication is for white people": Raising expectations for other people's children.* New York: The New Press.

DiAngelo, R. (2018). *White fragility: Why it's so hard for white people to talk about racism.* Boston, MA: Beacon Press.

Douglas, F. (1857, August 3). West India Emancipation (speech) Canandaigua, New York. Retrieved from https://www.blackpast.org/african-american-history/1857-frederick-douglass-if-there-no-struggle-there-no-progress/

Doyle, G. (2020). *Untamed.* New York: The Dial Press.

Duncan-Andrade, J. (2009). Note to educators: Hope required when growing roses in concrete. *Harvard Educational Review, 79*(2), 181–194.

Emdin, C. (2017). *For white folks who teach in the hood and the rest of y'all too* (p. 61–80). Boston, MA: Beacon Press.

Etymology Dictionary. (n.d.). Etymology of "coherence." In *Etymology dictionary*. Retrieved from https://www.etymonline.com/word/coherence

Evergreen School District. (n.d.). *Profile of a learner*. San Jose, CA: Evergreen School District. [chart] https://www.eesd.org/uploaded/departments/instruction/Profile_of_a_Learner/Profile_of_a_Learner_Chart_051120.pdf

Fanon, F. (1952). *Black skins, white masks*. New York: Grove Press.

Feldman, J. (2018). *Grading for equity: What it is, why it matters, and how it can transform schools and classrooms*. Thousand Oaks, CA: Corwin.

First Nations Education Steering Committee. (2015). *First peoples principles of learning* [Poster]. West Vancouver, BC, Canada. Retrieved from http://www.fnesc.ca/wp/wp-content/uploads/2015/09/PUB-LFP-POSTER-Principles-of-Learning-First-Peoples-poster-11x17.pdf

Freedman A. (Producer), & Wardrop, K. (Director). (1917). *Making the grade* [Documentary]. Ireland: Venom Films.

Freire, P. (1970). *Pedagogy of the oppressed*. New York: Continuum.

Fullan, M. (2009). *Motion leadership: The skinny on becoming change savvy*. Thousand Oaks, CA: Corwin.

Fullan, M., & Quinn, J. (2015). *Coherence: The right drivers in action for schools, districts, and systems*. Thousand Oaks, CA: Corwin.

Galloway, M. K., & Ishimaru, A. M. (2015). Radical recentering: Equity in educational leadership standards. *Educational Administration Quarterly*, *51*(3), 372–408.

Gallup. (2013). *State of America's schools*. Retrieved from https://www.gallup.com/services/178709/state-america-schools-report.aspx

Gallup. (2014, December 11). *Gallup student poll 2014 U.S. overall report*. [Poll] Retrieved from http://www.gallup.com/services/180029/gallup-student-poll-2014-overall-report.aspx

Gay, G. (2002). Preparing for culturally responsive teaching. *Journal of Teacher Education*, *53*(2), 106–116.

Gaymes, A., & San Vicente, R. (2020, March 27). Schooling for equity during and beyond COVID-19. *Behind the Numbers*. [Web log post]. Retrieved from http://behindthenumbers.ca/2020/03/27/schooling-for-equity-during-covid-19/

Ginwright, S. (2018, May 31). *The future of healing: Shifting from trauma-informed care to healing-centered engagement*. Medium.com. Retrieved from https://medium.com/@ginwright/the-future-of-healing-shifting-from-trauma-informed-care-to-healing-centered-engagement-634f557ce69c

Goldstein, D. (2019a, December 3). 'It just isn't working': PISA test scores cast doubt on U.S. education efforts. *The New York Times*. Retrieved from https://www.nytimes.com/2019/12/03/us/us-students-international-test-scores.html

Goldstein, D. (2019b, December 6). After 10 years of hopes and setbacks, what happened to the common core? *The New York Times*. Retrieved from https://www.nytimes.com/2019/12/06/us/common-core.html?smid=nytcore-ios-share

Gomez, T. (2019, December 19). *Making the grade: A 20-year retrospective reunion of Balboa–Main Academy* (BalMa). Education Equity Project [Live panel]. Oakland, California.

Gonzalez, J. (2014, May 1). *Know your terms: Holistic, analytic, and single-point rubrics*. Cult of Pedagogy. Retrieved from https://www.cultofpedagogy.com/holistic-analytic-single-point-rubrics/

Grossman, P. (2020, May). Making the complex work of teaching visible. *Phi Delta Kappan*, *101*(8). Retrieved from https://kappanonline.org/making-complex-work-teaching-visible-common-practice-grossman/

Guha, R., Wagner, T., Darling-Hammond, L., Taylor, T., & Curtis, D. (2018). *The promise of performance assessments: Innovations in high school learning and college admission*. Palo Alto, CA: Learning Policy Institute. Retrieved from https://learningpolicyinstitute.org/product/promise-performance-assessments-report

Gutiérrez, K. D. (2008, April/May/June). Developing a sociocritical literacy in the third space. *Reading Research Quarterly*, *43*(2), 148–164. Retrieved from https://doi.org/10.1598/RRQ.43.2.3

Hall, S. (1992). The West and the rest: Discourse and power. In S. Hall and B. Gieben (Eds.), *The formations of modernity* (pp. 276–320). Cambridge, MA: Polity and Open University.

Hammond, Z. (2014). *Culturally responsive teaching and the brain*. Thousand Oaks, CA: Corwin.

Hannah-Jones, N. (2019, August 14). Our democracy's founding ideals were false when they were written. Black Americans have fought to make them true. *New York Times Magazine*. Retrieved from https://www.nytimes.com/interactive/2019/08/14/magazine/black-history-american-democracy.html

Hatano, G., & Inagaki, K. (1986). Two courses of expertise. In H. Stevenson, H. Azama, & K. Hakuta (Eds.), *Child development and education in Japan* (pp. 262–272). New York, NY: Freeman.

Hattie, J. (2008). *Visible learning*. Routledge.

Herrnstein. R. (1973). *IQ in the meritocracy*. Boston: Little Brown.

Hodges, T. (2018, September/October). Not just a buzzword: Using survey data to foster engagement among students, parents, and teachers. *Principal: 98*(1), 10–13. Retrieved from https://www.naesp.org/sites/default/files/Hodges_SO18.pdf?utm_source=link_wwwv9&utm_campaign=item_244022&utm_medium=copy

Hulan, R., Eigenbrod, R., & Gorsebrook Research Institute for Atlantic Canada Studies. (2008). *Aboriginal oral traditions: Theory, practice, ethics*. Halifax: Fernwood Publishing.

Hurwitz, L., & Bourque S. (n.d.). *Settler colonialism primer*. Righting Relations National Hub. http://catherinedonnellyfoundation.org/national/resource/settler-colonialism-primer/

Immordino-Yang, M. (2016, February 18). *Ed-Talk: Learning with an Emotional Brain*. Retrieved from http://www.aera100.net/mary-helen-immordino-yang.html

IndEdu 200x. (2017, February 6). *Topic 3: Learning from indigenous worldviews* [Video]. Youtube. https://youtu.be/9I2LAWCHNsc

Jensen, A. R. (1969). How much can we boost IQ and scholastic achievement? *Harvard Education Review, 39*, 1–23

Jensen. A. R. (1980). *Bias in mental testing*. New York: Free Press.

Jones, K., & Okun, T. (2001). *Dismantling racism: A workbook for social change groups*. Change Work.

Jones, N. A., Ross, H., Lynam, T., Perez, P., & Leitch, A. (2011). Mental models: An interdisciplinary synthesis of theory and methods. *Ecology and Society, 16*(1), 46. Retrieved from http://www.ecologyandsociety.org/vol16/iss1/art46/

Kendi, I. X. (2019). *How to be an antiracist*. New York: One World.

Kirwan Institute. (2015). *Understanding implicit bias*. The Kirwan Institute for the Study of Race and Ethnicity. The Ohio State University. Retrieved from http://kirwaninstitute.osu.edu/research/understanding-implicit-bias/

Kleinfeld, J. (1975, February). Effective teachers of Eskimo and Indian students. *The School Review, 83*(2), 301.

Knight, J. (2015). *Better conversations: Coaching ourselves and each other to be more credible, caring, and connected*. Thousand Oaks: Corwin.

Knight, J. (2019, November). Why teacher autonomy is central to coaching success. *Educational Leadership, 77*(3), 14–20.

Kohl, H. (1995). *I won't learn from you: And other thoughts on creative maladjustment*. New York: New Press.

Ladson-Billings, G. (1994). *The dreamkeepers: Successful teachers of African American children*. San Francisco: Jossey-Bass.

Lead by Learning. (2020). *Leading by learning: Creating the conditions for adult learning*. Oakland, CA: Lead by Learning. Retrieved from https://weleadbylearning.org/playbook/

Lee, E., Menkart, D., & Okazawa-Rey, M. (Eds.) (1998). *Beyond heroes and holidays: A practical guide to K–12 anti-racist, multicultural education and staff development* (1st ed.). Nashville, TN: Network of Educators on the Americas.

LeFevre, D., Timperley, H., Twyford, K., & Ell, F. (2019). *Leading powerful professional learning: Responding to complexity with adaptive expertise*. Thousand Oaks, CA: Corwin.

Losen, D. J., & Gillespie, J. (2012). Opportunities suspended: The disparate impact of disciplinary exclusion from school. *UCLA: The Civil Rights Project / Proyecto Derechos Civiles*. Retrieved from https://escholarship.org/uc/item/3g36n0c3

Love, B. L. (2013). "I see Trayvon Martin": What teachers can learn from the tragic death of a young black male. *The Urban Review, 45*(3), 1–15.

Love, B. (2019). *We want to do more than survive: Abolitionist teaching and the pursuit of educational freedom*. Boston, MA: Beacon Press.

Maina, N., & Haines, S. (2008). *The transformative power of practice*. Retrieved from https://www.racialequitytools.org/resourcefiles/TransformativePracticeIndiv.pdf

McDougal III, S. (2014). *Research methods in Africana studies* (1st ed.). Black Studies and Critical Thinking (Book 64). New York: Peter Lang, International Academic Publishers.

McGee Banks, C. A., & Banks, J. (1995). Equity pedagogy: An essential component of multicultural education. *Theory Into Practice, 34*(3), 152–158. Retrieved from https://www.tandfonline.com/doi/abs/10.1080/00405849509543674?journalCode=htip20

Mehrabian, A. (1981). *Silent messages: Implicit communication of emotions and attitudes.* Belmont, CA: Wadsworth.

Mehta, J., & Fine, S. (2019). *In search of deeper learning: The quest to remake the American high school.* Cambridge, MA: Harvard University Press.

Mintrop, R. (2016). *Design-based school improvement: A practical guide for education leaders.* Cambridge, MA: Harvard Education Press.

Miranda, L. (2015). *Hamilton: An American musical* [MP3]. New York: Atlantic Records. (Aaron Burr, Sir lyrics)

Morris, A. (2019, January 22). *What is settler-colonialism?* Teaching Tolerance. Retrieved from https://www.tolerance.org/magazine/what-is-settlercolonialism

Morris, M. W. (2016). *Pushout: The criminalization of Black girls in schools.* New York: The New Press.

National Education Association. (2020). *History of standardized testing in the United States.* Retrieved at http://www.nea.org/home/66139.htm

Oakes, J., Wells, A., Jones, M., & Datnow, A. (1997). Detracking: The social construction of ability, cultural politics, and resistance to reform. *Teachers College Record, 98*, 482–510.

Okun, T. (2020). *White supremacy culture.* Retrieved from https://www.dismantlingracism.org/uploads/4/3/5/7/43579015/okun_-_white_sup_culture.pdf

Ortiz Guzman, C. M. (2017). *equityXdesign: Leveraging identity development in the creation of an anti-racist equitable design thinking process* (p. 45) (Doctoral dissertation). Harvard Graduate School of Education, Cambridge, MA.

Panorama Education. (n.d.). *User guide: Panorama equity and inclusion survey: Topics and questions for students and staff.* Retrieved from https://go.panoramaed.com/hubfs/Panorama%20Equity%20and%20Inclusion%20User%20Guide.pdf?hsCtaTracking=2cfdd1d0-1eb4-4829-94b3-1da7a8bcdc47%7C6b526b35-b3dc-4c4b-86e8-db3f55b3691b

Phung, H. (2020, March 9). MS bulletin. San Unified School District. Retrieved from https://docs.google.com/document/d/1GimIsN1SzFranciscoUf7NOYraqr8o_mIT9un4GSzlyvMvv6l1IE/edit?ts=5ee2bcf6

Pressley, A., & Morris, M. (2019, December 5). A just society doesn't criminalize girls. *Boston Globe.* Retrieved from https://www.bostonglobe.com/2019/12/06/opinion/just-society-doesnt-criminalize-girls/

Promise54.org and Galloway, M. K., & Ishimaru, A. M. (2015). Radical recentering: Equity in educational leadership standards. *Educational Administration Quarterly, 51*(3), 372–408.

UCSF Multicultural Resource Center. (n.d.). *Racial equity & anti-Black racism.* University of California San Francisco. Retrieved from https://mrc.ucsf.edu/racial-equity-anti-black-racism

Regional Educational Laboratory Program West (REL West). (2017, December). *What is improvement science?* Retrieved from https://ies.ed.gov/ncee/edlabs/regions/west/Blogs/Details/2

Relationship Centered School. (2018, December 12). Retrieved from https://caljustice.org/our-work/rcs/

Ross, L. (1977). The intuitive psychologist and his shortcomings: Distortions in the attribution process. *Advances in Experimental Social Psychology, 10*, 173–220. Retrieved from https://doi.org/10.1016/S0065-2601(08)60357-3

Safir, S. (2017a, March 23). Community walks create bonds of understanding. *Edutopia.* Retrieved from https://www.edutopia.org/blog/community-walks-create-bonds-understanding-shane-safir

Safir, S. (2017b). *The listening leader: Creating the conditions for equitable school transformation.* San Francisco: John Wiley & Sons.

School Reform Initiative. (n.d.). *Peeling the onion: Defining a dilemma protocol.* Retrieved from http://schoolreforminitiative.org/doc/peeling_onion.pdf

Senge, P. (2009). *The fifth discipline: The art and practice of the learning organization.* New York: Doubleday/Currency.

Senge, P. M. (2000). *Schools that learn: A fifth discipline fieldbook for educators, parents, and everyone who cares about education* (1st Currency pbk. ed.). New York: Doubleday.

Senge, P., Kleiner, A., & Roberts, C. (1994). *The fifth discipline fieldbook: Strategies and tools for building a learning organization.* Currency Doubleday: New York.

Showing Up For Racial Justice. (n.d.). White supremacy culture. [Web page.] https://www.showingupfor racialjustice.org/white-supremacy-culture.html

Sleeter, C. E. (1992). Restructuring schools for multicultural education. *Journal of Teacher Education, 43*(2), 141–148.

Smith, L. T. (2012). *Decolonizing methodologies: Research and indigenous peoples.* London: Zed Books.

Smith, P. (2020, August 26). *Listening and leading for equity: A restorative return to school.* [Keynote speech, opening remarks]. Abbotsford, British Columbia, Canada.

Snyder, C. R., Shane, J. L., Hal, S. S., Kevin, L. R., & David, B. F. (2003). Hope theory, measurements, and applications to school psychology. *School Psychology Quarterly, 18*(2), 122–139.

Spencer, S. J., & Steele, C. M. (1994). *Under suspicion of inability: Stereotype vulnerability and women's math performance* (Unpublished manuscript). SUNY Buffalo and Stanford University.

Steele, C. M., & Aronson, J. (1995, November). Stereotype threat and the intellectual test performance of African Americans. *Journal of Personality and Social Psychology, 69*(5), 797–811. doi:10.1037/0022-3514.69.5.797. PMID 7473032. Pdf.

Steingold, D. (2017, December 11). *'Are we there yet?' Children ask parents 73 questions a day on average, study finds.* Study Finds [website]. Retrieved from https://www.studyfinds.org/children-parents-questions/

Superville, D. R. (2019, March 12). *These students are doing PD with their teachers. Their feedback is candid.* Retrieved from https://www.edweek.org/ew/articles/2019/03/13/these-students-are-doing-pd-with-their.html

10 facts about school attendance. (2018). Retrieved from https://www.attendanceworks.org/chronic-absence/the-problem/10-facts-about-school-attendance/

Timperley, H. (2018, May). *Adaptive expertise and the spiral of inquiry: A different way of thinking about what it means to be professional.* Talk presented at NOIIE Symposium 2018. Vancouver, British Columbia.

Tunison, S. (2007). *Aboriginal learning: A review of current metrics of success.* University of Saskatchewan, Aboriginal Education Research Centre, Saskatoon, Saskatchewan and First Nations and Adult Higher Education Consortium, Calgary, Alberta. Retrieved from http://www.aerc.usask.ca/

Urrieta, L. (2010). Whitestreaming: Why some Latinas/os fear bilingual education. *Counterpoints, 371,* 47–55. Retrieved from http://www.jstor.org/stable/42980681

Wang, T. (2016, January 20). *Why big data needs thick data.* Ethnography Matters. Retrieved from https://medium.com/ethnography-matters/why-big-data-needs-thick-data-b4b3e75e3d7

Watkins, J. (n.d.). Deeper Learning Dozen website. Retrieved from https://www.deeperlearningdozen.org/

Wheatley, M. (2000). *Turning to one another. Kansas Health Foundation 2000 Leadership Institute.* [Keynote Address]. Retrieved from https://www.margaretwheatley.com/articles/turningtooneanother.html#:~:text=%22One%20of%20the%20things%20we,really%20concern%20you%20%2D%20requires%20courage

Yosso, T. J. (2005, March). Whose culture has capital? *Race, Ethnicity and Education, 8*(1), 69–91.

Yurkofsky, M., Peterson, A., Mehta, J., Horwitz-Willis, R., & Frumin, K. (2020, April 21). Research on continuous improvement: Exploring the complexities of managing educational change. *Review of Research in Education, 44*(1), 403–433.

Index

A SAGE Publishing Company

Helping educators make the greatest impact

CORWIN HAS ONE MISSION: to enhance education through intentional professional learning.

We build long-term relationships with our authors, educators, clients, and associations who partner with us to develop and continuously improve the best evidence-based practices that establish and support lifelong learning.

Keep learning...
Available for consulting

SPEAKING ENGAGEMENTS

We offer professional learning sessions on a range of topics and are available to speak at your next conference or educational event to bring the principles of *Street Data: A Next-Generation Model for Equity, Pedagogy, and School Transformation* to life.

COACHING

Leadership Coaching and Capacity-Building for Equity

My colleagues and I, including my co-author Jamila Dugan, provide leadership coaching at every level of the school system: for superintendents, central office leaders, site administrators, and teacher leaders who want to increase their impact and become more strategic and equity driven.

CONSULTING

My team and I consult around a wide array of strategy and design issues that meet your needs and help you achieve your goals.

Shane Safir has worked at every level of the education system for the past 25 years, with an unwavering commitment to racial justice and deep learning. She provides equity-centered leadership coaching, systems transformation support, and professional learning for schools, districts, and organizations across the United States and Canada and is the founding principal of June Jordan School for Equity (JJSE), an innovative national model identified by scholar and policy leader Linda Darling-Hammond as having "beaten the odds in supporting the success of low-income students of color."

Jamila Dugan is a leadership coach, learning facilitator, researcher, and former Washington, D.C. teacher and school administrator. She holds a bachelor's degree in psychology from California State University, Fresno, a master's degree in early childhood education from George Mason University, and a doctorate in education leadership for equity from University of California, Berkeley.

www.shanesafir.com